"The army of geniuses Brian Gresko has assembled to reflect on the beautiful, ridiculous, transformative, exhausting experience that is fatherhood does not disappoint. *When I First Held You* glows with radical honesty, and cuts through the hysterical noise of parenting chatter with incisive reflection and quiet revelation."

—Adam Mansbach,
#1 *New York Times* bestselling author of *Go the F**k to Sleep*

"Full of humor, heart, and brilliance, *When I First Held You* contains everything I wish I'd known (but probably wasn't ready to hear) about fatherhood before I became a father. Over and over again, as I read the essays Brian Gresko has deftly gathered here, I wanted to grab my wife, my son, and even strangers on the train and point emphatically at one line or another to say, 'This! This is what it's like.' The failures and triumphs of fatherhood have never sounded better than they do in the words of these fine writers."

—Kristopher Jansma, author of *The Unchangeable Spots of Leopards*

"Reading these essays confirms my belief that being a father is not only the most important thing a man can do in life, but also that it's one of the hardest damn undertakings under the sun. That is, with the possible exception of writing about it honestly, which is what the authors in *When I First Held You* do, with humor and grace and sadness, to a striking, unflinching degree."

—Donald Ray Pollock, author of *The Devil All the Time*

continued . . .

"Brian Gresko's superb collection captures the singular weirdness that befalls the male of the species: a woman expels another human from her body and, with that act, somewhere, a man becomes a father. With great intensity and thoughtfulness, and with no tigers and no French anywhere in sight, these accomplished writers wrestle with the fears, failures, and fears of failure that mark this transformation at a remove. These carefully vetted, entertaining tales vary wildly; from the anxious Park Slopians to the gay sperm donor afflicted with ALS, *When I First Held You* is a platinum album of reflections on modern fatherhood."

—Daphne Uviller, coeditor of *Only Child*
and author of *Super in the City* and *Hotel No Tell*

When I First Held You

22 CRITICALLY ACCLAIMED WRITERS TALK ABOUT THE TRIUMPHS, CHALLENGES, AND TRANSFORMATIVE EXPERIENCE OF FATHERHOOD

EDITED BY

Brian Gresko

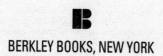

BERKLEY BOOKS, NEW YORK

THE BERKLEY PUBLISHING GROUP
Published by the Penguin Group
Penguin Group (USA)
375 Hudson Street, New York, New York 10014

USA • Canada • UK • Ireland • Australia • New Zealand • India • South Africa • China

penguin.com

A Penguin Random House Company

This book is an original publication of The Berkley Publishing Group.

WHEN I FIRST HELD YOU

Berkley trade paperback ISBN: 978-0-425-26924-4

An application to register this book for cataloging has been submitted to the Library of Congress.

PUBLISHING HISTORY
Berkley trade paperback edition / May 2014

PRINTED IN THE UNITED STATES OF AMERICA

10 9 8 7 6 5 4 3 2 1

Cover art by Warren Goldswain/Shutterstock
Cover design by Diana Kolsky
Interior text design by Kristin del Rosario

For Sara and Felix, with much love

It's the most terrifying day of your life, the day the first one is born. Your life as you know it is gone, never to return. But they learn how to walk, and they learn how to talk, and you want to be with them. And they turn out to be the most delightful people you'll ever meet in your life.

—DIALOGUE SPOKEN BY BILL MURRAY IN *LOST IN TRANSLATION* BY SOFIA COPPOLA

CONTENTS

Foreword

DARIN STRAUSS

You catch me at an interesting time.

Yesterday I may have failed my son—actually one of my twin sons, who is now almost six. He has a medical condition, which I don't want to specify here, and the thing is, yes. I did something that my wife thinks jeopardized his health. Not jeopardized in a huge way. But any jeopardy is more than enough jeopardy.

Well, here's the thing with me and fatherhood. I'm a keen learner, sure—but mostly I'm an expert fuck-up and apology-offerer. And you probably are too. Michael Chabon says something to the effect of "Every day you are a father is a day you fail." Ah, hindsight, hindsight.

It's not that nobody tells you this beforehand. They do. *It's hard*, they say when your wife gets that first ultrasound. ("They" is everybody.) They say, *It will change your life*. We hear those words, we think we know what they mean. We don't, we really don't. And after the unheeded words, we actually *have* the kid. (Or, in my experience, kids.) So, what happens? After the opening scenes of childbirth get acted out (after your days and your nights morph into thickets of wiping and swathing), you realize parenthood is an executive position. And a mid-management job. And entry-level. Decisions, hundreds of decisions a day—then the attempts at implementation. And the plastic Optimus Prime is always hiding behind the divan, the dainty chin is always pointed right at the hard pavement, the ambulance is always revving just outside.

You may see me and my kids walking into a kindergarten class. But what do I see? I see not them, exactly, but countless reminders of countless mistakes—tears, yellings, cracks in the playroom wall.

So: why do we do it, and why are you here, reading this book? I think you are here to laugh about how hard other dads find things, but also to have something else—a hard-to-describe contentment—described to you. Because the joys of fatherhood are real but not often put into accurate words. There is an intensity of some emotion—not happiness, definitely not happiness—but something like contentment, only more profound than that. Sometimes I feel it in my chest when I am with my kids: a warm fullness around the heart, like a water heater squirting everywhere inside the rib cage. That is not the kind of thing I've seen elucidated very well, or often. Until I picked up this anthology. There are great essays here, wherein great writers do just that.

Here's Ben Greenman, telling us "It is rejuvenating to locate yourself near the start of things, whether a child's life or an essay. There is so much left to do. There are so many chances to get it right." And Andre Dubus III, explaining that being a dad is knowing that "*something* is here among us: something I cannot see but feel; something I cannot hear but sense; something I cannot

smell but know." This mystery feeling comes up again and again, as with Chris Bachelder, who tells us "I don't pray, but I pray every night in the dark silence of my daughters' bedroom."

That's worth feeling: men learning about the astonishments and awes of fatherhood. And anything worth feeling is worth reading, if it's well articulated.

The same night when my wife told me (wrongly, I think) that I had jeopardized my son's health—after a stomach-twisted, head-down day spent wondering if I could do this for the rest of my life, and *why had I chosen to do it*—my twin boy, the one I had worried about, asked me if I might come observe him and his brother do a "somersault show" on the bed.

"Watch, Daddy," the boys said, rolling into each other and into my arms. And I smiled and felt the tears come. "Watch."

Introduction

BRIAN GRESKO

Before spending back-to-back days at my neighborhood play-ground, chasing my toddler son, I was that guy—the young man who swore never to be penned in, domesticated, anchored to a wife and children. I claimed to be a free spirit. The thought of commitment and responsibility left me trembling with panic, my eyes darting to find the nearest exit. These days, when I browse my Instagram feed, rife with photos of me and my son, Felix, I'm often surprised at how I never thought I'd be here.

Felix was born five years ago. He did not come easy, and spent the last few hours of a long labor stuck in the birth canal. When the heart monitors made clear that both his and his mother's lives were becoming endangered, a vacuum device pulled the baby into the cold glare of the birthing room. A doctor cut the cord without ceremony, and, instead of placing him on my wife's breast, a trio of nurses in blue scrubs buzzed about his body on an infant-sized table. I couldn't see what they were doing exactly, but when I caught a glimpse of my son's arm, it looked mottled with bruises, the skin tinged with a sick, purplish hue. "Why won't he cry?" my wife whispered.

Only then did I become aware of the room's silence. The midwife and our chipper, amazing nurse, who had been a cheerleader throughout the whole ordeal, had found cleaning chores to keep their hands busy and eyes cast away from us. They were attuned, I sensed, to what was happening on that little tray. I stood next to my wife, emotionally poised between exaltation and upset, on the shore of a great sea of fear, unsure whether the tide was running in or out. Seconds elongated in brittle quiet till a doctor announced, "We have a heartbeat, and it's strong."

After the attendants syphoned mucus out of my son, my wife received him. But the midwife took him after only a minute, flipping Felix over and banging his back with a cupped hand as if he were a doll, not a baby. "Give him to the dad," someone said. I nodded, not realizing this meant me. In the moment I held his tiny body, he snorted wetly and frothed a bit at the mouth.

"Is this normal?" I asked the midwife.

It was not, and pediatricians whisked him away to Neonatal Intensive Care. For a while, my wife and I sat together in the delivery room, scarfing sandwiches to fill stomachs that hadn't been fed in twenty agonizing hours. We talked about the scary, intense labor, but, strangely, didn't discuss the baby in any detail— not what he looked like or how he felt in our arms, where he had rested for less than a minute. I felt only an abstract anxiety for the boy, as I might for any child in distress, more a sense that I should be concerned than concern itself. Why, I wondered, was I so cold? I worried that maybe I lacked a gene, a mutation passed along by my biological dad.

When I was ten years old, my parents revealed that the man I thought of as my dad was not in fact my "real dad." My real dad was out there, somewhere, though who he was and why he didn't want to be a part of my life, my parents wouldn't say. It was obvious to me that the circumstances of my birth caused them great pain and distress, a discomfort they broadcast with teary eyes and pinched expressions, so I swallowed my questions.

I now know that my fear of fatherhood stemmed from that silence, a fear I brandished into adulthood with pride, as if I was tough and hard-boiled, though on the inside I still felt like that confused ten-year-old boy. Even sitting in the delivery room, my unknown paternity turned what should have been declarations of love and support into question marks of self-doubt.

Later, the doctors allowed me to see Felix in the NICU, recovering, they explained, from inhaling fluid on his slow way out. He looked sickly and small laid out on a table beneath a warming light. A breathing tube obscured his mouth, monitors tattooed his pale chest. Some, in a gesture I found ironic and completely inappropriate, were adhered by cheerful, rainbow-colored stickers.

"Hey, kid, it's your dad," I murmured.

I stroked his arm with my finger, and then he wrapped his little hand around it and locked his striking blue eyes on mine. That's when it hit me: the intense love, the desire to be the best father I could for this boy. I promised him then, no secrets. One day I would tell him the story of my origin and provide him clear answers when he asked about his roots. Most importantly, I vowed to raise him with an uninhibited, open heart.

A few weeks after arriving home with Felix, I talked to my biological father for the first time by phone. Beset by financial problems, he had had a tense relationship with his own emotionally distant father, wrecked two marriages by womanizing, and sired three other kids, who hadn't quite believed him when he came clean to them about me a couple of years before. "My son," he had the nerve to address me. "Can you forgive me?"

Actually, I could, because I realized that I didn't need him, neither as a child nor now, as an adult. I already had a dad, the man who had raised me as his own son. There's a photo of him just moments after my birth, his eyes big, their hazel tones brightened by his green scrubs, his face washed in emotion, my tiny form nestled in his arms. He didn't have to be my father, he chose to be. "When I first held you," he told me, "I knew. I wanted to be there to see this kid grow up."

I wanted the same, but I wanted to view my son's childhood in extreme close-up, with emotional X-ray vision. I felt an almost physical urge, after years of ambivalence, to get as deep in the muck of daddy-hood as possible, to not just be there, but breathe in every moment, good or bad. So, after about three months, I became my son's primary caregiver for eight hours a day. As with all things parenting, a financial consideration weighed on this decision as well: Felix was born a week after I graduated with a master's in Fine Arts in Creative Writing and I had no job, while my wife wanted to go back to work. Being a stay-at-home dad made sense both for my heart and our budget.

One might expect minds to be open and conventions challenged in Brooklyn, where families come in all shapes, sizes, colors, and makeups, and where I've lived for fifteen years. And yet, the stereotype of the male as financial provider, as the stoic, tight-lipped cowboy or the predatory, besuited businessman, loomed large. "A year off with the kid? That sounds like fun," one acquaintance said when he first heard of my situation. Another asked if I did chores around the house, and then revealed that he *once* folded laundry for his wife, smirking at me all the while. Often strangers offered their advice on the street about my son's behavior, his clothing, even the direction I had the stroller oriented ("You know you're getting the sun in his eyes, Daddy?" one well-intentioned nudge-nik told me. "His little eyes are very sensitive, you have to take care."), solicitations my wife didn't receive, since she wasn't the "clueless dad."

My first winter alone with a not-yet-walking baby drove me stir crazy, especially when frigid temperatures kept me housebound. I longed for company, specifically another stay-at-home dad who might be going through a similar experience, yet I wasn't sure I wanted to meet the kind of guy who would cop to the title even if I spotted one. (Like many parents, I bristled at the term "stay-at-home" because it boiled my entire identity down to parenthood.) What would we talk about? Bottle feeding and diaper changing?

It turned out, of course, that other dads were out there, though these lone wolves largely kept to themselves on the playground, eschewing the packs of nannies and mommies. Maybe, being men, we're of a more solitary nature about our parenting because paradigms of engaged, active fathers are hard to find, or because men, encouraged to be strong, brave, and authoritative, find themselves shy or uncomfortable discussing the intensely emotional world of parenting, a place where our sense of control can be illusionary. Perhaps men of a certain age are wary of making friends with one another in general, or these guys shared my fear of having dad buddies who would only want to talk baby. But I knew dads were out there, in greater numbers than ever, in fact. The census bureau estimates that the number of men acting as primary caregivers has more than doubled in the past ten years. And surely the amount will continue to grow in the next decade as the assumption that men belong solely in the workplace and women at home recedes in our cultural rearview mirror.

As I met other dads, both working and stay-at-home, I found that many men had struggled with inhibitions and anxiety around having kids—only the specifics of my story were unique, not the sentiment. I learned that the majority, like me, discovered fatherhood to be both a transformative space and also one thick with dark matter. I'm not talking about in the abstract—the societal stereotypes I touched on already—I mean on the ground, in the nursery, and especially on the changing table. Seeing your children's growth up close and observing their personalities spring forth in fits and bursts, with new traits emerging almost overnight, as if all this time these little beings harbored much older, more developed selves within, is akin to a miracle. I remember the first time Felix smiled at his own reflection, the first conversation we had (in which, of course, he wanted to know when Mommy would be home), and the first time he said goodbye and walked off to class on his own, a self-proclaimed big boy. Hugging your child, smelling his or her scalp, might raise the hairs on the back of your neck and cause a pleasant light-headedness, a buzz not unlike the one you experienced during the early, most innocent phases of a teenage love affair. Your kids will run to you in distress and cry for you at night, and you'll feel not just loved but needed, truly important in their life. Even today, I frequently wake to find my little boy curled beside me in bed. "Can you put your arm around me, Daddy?" he'll ask, knowing the answer will never be no.

This, however, is what we generally talk about when we talk about parenting—how it's "wonderful" or "a wild ride!" We don't discuss the manner in which the intense positive and negative

impulses of paternity—of contemporary parenting at large—
revolve around one another as electrons do protons, antithetical
and yet concurrent. Parenting is challenging work because of what
it requires physically and mentally, but also because of these constant contradictions. Alongside the day-to-day joys, you'll find
your attention span wrung out, your intellect understimulated.
Kids demand so much, especially when young. Patience will be
lost and breaking points reached for both parent and child. Inevitably, every man asks himself, *Am I a good father? Or a good enough
father?*

This anthology provides stories of men speaking with unflinching honesty about their experiences as fathers—full disclosure, no
secrets or candy-coating. I turned to twenty-two of our most
beloved and accomplished contemporary male writers to pen these
essays, authors whose work I've reached for before when seeking
both entertainment and something else, something more—
nourishment, let's call it. Grist for thought, octane for the spirit.
Vital, primal stuff. A multitude of voices are included from men
of different ages, with children at all stages of life. Apartments are
made crowded by the addition of a baby, and then rooms go empty
when children leave for college. Taken together, the essays create
a nuanced mosaic of fatherhood, the darks and grays amid the
highlights. No father's story is simple, or monochromatic. But
that's life, isn't it? Especially life with kids.

Though one would rather not be caught in the midst of the
nastiest crisis, here you'll find reassurance that help will appear.
Andre Dubus III takes comfort from his father's wisdom, and
strength from his wife. In Stephen O'Connor's case, a Russian
cabdriver provides advice and, later, lends a hand. For Steve
Edwards, a doctor proves willing to go to extra limits to put Steve

and his wife's minds at ease. These essays illustrate how a father is never alone, whether facing an accident, illness, surgery, or, in Garth Stein's case, buckets of vomit. And while these are the sorts of things you'd like to put behind you, like the winter when Felix was two and caught every germ known to mankind, you may find yourself feeling as Ben Greenman does: recalling things that didn't exactly happen, while the things you expect to remember forever slip away.

What is clear is that having a child clarifies the passage of time, the family line, and a man's sense of himself in the world. A few of the essays, most explicitly Justin Cronin's, address how fatherhood has led to a renewed faith in the divine. Karl Taro Greenfeld finds genetic traits coming into clearer focus, for better and for worse, while Benjamin Percy and Anthony Doerr each consider their own mortality, less with paralyzing sadness and more with a sense of life's great movement.

In other pieces, the guys get into the nitty-gritty of parenting, talking about anger and frustration. Marco Roth struggles to figure out his role as an authority figure in his daughter's life, Bruce Machart would rather do anything than play pretend, and Chris Bachelder loves his daughters but sometimes wishes they would shut up and allow him a moment's peace. In these, one finds the daily struggles amid the many joys of parenting—the fight to keep a sense of self, of independence, of personal space, of private imagination, a semblance of cool, while also being a responsible father. To paraphrase Alexi Zentner's eloquent essay, fatherhood is like learning to breathe underwater. Painful, but not without its pleasures—primary among them laughter. Fatherhood strips a man of certain delusions about himself, some of which Dennis Lehane lists with insight and humor. Though at times, your laughter may be thick-throated and bittersweet, such as when comedian and novelist Bob Smith cracks jokes in the face of his life-threatening illness, ALS, which has taken his ability to speak to his two children.

Several pieces examine the great personal challenges of fatherhood, how, as Darin Strauss writes in the foreword, a man faces failure every day. Lev Grossman and Peter Ho Davies specifically discuss the impact fatherhood has had, or not had, on their writing. In one magnificent sentence, the astute Rick Moody puts his finger on the crisis of contemporary fatherhood, how dads today are asked to play a multitude of roles, some of which seem at odds. Moody's essay, and several others, talk of divorce and separation; and yet the child is never to blame. I challenge you to hear Matthew Specktor telling his daughter how she is the one thing he will not fuck up in his life, and not find your heart swelling with promise for your own child.

For all the obstacles each author faces—and parenthood certainly brings with it a good number of problems and conundrums, the type men and women have never dealt with before, the kind you just can't practice for (because if you could, you probably wouldn't choose to have a child!)—for all the bullshit and heartache, each essay sings of joy and love and of a life lived fully. Spending time with your child, even a boring, snowy Saturday morning in February, leaves you feeling, in Frederick Reiken's words, like "nothing is happening and everything is happening." The world moves so slow and yet too fast, which André Aciman also acknowledges in his contribution. Let the essays here provide a moment to catch your breath, to stop and reflect and commune with the voices of guys who might not know exactly what you're going through, but probably get the gist of it.

I hope that these narratives inspire you to be the best parent you're capable of being, knowing that you'll never be as good as you want to be. Forgive yourself for your failings. Don't let fear silence you. Or frustration cripple you. These may be understandable emotions to feel when it comes to our children, but it's totally useless to hold onto them. Instead of shying away from the fire or becoming consumed by it, tame it, let it reforge you.

After all those years of deploring fatherhood, I can't imagine my life without Felix. My love for him comes from the gut. It's indelible. A constant. Even the most difficult of tantrums, thrown over the smallest of stakes—bedtime, say, or finishing his peas—end in a warm hug. Being a parent is confusing, complex, and challenging, but as Andre Dubus III puts it, "It's as if my deepest, truest life could only begin once I became a father." Amen to that, sir.

On Love and Incompetence

DENNIS LEHANE

Since I had children, trips to the supermarket have become ubi-
quitous. Twice in one day is not out of the norm, the second time
usually to pick up something I forgot to grab the first time; three
times isn't unheard of, usually to pick up something I forgot the
second time. After a recent trip, I pulled a packet of yogurt bites
out of the bag and my wife said, "Um, are those the organic kind?"
My wife and I don't want hormones pumped into our daughters'
bloodstreams from birth, so, embodying every yuppie cliché about
well-meaning, left-leaning urbanites, we usually shop at Whole
Paycheck or Raider Joe's. But I'm also from a working class background where I'm fully aware how much fun *I* would have made
of people like me back in the day, so I'm not above giving my wife
a hard time for her organic obsession, which far outweighs mine.
("I promise these paper towels come from organically cut-down
trees," I'll say, "and this aluminum foil was harvested in a field in
Vermont.") So I'm fairly certain my response to her question about

the yogurt bites fell along the lines of "They're *yogurt bites*. She'll survive a chemical or two this one time." My wife forgot about the exchange and I forgot about it and we moved on to the next phase of our day.

My youngest daughter, Keera, was just short of one. A few weeks later, at a family gathering in a restaurant, my wife and I laid out some food for Keera, and she ate it, as she usually does, two-fisted, shoveling in pieces of cut-up pear and cut-up grilled cheese and cut-up grapes so fast we've been forced to question whether the cutting up can keep up with the speed with which she ingests. We also dug those yogurt bites out of her diaper bag and laid a few out for her. A moment later, when I saw a couple of the yogurt bites heading toward her mouth, I registered a clear and quick thought—*Those seem big, even for her*—and my wife said she registered a similar thought—*The non-organic ones don't melt as well*. (The built-in safety measure of yogurt bites is that they dissolve almost instantaneously once they hit the tongue. Well, the organic ones do anyway.)

So when my daughter, 364 days old at this point, began to choke, my wife and I knew exactly what had caused it. And we knew to remove her from her high chair and bend her forward and pat her back in an upward motion with the heel of a hand. Still, she kept choking. And her eyes rolled back in her head. Then she vomited. And I thought, "Okay, that's good. Vomiting means she's exhaling." And I told my wife this, which worked to calm her down.

But my daughter continued to choke. The color changed in her face, her eyes rolled even farther back, to the whites, and my wife and I exchanged a blink-and-you'd-miss-it look of dire and intimate helplessness. We kept patting our child's back, we kept her pitched forward, we kept doing everything we'd been taught in

Baby CPR class, including tamping the impulse to reach down her throat. And just as we were reaching what felt like a point of critical mass, after which would come the lurch into full-fledged panic, my daughter vomited again. And wailed with fear and outrage and took in copious amounts of oxygen through a suddenly cleared windpipe and then continued to rage against the indignity of her first choking experience.

I say "first" because my older daughter, when she was around the same age, choked twice within one month. Both times the culprit was a grape, which is why her younger sister gets grapes so sliced up they're practically puree. Talk to older parents or grandparents and they say, "Kids choke. You gotta watch 'em." It's the *Shit happens* of the parenting world: Kids choke.

The look my wife and I exchanged during our youngest child's choking episode was one we've exchanged a few times since becoming parents. It's a look so loaded with the worst truths that, within it, I can feel at risk the foundations of everything we are as both a couple and individuals. And that truth is: We don't control anything.

Nada. Niente. Nothing.

If Fate or the gods or God or Lady (Bad) Luck decides to shine unfavorably on you and all you love, there's very little you can do about it.

As a man who reached his forties a resolutely independent, happily childless, responsibility-free being, the experience of becoming a father first at forty-three and then at forty-six has shorn me of any number of delusions. Some of these delusions were minor—*Of course, I can sleep late when I feel like it*—but others were the bricks and mortar of my self-image. Watching my daughter choke and being, if not helpless, certainly limited in my available responses should that fucking yogurt bite (and that's how I'll describe it for the rest of my life) not have dislodged due to our incessant patting on her back, I was stripped of delusion #1:

1. We Have Nothing to Fear but Fear Itself

I'm a big FDR fan, and I've often used this line to buck myself up when attempting something out of my comfort zone. Whenever I've taken risks in my career, in fact, risks that have left many people staring at me in a kind of apprehension and/or befuddled respect. And maybe I grew a little smug, because it's true that creative failure has never frightened me. And if you're not afraid of the things that most people are afraid of—creative failure, heights, snakes and spiders—it's possible to believe you're not afraid of most things.

Since my children were born, I fear everything. At its worst, the fear jolts me awake in the gray just before dawn, heart thumping away. At its best, it lurks, as politely as something can lurk, behind most of my thoughts. I don't see electrical cords anymore; I see electrocution. I don't see dogs walking on the street; I see beasts that could turn feral without warning and launch at my oldest daughter's head, which is often at exactly the same height as their teeth. Cars drive way too fast on all my local streets, and the drivers of those that don't drive way too fast make up for it by texting with their heads down, foot on the gas. In crowds, I see potential predators. In empty spaces, I wait for an unknown mass of something heavy or sharp to drop from the sky. I don't voice these thoughts to anyone, of course, but that doesn't mean they're not there.

I understand the completely contradictory impulse to bring a newborn home and then go out and buy a gun. I understand the impulse to seek safety in the most boring place one can find, severing all ties with a stimulating culture, with multi-ethnic interaction, with the give-and-take of a large metro area that I've always believed "builds character." *Screw character*, the voice in my head says, *just ensure their safety. Even if you have to lock them in a tower.*

On a recent trip, my older daughter, Gianna, accompanied me out onto the fifth-floor balcony of our hotel. She's almost four, well traveled, and knows the dangers of falling from a great height. The railings on the balcony were taller than her and didn't have gaps big enough for her to slip through; even so, I went around and surreptitiously pulled hard on the wrought iron at every conceivable juncture to make sure it was soldered so tightly to the building that the ratio of give was zero. My daughter and I talked about how she was never to go out on the balcony without Mommy or Daddy. At night, I engaged the upper lock on the door leading to the balcony, a lock so high my wife had to stand on her tiptoes to reach it.

The next day, with three adults within arm's reach, Gianna managed to push a foot rest to the rail and stand on it so that she could look over the ledge at the pool below. Was she capable of falling over the railing? No. But she *was* capable of pulling herself over quite easily. The three adults reacted quickly and forcefully as soon as they saw her—*Get down.* But, even so, in what I later judged to have been fifteen seconds, she managed to pull a foot-tall object to the railing of a fifth-story balcony and step up on it.

Just before Gianna was born, a friend of mine told me, "Say goodbye to your peace of mind."

That pretty much sums it up.

2. I Am Cool

I write a lot about people who are far braver than I am. They're usually cooler too, if for no other reason than they have me spending hours to think up their "instantaneous" retorts for them. But I also spent a good portion of my own twenties and thirties cultivating a fairly cool persona. It wasn't all that hard; it mostly involved flashing a soft, wryly amused smile and wearing a lot of dark clothes. It's fairly easy to pull off actually, unless you're lugging car seats, a stroller, and several bottles of formula through an airport security checkpoint, covered in a sheen of flop sweat before you even reach the gate.

My Single Guy Speed Through a TSA Security Checkpoint was somewhere near the George Clooney *Up in the Air* time of a minute-thirty from shoes-off to belt-back-on. But when my daughter drops my hand to take off her shoes too—she doesn't have to; she wants to—and our stroller jams up every piece of luggage on the belt because even though it meets TSA requirements, not every security belt canopy is built to the same height and width, and the woman behind me lets out a sigh louder than a winter gale (even though she clearly saw me, my brood, and all my equipment in the line before she stepped into it), and I set off the alarm because I left my watch on—and Single Guy *never* left his watch on, not in twenty years—and the woman sighs *again*, I realize—

I'm only as cool as my pressures allow me to be.

Or my clothes allow me to be. And the other daughter—the one-year-old—just drooled a combination of milk and quite possibly battery acid all over the shoulder of my once-cool leather jacket. At least I think it's battery acid, because normally milk doesn't burn a permanent mark in leather.

3. I Will Live Forever

Our own death surprises us. Hence the whole cycle of denial that greets imminent news of it. In the back of our minds, we think, *Yeah, yeah, it's gonna happen. Someday. I get that.* But we don't. Not most days anyway. And rarely when we're single.

The moment I held my firstborn in my hands I knew I was going to die. There was no sentimentality attached to it, no woe-is-me. Just this: *Holy shit. I have to provide. Not just for now, but for the rest of her time on Planet Earth.* The veil dropped—I was going to die. On any number of levels, big deal. But it would be a huge deal if I died without my wife and children having been taken care of.

Gianna likes to go into the room where I keep most of my books and play "library." She pulls a book off the shelf, brings it to me so I can check it out with an imaginary stamp on the back, and then goes to hide the book God knows where (the dishwasher once) before returning for another one. I recently pointed out Daddy's books to her. She said, "You wrote all dose?" I said, "Yup," the peacock's feathers rising until she pointed to the novels which happen to fall alphabetically after mine, those of one of my favorite writers, Elmore Leonard. Gianna said, "How come you don't have as many books as him?" Now I was, of course, proud that my almost-four-year-old grasps the written word enough to recognize Elmore Leonard's name repeated on thirty hardcover spines, but I was also dismayed because that's a frightening question if you're thinking in terms of consistently providing for your family. I don't write a book a year. I wish I knew how, believe me, now more than ever. And since my daughters entered the world, I've tried to pick up the pace only to fail miserably because my books simply wither when placed under the duress of hastily chosen words and half-baked structure. And that's all my paltry imagination is capable of if I have only six months or so in which to work.

But, as noted, I won't live forever. And an extra book every four years, say, could make all the difference to my family's future. If I continue to work in sound mind and body for the next twenty years, I'm sure the future will be rosy, yes, but I'm more concerned with the cataclysmic event, the plane that falls out of the sky, the car that skids on the ice, the inoperable and terminal Something Bad.

4. I Am Competent

Over the years, I've managed to convince a surprising number of people that I'm a competent human being. I've done this by playing exclusively to my strengths. You'll never see me publicly attempt anything that I'm not good at, from volleyball to martini-drinking to tai chi. I won't even attempt something I *might* not be good at.

So imagine my surprise when I discovered just how utterly incompetent I was as a husband and father. I was in the parking lot of a Target, waiting for my wife, when my two-month-old firstborn woke from a nap and immediately set to wailing. The binky wouldn't work; neither music nor my touch would chill her out. We were in Florida at the time, in August, where the temperature and the humidity both hovered around ninety-eight, so opening the windows was not an option. And this chick has *lungs*. Banshees travel from far-off lands just to study the movements of her diaphragm. All glass trembles in her wake. Those kind of lungs.

And the only thing that could bring her back from DEFCON 4 in these circumstances was on my wife's person, was actually part of my wife's person, and my wife was in Target. And I'm thinking, *Remember when I used to be cool? Remember when I used to be competent? Remember when some people actually envied me?* Because not only was my daughter not stopping, she had apparently just been warming up. She found a new pitch and celebrated the discovery by reaching for higher decibels. I reached back and gave the binky one more try and she stiff-armed it like she was posing for the Heisman. And SCREAMED.

I turned in my seat, looked out the windshield with eyes widened, I'm sure, by helplessness, and there I saw my wife stepping out the front door of the megastore. The answer to every prayer that had ever passed my lips. And I snatched competency back from the ether. I clenched it. Because one of the few things I'm good at—and it's a small list—is driving. I did it for years, even had a Class 2 truck driver's license before I was old enough to legally drink. I've driven stretch limos, delivery vans, and those shuttle buses you take from airports to the local hotels. When I was a parking valet, driving upward of two hundred vehicles on a given night, I could make cars perform magic tricks, slide them into spaces you couldn't slip a razor blade, without ever touching the brake or readjusting my original path.

So I took competency in hand with my child screaming in the back of my car, and I drove forward toward my wife. What I'd forgotten was that I was angled into a parking space with my wheels pressed against one of those yellow parking barriers; you know the ones—short and long, in the shape of a Fort Knox gold bar. Drove right over the first one and hit one on the other side as well. So that was two parking lot barriers I was perched on. As my wife watched in horror—and, I swear to this day, some amusement—I dragged the underside of our car in a series of spasmodic lurches over two loaves of cement with my baby screaming from the back.

"I don't even know what to say to that," my wife said when she got in the back of the car and took the baby to her breast. "I've never seen you act so . . ."

"Stressed?"

"Dorky."

She followed the description up with a thousand qualifiers, including those meant to paint it as a compliment ("You've normally got it so together that it's nice to see you flail around like normal people"), but I assure you, my wife's seen me flail around too many times for this "compliment" to be genuine.

In the ensuing months, I would prove that my incompetence was no flash in the pan—I overheated bottles, left full diapers sitting atop the changing table, pinched my child's thighs with the seat belt of her car seat—twice—opened the door to the refrigerator when she was just starting to walk and heard a suspicious thump from the other side of the door that made me ask, "Where's Gianna?" a half second before her stunned cry answered the question. I've lost my temper and lost my cool. And I believe I officially lost my dignity when I begged a nine-month-old to just please, for the love of God, just please, please go to fucking sleep.

I have never been worse at anything in my life.

And yet . . .

You'd find it hard to believe from this essay, which concentrates on the internal basket-case me, not the external "I got it" me, but I'm the hands-off parent, the one who lets the girls go hog wild at the playground in the belief that it's through falling that you learn to pick yourself up. My wife is far more protective, far closer to the helicopter parent variety (though she keeps it admirably in check most days).

One of the ways we differ in our parenting lies in our approach to the metropolises in which we often find ourselves. I grew up in the city, my wife in a small town. My love of the urban is manifest and clear to anyone who reads a page of my work or spends ten minutes in my company. When I was growing up, it was common to hook up with your friends, gang-hop the turnstiles and joyride the subway for the day. Sometimes we just spent days running through multi-tiered parking garages downtown because all parking garages of a certain height had great views from the roof and security guards could only catch so many of you. I find myself unable to help trying to engage my girls on this level. I want to show them that kicking a can is almost as fun as kicking a soccer ball or that there's as much wonder to be found staring at a city skyline as at a Hawaiian sunset.

It was with this in mind that during a trip to NYC a couple years ago, I took my eldest daughter into Times Square. She was a few months shy of two, and she loved the lights and the noise and the way the neon reflected off the buildings in a sherbet wash. The traffic was clogged around Times Square that night, far worse than normal, and outside of what appeared to be a convoy of mint-condition, souped-up muscle cars stuck bumper-to-bumper on 48th Street, I couldn't guess what was causing the holdup. Lots of police around, maybe more so than usual, but it was hard to tell. In any case, all those lights, all those buildings, all that vibrancy—my daughter ate it up.

When I told my wife where we'd been, she said, "Is that safe? Times Square?" To which I replied, "It's not 1977 out there, honey. It's practically Disney World."

This version of Disney World, as we discovered the next morning, had been infiltrated by a Kramer jihadist in a smoking Nissan

Pathfinder that was primed to blow up a good section of the block it was parked on. Which was half a block over from the point where my daughter and I had decided to return to the hotel.

So it would seem that strolling your daughter around Times Square the night a terrorist tried to blow it up would be the height of parental incompetence, but I would argue that the terrorist is no different than the great Piece of Unknown that could fall from the sky if I were walking across a meadow with her. It's the Anything Could Happen at Any Time Chunk of Fate that, yes, wakes me up at night and is related to the fear.

But not the competence, or lack thereof. The next time my daughter was in Times Square, she said, "This looks like the place you took me with the girl and boy on the building." It took me a minute to get it—the girl and the boy were the images of Tina Fey and Steve Carell projecting out from one of those three-story-tall, half-block-long neon ads for *Date Night*, a movie they were starring in at the time. My daughter, for clarity, said, "The girl had messy hair." (In the ad, yes, she did, though Ms. Fey has always seemed otherwise perfectly coifed in public.) My daughter said, "Daddy? I like this place."

Which made me feel vaguely competent.

Which lasted right up until I put her sneakers on the wrong feet. And didn't notice until ten minutes later. When she told me.

5. Single Life Is Better

It's always struck me as ridiculous how we, in this society, exalt parenthood to the point that the childless among us are deemed somehow inferior to those of us who choose to have progeny.

Many people who choose not to have children are heroes when compared to people who clearly shouldn't bring children into this world but do just that and make a mess of things. They raise offspring who channel their compendium of issues into violence or white collar robber barony or low class welfare fraud. They help make the world an often terrible place, these maladjusted, poorly or corruptly raised "miracles of life." So those who choose not to propagate that cycle because they fear it's just not something they'd be good at or because, as one childless friend of my mine proudly put it, they "don't like being interrupted," I applaud you.

Having said that and having been a member of that cohort for most of my adult life, the most surprising aspect of parenting has been how much my pre-parenting life looks like a cloud in the rearview. I can't imagine what I ever did there or why I got up in the morning (as opposed to getting up at 3 a.m. to change a diaper) or why I didn't do this sooner. (Well, actually, as to the latter, I know why—I hadn't met my wife yet.)

Recently, on yet another plane, we asked our older daughter to entertain the younger one. My older daughter is endlessly exuberant. Sometimes, this is quite frankly a pain in the ass because high energy without an off switch can wear a middle-aged parent out. But her exuberance is also undeniably charming, if only because it's so pure. She's not a show-off or attention-starved; she simply likes to engage or be engaged. Do so, and what flows out of her is often inspired and definitely interesting most days. So she sat beside her little sister, who's so serene we often wonder where she came from. And Gianna opened up the in-flight magazine, which is mostly filled with glossy ads, and commenced to tell a story to Keera. The doctor in one ad was going home to meet his wife (the woman in the Whirlpool ad), and they were going to drive their car (Mercedes ad) to pick up his mommy (Alzheimer's ad) at her house, where she was looking out the window at her flowers. And then they were going to visit Princess Gianna, who would tell them, uh, some things about pink. Then she looked down at her little sister, closed the magazine, and said, "I love you, Keera. You're my favorite baby I ever had."

Now, a few minutes later, during takeoff, Keera was screaming because of the pressure on her ears, and Gianna was asking why she couldn't watch something on the iPad, and both of them were acting pretty hungry and irritable, and we still had a lovely six and a half hours of air travel to go.

But if the clichéd sentiment to be found here is one my old man was fond of saying—*For all the headaches, I wouldn't trade this for the world*—then maybe clichéd sentiments occasionally have their place. Because, as I watched my oldest daughter tell my youngest a story using nothing but a collection of ads, I felt a pride I never felt in association with my own meager accomplishments. I never knew pride like that existed actually. I never knew love could feel quite this way. And that's worth no longer being cool, no longer being competent, and no longer having peace of mind ever again.

Daughter Pressure

LEV GROSSMAN

It wouldn't literally be true to say that I come from a long line of childless couples, but there's a grain of truth to it. My ancestors did manage to reproduce, obviously. But breeding has never been a major priority in my family. I would even go so far as to say that it's frowned upon.

The definitive story on this subject stars my paternal grandfather, who ran a car dealership in St. Paul, Minnesota. Late in his life he developed Alzheimer's disease, and he forgot that he had a family. My dad would visit him, and they'd have these heart-to-heart conversations, and at the end my grandfather would clap my father on the shoulder and say, "You know what I'm really proud of, Al? I'll tell ya. *Never had kids.*"

Before they retired, both my parents were English professors: my father taught at Brandeis and Johns Hopkins, my mother at Smith and later UC Irvine. They were also writers: my mother wrote fiction, my father poetry—he published about a dozen books of it.

Above all they were both intellectuals: they lived the life of the mind. What mattered to them was reading and writing and art. In our family Samuel Johnson was considered an excellent role model. Beethoven was too—it was a little like being raised by Schroeder from *Peanuts*. Johnson and Beethoven were both admirable men in many respects, but neither of them was especially interested in parenthood. As far as I can tell Beethoven never even had sex.

No one talked about having children. In our family what people talked about was your "life plan." A life plan was, essentially, the stuff you wanted to do before you died, and your success was measured by how closely you managed to stick to it. Music, writing, teaching, politics, travel, money—those were fit subjects for a life plan. Children were not. People who got distracted by children, sidetracked and bogged down and time-sucked by them, had wandered away from their life plans. Therefore they had failed.

My personal hero growing up was James Bond. He was no Samuel Johnson, I'll grant you, but you can't deny that he stuck to his life plan. He had plenty of sex, but if Bond ever got close enough to somebody to even consider marrying them, that person would immediately be killed by SPECTRE before anything so uncool as procreation could occur.

Our family was a bit weird, but I can't help but feel that in some ways we were a reflection of a larger cultural reality. Even as a child I could see that appealing depictions of fatherhood in popular culture were, at least in the 1970s and 1980s, thin on the ground. There didn't seem to be a cool way to do it: fathers were schlubby suburbanites who were either pussy-whipped for changing diapers or assholes for not changing diapers. Fathers were most often seen taking out the trash in sitcoms. They were almost never seen composing works of genius, or walking away from buildings in slow motion as those buildings exploded behind them.

(Not that things were any kind of a picnic for mothers either. I got a strong sense, when I was growing up, that my father blamed my mother for the fact that we children existed at all, and now that we were here, it was up to her to make damn sure we stayed out of the way of his life plan.)

The training took. My brother doesn't have children. Neither does my sister. I never expected to have children either.

Having grown up in a home of, at best, middling happiness, I went on to create a fairly unhappy home of my own. I was married at thirty, and by the time I was thirty-five, my first wife and I were already in a downward spiral. In the middle of that spiral, we had a daughter. I wish I could say that having a child was an act of rebellion against my upbringing, but the unflattering truth is that it was more the result of passivity on my part. My wife wanted a child very badly, and I wasn't sure how I felt about it myself, but I wanted her to have what she wanted, so we had Lily.

My parents hadn't provided me with much of a model for how to be a parent, or for that matter how to be a spouse. My plan for being a father was to act like Christopher Plummer in *The Sound of Music*, all the time.

Lily was born by C-section, so the doctors handed her to me first, all wrapped up in a hospital blanket. Up to that moment in my life I'd had very little contact with children, at least not since I'd been one. I had no younger siblings. I'd never even babysat. With her triangular face and deep violet eyes, Lily looked to me like a tiny alien creature. The most beautiful alien creature I'd ever seen, but still: a visitor from a foreign planet. A planet of which I was now, suddenly, an inhabitant.

I can clearly remember changing my first diaper in the hospital and thinking: That can't be how you do it. It can't. There must be some other way. Surely somebody's cracked this problem. But no. That was how you did it.

One of the first things I discovered about fatherhood was that my father was right: it was hard, and it kicked the shit out of your life plan. I had a full-time job at a magazine, but what I really wanted to do was write novels. That's what was on my life plan. I'd written and published two already, but I wasn't satisfied with them, and from what I could see of my Amazon reviews I had the sense that other people weren't satisfied with them either. I hadn't found my voice yet. My second book had sold well, well enough that the publisher was interested in another one, but it had an oddly chilly quality to it that I couldn't seem to shake. In between the words, there was an awful lot of blank emotional space.

It had been hard to write too—too hard. I'd worked on it for six years, and those years were like breaking rocks. They'd paid off, in the end, but there are books that should take six years to write, and that wasn't one of them.

My wife worked on Saturdays, and before Lily was born I would spend my Saturdays writing my books. Now I spent them looking after Lily. As far as fiction went, my output slowed to a trickle—whatever I could do in the evenings or during Lily's naps. Instead of writing, I changed diapers. I made lunches. I played games. I gave baths. I sang songs. I strapped and unstrapped Lily in and out of car seats. I did all the things parents do. They'd never sounded especially hard; frankly, I'd always thought that parents were a bit whiny about them. It wasn't till I did it myself that I realized that being a parent was harder than anybody let on. The reality was, people weren't whining nearly enough.

It wasn't that I didn't love Lily. I can honestly say that I loved my daughter more than I'd ever loved anyone or anything in my life. But child care reduced me to a state of boredom that was practically hallucinatory. I lived in fear of those Saturdays. The minute my wife got home on Saturday I started in dreading the next Saturday. When— probably as a result of sheer stress—I came down with shingles a few weeks after Lily was born, and the doctor told me I had to minimize contact with the baby for a while, I was actually kind of relieved.

I realize now that I was probably making it harder on myself than I had to. For example, I shouldn't have been trying to take care of my daughter in total solitude. But I didn't have many friends with children, and none of them lived nearby. My wife belonged to a moms group in the neighborhood, and they had playdates and hung out together and chatted about being moms. They liked one another. There was a dads group too, and I would absolutely have joined it, except for the fact that I would rather have died.

It got to the point, six months in, where I was preparing to hold a wake for the writer I had hoped to be. I felt like I'd sacrificed my writing life on the altar of this poor, helpless, weeping little creature. My life plan was screwed. All the time and energy I'd hoped to put into my books, I was putting into meeting Lily's many and varied needs. And I accepted this.

But not gracefully. In fact I started acting out. I became a bad person, or maybe just a worse one than I already was. I recited little assholic monologues in my head, along the lines of Marvin the Paranoid Android in *The Hitchhiker's Guide to the Galaxy*: "Brain the size of a planet, and they expect me to empty the Diaper Genie . . ." I ogled the beautiful moms at the playground, as they squatted and bent over to take care of their offspring. I drank too much. Wine with dinner, then wine without dinner, then binging with childless friends.

Any man who has to take care of a baby while nursing a hangover, on two hours of sleep, deserves what he gets, and I got plenty. It wasn't appealing, and it wasn't sustainable. Something had to give.

What gave, it turned out, was me. Something inside me—the psychic equivalent of R2D2's restraining bolt—snapped.

I noticed it first in my writing. I'd spent the eighteen months before Lily was born working on a vast, layered, galactically ambitious novel, a glittering labyrinth of moving parts and nested stories. An American *Cloud Atlas*, you might say, or that was the idea anyway.

When I came back to my book, after Lily was born, I saw it for what it was: cold, dull, lifeless, massively overthought—a labyrinth with no minotaur inside. I told myself I was just taking a break from it, but the truth was I binned it and started something new. I picked up an idea I'd had years before but hadn't taken seriously at the time, because it was fresh and weird and risky and different from anything I'd ever tried before. Six months after Lily was born, I took a week off from work to explore it, and I wound up writing twenty-five thousand words in five days. I'd hit an artery, and the story came surging out hot and strong. Not only was it the most productive week I'd ever had, I enjoyed it more than I'd enjoyed doing anything for literally years. I was more proud of it than anything I'd done in my entire life.

Something was afoot. I was waking up. Somewhere inside me the emotional pack ice was cracking and melting, ice that had formed long ago in the Fimbulwinter of my childhood, and feelings that I'd been avoiding for decades were thawing out and leaking through, both good and bad: joy, grief, anger, hope, longing. I was like some frozen extrasolar planet, where even gases exist only in neat, handy solid forms. But now I was warming up, and buried things were surfacing.

The cause of this cosmic disturbance was Lily. I didn't see it at the time, probably because I had the emotional intelligence of a sea slug, but it was all her—she was the sun that was warming me. I couldn't stay frozen around her. She wouldn't have it.

I was raised by cool, distant parents to be a cool, distant person, but there's no point in trying to be cool or distant around a baby. There's no point in holding things back. Babies don't hold anything back. They have no filters, and around Lily I was losing track of my filters too. You can't bullshit a baby. Who would even do that? I couldn't bullshit her, and I was losing my ability to bullshit myself. It was as if she generated a weird truth-telling field. Lily set the bar high, as far as honesty was concerned, and I was damned if I was going to disappoint her. There are few worse feelings than disappointing a baby.

For the first time in life I felt like it mattered what I did, and who I was. It was all well and good for me to fuck around and write mediocre fiction when I was just some asshole. But I wasn't just any asshole anymore: I was Lily's father. I could let myself down all I wanted, all day long, year in and year out, but I was damned if I was going to let her down. Any time I wrote a sentence that was less than true I could feel her looking over my shoulder and shaking her head, slowly and sadly: *Come on, Daddy. We both know that's crap.* Having a child didn't make me wise or mature, but it did make me realize how unwise and immature I was. It was a start.

With all the cracking and melting that was going on, there were bound to be some catastrophes—tropical storms, rising sea levels, mass extinctions. And there were. I went to therapy, something that until then had seemed too embarrassing and Woody Allen–ish to me to be even remotely bearable, but suddenly taking responsibility for my mental health seemed more important than avoiding embarrassment. Once I sat up and took a good look at what my life was really like, it was painfully obvious that I had to change it. I realized that I had to leave Lily's mother. I tell myself every day that I did that as much for Lily as for myself—that Lily wouldn't have been happy growing up in a house with two miserable parents who didn't want to be married to each other. I think it's actually possible that I was right.

That was nine years ago. My life now only distantly resembles what it was when Lily was born. Having learned what it was like to love my child—to love anybody, really—and having had tens of thousands of dollars worth of psychotherapy, and a few mood-altering drugs, I got to the point where I was ready to fall in love with an actual grown-up, and I did. I got remarried, for good this time. Now Lily has a younger half sister and an even younger half brother. I've started to think that the business of making new people is actually pretty important—important enough to go on a life plan, even. Because otherwise where would new people come from? My only regret is that my parents never taught me how to be a father, so my daughter had to teach me instead. It's a lot to ask from a little girl. Fortunately, my little girl is tough as nails.

Not only that, she taught me how to be a writer. It took me five years to finish the book I started after she was born, writing nights and weekends and naptimes, but I did finish it, and eventually it was published. It became a bestseller, and the sequel was a bestseller too. In a way, having children did screw up my life plan, well and good. Probably I would have written a hell of a lot more if I'd never had kids. But I would have been miserable doing it, and I'm pretty sure that what I wrote wouldn't have been worth a damn. It wasn't that I'd finally, at long last, found my voice. It's that Lily had found it for me.

First Child

DAVID BEZMOZGIS

Two weeks before the birth of my first child I was seized by an acute attack of abdominal pain. The pain started in the evening and built slowly, like an orchestra tuning up. By midnight it had attained full intensity. I'd had attacks like this before, and each time, when I felt the onset, I held out the faint hope that the pain would subside on its own. It never did. The first time it had happened was in the fall of 2002 when I had gone to New York to meet the editor who had offered to buy my collection of stories. I had spent the night before my return home hooked up to a morphine drip at St. Vincent's Hospital in Manhattan. Over the years, the attacks recurred intermittently and inexplicably. Doctors and friends proposed reasons, none of which sounded convincing to me. I could discern no pattern behind the attacks; they descended like some dreadful force of nature.

That night, not wanting to disturb my pregnant wife, I crept out of bed and went to writhe quietly in another room. Pain is a strange phenomenon, a fact I'm hardly the first to note. It defies quantification, and yet, when you are in the grip of it, you feel an obsessive need to quantify it. It's as though, if you could only fix a value on it, the pain would become, if not governable, at least subordinate to intellect. Gritting my teeth and trying to breathe around the pain, I attempted to compare this attack to other ones. Was this one worse? But recalling pain is even more impossible than quantifying it. Which is why women consent to having second children and writers embark on new books.

I suffered like this for several hours before I finally surrendered and woke my wife. At four in the morning, we were in the car making the ten-minute drive from our house to Mount Sinai Hospital in downtown Toronto. The irony of my pregnant wife rushing me to the hospital did not escape either of us. But since I found it hard to speak or move, let alone laugh, it wasn't as funny as it should have been. For the duration of the drive, and really for much of the night, I contemplated how people lived with extreme pain. I wondered how long I could hold out if I was condemned to my pain indefinitely. Though, more specifically, I thought about my father. Two years before, I had watched him die a tortuous death. He had endured terrible pain with a courage and dignity that made everything the more heartbreaking and unjust. Seeing him in his final days, I understood that I was receiving my father's last lesson. This had taken place at Toronto General Hospital, across the street from Mount Sinai and just south of Women's College Hospital, where my wife was due to give birth. Since my father's death, I had tried to avoid this part of the city. The associations were too raw, too powerful. The mere sight of Toronto General unsettled me. The child my wife was carrying—whose sex we had elected not to know but who we nevertheless believed was a boy—we planned to name in honor of my father.

Previous visits to Mount Sinai had taught me what to expect. Hospital clerks and nurses rarely move with an urgency commensurate to the pain you are feeling. Then there is the interminable period of waiting, spent hunched over and motionless, mentally willing time to move faster.

Eventually, a doctor examined me, took blood, and provided a dose of morphine, which, though it made me throw up, quieted the pain. He then diagnosed me with appendicitis. A scan confirmed it. The whole thing seemed strange to me. Was it possible for a person to have recurring attacks of appendicitis over a span of six years? Strange or not, I was soon being wheeled along a cold corridor toward the operating room. A nurse and an anesthesiologist walked beside the gurney. Trying to sound conversational, I told them my wife was expecting our first child. "Will I be able to pick him up?" I asked. The question—which I'd intended to come across as sober and practical—came out instead sounding panicky and ridiculous. I was assured that I needn't worry about that. My more morbid worries I kept to myself.

A few hours later, I awoke in a hospital room. My wife and mother were there. Later, other relatives came to visit. I was on painkillers and somewhat hazy, but I didn't feel too badly. The next day I was released.

Though the operation had been performed laparoscopically, I wasn't quick to recover. For at least a week, walking was difficult, so was getting up, and laughing doubled me over with pain. What's more, I also contracted a bladder infection, a condition I had previously considered exclusive to women. I'd heard about the couvade syndrome where men exhibited symptoms in sympathy with their pregnant wives—weight gain, fatigue, insomnia—but what had happened to me, at least to my mind, seemed worthy of some sort of special prize.

By the date scheduled for my wife's C-section, I was capable, as promised, of lifting an infant-sized weight. Very early in the morning, at the appointed hour, my wife and I loaded her suitcase into the car and repeated our drive of two weeks earlier—only more calmly. Making the turn into Women's College Hospital, I felt again the grim countenance of Toronto General. And from the other side of the street, I also felt the gaze of Mount Sinai, less grim and more philosophical. Women's College, where nothing had yet happened to us, received us blankly.

Since life seldom unfolds according to plan, it was not until early evening that my wife was taken into surgery. Before I was called in, I waited with my wife's parents and with my mother, who had all arrived by then. From time to time that day, and particularly when I took notice of my mother sitting by herself, looking unnaturally alone, I keenly felt my father's absence. I remembered his words from when he was already ill, how he wished to live to see his grandchildren, to teach them to ice skate. When I thought of the imminent birth of my child, I thought also of my father's words, and of what would and would never be.

In time, I was called into the surgery where my wife, having been given her epidural, was awaiting the grand finale of her nine-month enterprise. A so-called screen—really just a blue hospital sheet—had been draped and clamped in such a way as to conceal most of what was taking place below my wife's waist. I was provided with a chair at the head of the operating table, where I could hold my wife's hand, and be otherwise present. Like a proper modern Western husband and father, I had donned the paper overshoes, scrubs, and shower cap, and brought the digital camera. Other than to be a source of comfort for my wife, my function was to officially announce of the sex of the child.

Of the surgical procedure itself, there is little I wish to say, other than that it demanded more physical vigor than I had expected. At one point, some sort of medieval suction cup device was introduced. The screen, though it obscured much, could have obscured more. And then my moment came. The obstetrician held the child aloft. I rose to gain the proper vantage. I saw a baby, its color a deep violet, its dark hair matted, its mouth open to emit its first cries. I saw the decisive part. "That's a girl," I said, with an undeniable trace of disbelief, so certain had we been—for no rational reason—that we were going to have a boy.

This was our daughter. We named her Mae, according to Jewish tradition, giving her the first initial of my father's name, Mendel.

It is a truism to say that my life changed, but that doesn't make it less so. My life changed in all the predictable ways, but also in one unpredictable way. To mention this change might sound peculiar or trivial in the grand scheme, but I was struck by it. My daughter's birth changed the way I regarded myself, my wife, and much else, but it also changed my relationship to the city I call home. A part of the city that I had come to dread was redeemed for me. The joy of my daughter's birth did not erase the pain of my father's death, but the two became connected, as a namesake is connected to its predecessor, the new joy making the old pain more bearable.

Hurtings

ALEXI ZENTNER

My daughter wants waffles.

I know this because it is 5:14 in the morning and she is in her bedroom yelling the word "waffles," over and over again. Each time she yells "waffles," she says the word differently, as if she is making a meal out of the letters. She tries the word on for fit: *waf*fles; wa-*full*-s; wa*ff*les; wafflewafflewaffles; waf*fles*. It doesn't matter to her that it is 5:14 in the morning or that her mother and I are trying to sleep, or that her older sister, Zoey, is also trying to sleep, or that our dog, Hopper, who has overnight turned into the only living being in our house who seems to get as much sleep as he needs, is curled comfortably at the foot of my bed, his weight an anchor on my body. The only thing that matters to my youngest daughter, Sabine, is this: she wants waffles. I do not want to be awake.

I am awake.

. . .

The tiredness is overwhelming. It has a gravity of its own. I fall asleep watching television. I fall asleep stopped at a red light. I fall asleep reading a picture book to my daughters; I can hear my words slow and slur in the middle of a sentence, my eyes closing no matter where I am on the page, and there is nothing I can do to hold it back. One day, my wife comes out of the bedroom and finds me asleep on the living room floor: Zoey is playing with her doll and sitting on top of me like I'm a beanbag. There are nights when Laurie and I are asleep by eight, by seven-thirty. There are nights when I put one of the girls to bed and I'm pulled into the orbit of her dreams. One second I'm trying to get her to fall asleep, the next second I'm waking up in the middle of the night, her breath on my neck, her hands curled against my face, the heat of her body leaving my shirt damp with sweat.

Worse, still, is the sleep that has been interrupted. My children have stolen my dreams in a very literal sense: I've lost months in the minutes and hours that Sabine and Zoey have needed me at night, their thin, butterfly-beating hearts pushed against me in the darkness. Sometimes there are nightmares or coughing fits or vomiting. I'm brushing my fingers against their hair, their cheeks, telling them that I'm here, that it's okay. I'm pounding on their backs and giving them glasses of water. I'm changing sheets and cleaning vomit from the wall, starting the washing machine because I know I'll need more sheets later. It's two in the morning, and I'm awake to get a bowl for them to be sick into. It's three-thirty, and I'm awake to pick their blankets up off the floor. It's five-fourteen, and I'm awake because Sabine wants waffles. I'm awake.

This is seven years ago, when Sabine is two and Zoey is four and I am thirty-two and a stay-at-home-father, and no matter how tired I am, there are some days when I feel like it is the first time in my life that I am truly awake to the sudden realization that my life is no longer my own.

This is also seven years ago: I am sorting out the last dregs of my father's estate when I find the letter that he wrote to his mistress, complaining that my brother and I were the anchors that prevented him from sailing for new waters. He resented us, he wrote, because we would never let him be truly free. The nakedness of the letter is not a surprise to me. I know about the mistress and know that my father had, at least for a time, thought of her as the answer to the question he had never thought to ask, but the weight of the obligation that he felt for my brother and me comes almost like a physical blow. As I read the letter again, Zoey and Sabine are napping upstairs, and this time I am grateful for the quiet, because I am undone. I am not bothered by the complications of my father's love life, his statement that he never wanted children, or his desire to be unfettered from my brother and me, but rather by the knowledge that the tie binding him to us was strong enough that he could not break it.

It is the early afternoon and my daughters are upstairs sleeping, and I am in the basement reading this letter, and I am fully awake to the understanding that there is at least one thing I have in common with my father. It is the knowledge that I too am tethered to my children. I am anchored.

Now Sabine is nine. On the weekends, if my wife and I are still sleeping, my youngest child will slide out of bed and down the stairs, open the freezer, operate the toaster, and then drown her waffle in an unruly river of syrup. Zoey is almost eleven. On Saturday mornings she fixes herself a bowl of cereal and gets herself ready for swim practice. Laurie and I are allowed to sleep, to read, to do as we please. On the weekdays, the order is inverted and my daughters are the last ones to rise. I'm up at five for a run, Laurie working out in the basement and then getting lunches started. The two dogs that have replaced Hopper tumble down the stairs in a havoc, eating and visiting the yard, and then spending the next hour roaming through the downstairs of the house, alternating between quiet contemplation of the day ahead and the violent, toothed fighting that passes for play between them. By six-thirty I'm back from my run and sitting on the bedside of first one child and then the other, rubbing backs, calling their names, cajoling, trying to ease my children through the barrier between night and morning.

This morning, the girls come downstairs with a grace that I don't deserve. My throat is sore—it actually hurts and will continue to do so for another day—from how loudly I screamed at them the night before. It was the same small thing it always is, which is to say that it was nothing. Coats on the floor instead of on a hook, a door left open for the dogs to run outside, the daily coaxing of homework and piano lessons, and then an escalating fight between the girls over who was reading that book, over which one of them needs to finish cleaning up the mess on the table. It's a small splinter worrying its way into my chest. I spend the evening giving warnings and lectures and the directed consequences and encouragements that are designed to get them pointed in the right direction. I don't even remember what it was that caused me to finally send them to their rooms, Zoey, as always, stomping up the stairs and slamming her door, Sabine crying and saying, as always, that it wasn't her fault, that she had done nothing wrong. These actions are the trigger: I raise my voice to the breaking point, yelling as if that will be enough to make them bend. Later that night, with Laurie home, we sit around the kitchen table and talk of expectations and consequences. Zoey tries to apologize, but I'm still angry and I cut her off.

"I appreciate you saying it," I tell her, "but you are old enough that you need to understand that what you do, what you say, makes a cut. The apology doesn't make it better. The cut still leaves a scar behind. It never fully heals."

This morning, I'm embarrassed to see them. And Zoey makes it worse when she hugs me and says she's sorry, because I remember what I said to her when she tried to say she was sorry the night before. It's not that she or Sabine is blameless in the way she acted, but rather that they are children; they are supposed to make mistakes and then learn from them. I'm an adult; I should have already learned. I hug her back, pulling her tight, and tell her that I am sorry too, and that it is a new day.

Sometimes there is nothing else to do but to say that you are sorry and hope that the scar fades.

Sabine comes into the kitchen, bleary and clutching a blanket, and she leans against me with no thought that I could ever be anything other than a solid presence in her life. I'm reminded of all of the times she has leapt from stairs and ledges and chairs and playground structures and benches and rocks and fallen trees, knowing that I will be there to catch her. They are good kids, Zoey and Sabine. Great kids. Better than I have any right to expect. Both of them smart and curious in ways that stagger me: Sabine making it through the entirety of second grade without missing a word on her spelling tests, Zoey telling me that she wishes she could have an entire day of reading, a day when she didn't even have to put down a book long enough to eat. They can be thoughtful and kind: I'm sick and I wake up with Duck, Zoey's stuffed yellow unicorn—the most precious thing she owns—tucked in next to me on the couch, or I overhear Sabine talking to one of the dogs with a tenderness that I want to believe she has learned from her mother and me. There are moments when I look at one of them and I feel physical pain, an actual ache that travels from the base of my neck through my chest, at how much I love them.

And there are moments when I understand why my father wrote that letter.

I want to explain to Sabine and Zoey that my family has a history of anger. My great uncle killed a man in a bar by hitting him in the head with a glass pitcher. My mother, barely larger than Zoey is now, was a pinched tightness of fury when she felt she'd been wronged, scaring the hell out of men three times her size. My father pinned the second grade teacher against the wall and promised to kill him if he ever grabbed my brother by the neck again, if he ever hurt my brother in any manner.

A friend of mine once told me that I was the most terrifying man she had ever met. I told her that I didn't understand: she knew I'd never done anything worse than level a cutting remark, that I wasn't physically imposing, that she had not seen me do violence or even threaten it.

"But it's there," she said. "I wouldn't want to get between you and the kids."

Her remark startled me, not because I didn't think it was true, but because I thought I'd done a better job of hiding it. I remember my father telling me that my temper was something that I needed to keep a handle on: you can't un-pour boiling water. I also remember my father's advice when it came to fighting: if you can avoid a fight, avoid a fight, but sometimes violence is the only language. Break his collarbone, break his nose, break his spirit, break his will. Use the darkness, use a bat, use a blowtorch. It is probably too obvious to state that my father had a rougher childhood than I did.

I think of his advice when I think of the kinds of savagery I would commit to keep Zoey and Sabine safe. The protectiveness I feel for my daughters can stun me. I do not understand fathers who might hesitate in the service of their family. To threaten my daughters is to declare that the rules of civility have been disengaged. To hurt them is to understand that I am my father's son: start the drill at the back of the kneecaps so the bone splinters when the bit emerges from the front.

And yet. And yet. And yet, while there is nothing I would not do to keep my daughters safe, there is also nothing in the world that can anger me as much as they can. I struggle with that inconsistency, that I would do anything to protect them, but that Sabine and Zoey are also the two people who can most easily make me lose my temper. And worse, the things that anger me are always so small: the repeated inconsistencies of childhood. Zoey getting distracted when she is supposed to be putting on her shoes for school. Sabine complaining that she does not like a food even though she hasn't tasted it yet. Interrupting. Impatience. Impulsiveness. Traits I recognize in myself. Things that every parent recognizes. Behavior that should not make me furious.

This anger, of course, is not something I'm supposed to acknowledge or even write about. It doesn't matter that I have never physically punished Sabine or Zoey and will never do so; just acknowledging how mad I get at them feels like breaking a glass in my hand, and I want to shake the blood and shards to the ground. I can write about my father and the scar on his wrist from when he fought with knives, or about my grandfather and arson, but when it comes to anger and Zoey and Sabine, the specifics spill away. Even here, alone in my office, the words slip through my fingers and all I can do is write in abstractions when it comes to anger and my relationship to them. Father. Daughter. Parent. Child.

Some of my hesitation is simple fear: I know there will come a day when Zoey and Sabine turn to my work to try to understand me, and one of them will come across this piece of writing in the same way that I came across my father's letter. There is no good in this, no sense in trying to explain away the times I have felt angry, the times I have had to swallow down the desire to lash out at one of them, because the truth is that it is not their fault and has never been. The truth is simple and will not salve any wound: I am not as good a father as I want to be.

There is a brutal pleasure to waking up early. Five in the morning and streets are a sea of darkness, street lamps far enough apart that they do little more than serve as waypoints. I'm two miles into my run when it starts to hail, the shards of ice feeling like a windshield shattering in my face with every step. I could do without the hail. I'm running without music, so the only soundtrack is the skittering weather, the slow, heavy slap of my feet. I'm exhausted: Zoey has decided that she is old enough to wake herself in the mornings, but last night she accidentally set her alarm for 1:47 a.m., and I was the only person in the house for whom the alarm seemed to fulfill its intended function. She didn't wake up until I'd already turned the alarm clock off. "Sorry," she said, sitting straight upright in her bed, a sort of tired desperation in her voice, her eyes wide, as if she was unsure if she was still dreaming. "It was an accident," I said. What I didn't say was that I'd told her the day before to stop screwing around with her alarm clock, to set the time and to leave it alone so just this thing wouldn't happen. What I didn't say was that I was angry again. Another night slipping away from me, another night when I'd been fished out of the deep, warm, ocean of sleep. "Close your eyes," I said. "Go back to sleep." She leaned forward and hugged me, and I was startled by how tightly she pulled herself against me. "Sorry," she said again, but this time her voice was quieter, and she lay back down and was asleep before I'd left the room.

I'm running and I'm tired and I'm out of breath and the hail is coming down hard enough that I have a hand shielding my eyes, and suddenly I am fully awake, because I realize what has been bothering me about my father's letter: I can't quite make sense of the dates, but I think when he wrote the letter to his mistress, the letter complaining about how my brother and I were anchors around his neck, his mistress was already pregnant with the half sister whom I have never met. He might have been unable to leave my brother and me to fend for ourselves, but my father apparently had no compunction about leaving my half sister fatherless. A drowning man does not reach for another anchor. What was it that allowed him to walk away from her but kept him tied to my brother and me?

And I realize something else as I'm running: the night before, in the darkness of 1:47 a.m., when Zoey's alarm clock went off and she woke up to find me standing by her bed, she was worried that I'd be angry.

There is a feather of ice on the street, and one car and then a second pass me in quick succession, the first proof that there is anybody else awake at this hour. The hail, which I'd expected to pass, is punching down even harder. It's small and sharp and hateful enough that it's difficult to breathe without choking, and I'm almost exactly halfway through a fifty-minute loop. There is nothing to do but push forward. But I worry that my daughters will come to think of me as someone—like my father—who simply pushed forward because I could not turn back.

Perhaps I am being too hard on myself, and perhaps when they are older they will have no cause to question my love for them. Perhaps they will read this someday and have no memory of me being angry at them, have no idea of me as anything other than a father who loved them as constantly and as calmly as they deserved. Perhaps they already understand why I'm out of the bed at two in the morning, at three-thirty, at five-fifteen. Perhaps I should have written about all of the ways in which I delight in my daughters, how, next to meeting my wife, being a father has been the greatest thing that has ever happened to me.

But as I'm turning the corner, the hail finally loosening up, the idea of home becoming something tangible again, I know that the truth of my love for my daughters is in how my failures hurt me more than anything. To protect my family I could set a match to every other relationship in my life, but that does not mean that every moment of being a father is an easy one. And that's what I hope Sabine and Zoey understand about me: there are certain kinds of hurtings that can be wonderful, and every failure I've had as a father has been worth more to me than every success I had before they were born.

When my father wrote that letter to his mistress, he was angry because he'd discovered that no matter how selfish he wanted to be, being a father was the only relationship from which he could not fully walk away. My brother and I were anchors, and we didn't just keep him from sailing for new lands: we kept his head below the water. What I want to explain to my own children is that I am exactly like my father in that I see them as anchors too, that for the rest of my life my head will be below the surface of the ocean. But what I would also say to Sabine and Zoey is that the difference between my father and me is this: he never understood the joy of breathing underwater.

Nine Times (Among Countless Others) I've Thought About the People Who Came Before Us in My Brief Career as a Father

ANTHONY DOERR

1.

We're in New Jersey, my wife is pregnant with twins, and I'm walking home from the library on a dark and relentlessly cold afternoon. The row of brick-and-siding apartments we live in comes up on my left, originally built as barracks, old railings and old steps, a capsized tricycle in a snowbank, door after identical door, window after identical window, apartments built with GIs in mind, their cigarettes, their wives, their red-white-and-blue children.

I have spent the morning reading about some footprints in Tanzania, seventy impressions fossilized across twenty yards, left by three bipedal hominids trudging barefoot through volcanic ash three and a half million years ago. Two runty adults and someone smaller.

"It is tempting to see them as a man, a woman, and a child," Mary Leakey, who found the footprints, writes. One of the walkers veers to the left momentarily before continuing on.

The spatters of raindrops have been preserved in the mud around the tracks.

A wet day, a volcano erupting nearby, mud pressing up between their toes, and someone—a father?—has a second thought, or stoops to pick up something, or looks back at what has been left behind. Then they're gone.

In New Jersey twenty yards of ice crunch beneath my shoes. I climb our three steps. Through the front window I can see Shauna inside, bearing her huge abdomen from kitchen to couch, her feet swollen bright red, her body stretched to its limits. The two creatures that will be our sons are crammed against the underside of her skin, twisting, she tells me sometimes, like snakes.

I stand in the cold and a flight of geese cruises overhead, honking above the trees, and I think: My sons might see Paris, Cape Town, Saigon; they might get in fights, swim the English Channel, cook banana pancakes, join an army, fix computers. They might kill someone, save someone, make someone. They might leave tracks in the mud to last three and a half million years.

2.

Owen is born with acid reflux and has to be given Zantac every few hours. Henry has to be strapped to an apnea monitor the size of a VCR that squeals like a smoke detector anytime his breathing pauses or the adhesive on a diode slips off his chest. The doctor makes us put caffeine in his milk to stimulate his breathing.

They are five pounds, fraternal, wormy-armed, more blankets than flesh, no eyebrows, no kneecaps, and they need to be fed every three hours: three, six, nine, noon, three, six, nine, midnight. Most nights I take the shift from midnight to 3:00 a.m. I change diapers, fill bottles, listen to the BBC. The traffic light out the back window makes its mindless revolutions, green, yellow, red, green, yellow, red. No cars pass for hours.

One April night, two in the morning, I come out of a half dream on the sofa. Henry and Owen are in their Moses baskets on the carpet beside me. They're lying on their backs, wearing cotton hats, eyes open, neither making a sound, their gazes trained on some middle distance in the gloom. Henry's monitor flashes green, green, green. Owen shifts his eyes back and forth. In the dimness I can watch expressions flow gently across their faces; they assume enchanted, glassy, mysterious looks, then frowns, then their eyes widen. They are partly me and partly their mother, but they are partly strangers, too, tiny emissaries from forgotten generations, repositories of ancient DNA; there are genes in them from Shauna's great-great-grandfather, from my great-great-grandmother. Who are they? They are entirely new human beings, genetic combinations the universe has never seen before and will never see again. They are little brothers arrived from the mists of genealogy to lie in wicker baskets on the floor of our apartment.

As I lean over them, watching, they blink up at me at the exact same second.

3.

We move to Rome, Italy, for a year. I research stratigraphy, excavations, the accumulation of sediment. Mud, ash, sand, pollutants, and bits of architecture rain down over the city at a rate of something like a half inch per year. Emperor Hadrian would have entered the Pantheon by climbing stairs; now we have to brake the big double stroller as we coast down toward it. Today's Romans cannot dig a subway tunnel, swimming pool, or basement without stopping construction to call in archaeologists. In some sites researchers find ten, fifteen, twenty different layers of human settlements.

Emperor Nero built a three-hundred-room, hundred-acre party villa in the first century AD, and fifteen centuries later it had become a series of underground caverns. Renaissance painters used to rappel into the rooms to study the frescoes by torchlight.

On Thanksgiving morning I take Henry and Owen to a Roman landmark known as the Protestant Cemetery. Inside the walls are umbrella pines, box hedges, headstones in clusters. The pyramid of Cestius, a magistrate's tomb a hundred years older than Nero's party villa, looms half inside the walls, its marble-faced blocks mottled with weather and lichen. Crumpled leaves roll across the paths, and big, dusky cypress trees creak like masts.

John Keats, whose grave we've come to see, is buried near the corner. The stone reads:

This Grave contains all that was mortal, of a Young English Poet, who on his Death Bed, in the Bitterness of his heart, at the Malicious Power of his enemies, desired these words to be Engraven on his Tomb Stone: Here lies One Whose Name was writ in Water.

The tombs sleep heavily in the grass. Henry and Owen squirm against their stroller straps. I gaze down rows of memorials into silent corners. We are hemmed by brickwork, ivy, history; we are the only living people in the cemetery. I begin to feel outnumbered. A breeze drags through the trees, the lawn.

On the bus home I hold Owen at the window, put my thumb in Henry's palm. For every living person on Earth, I wonder, how many dead people are in the ground? Do they care that we walk around on top of their heads? Do our ancestors follow us around throughout the day and do they shake their heads at us when we repeat their mistakes?

We get off the bus in Monteverde; I wheel the boys home. In the old cage elevator they smile into the mirror from beneath their hoods. We rise through the stairwell. Owen reaches for the bakery bag in my fist. Henry fumbles for the keys.

I heap the boys onto their mother. They laugh and laugh. We eat croissants; we drink pineapple juice from a box. Yesterday, Shauna tells me, Owen clapped his hands twice. Henry can now roll halfway across the room.

It is a strange thing to bring five-month-old twins to a city stamped so indelibly with age and ruin. Every street corner rings with decline; decay of republic, disintegration of empire, the ongoing crumble of the church—decay is the river that runs through town, driving along beneath the bridges, roiling in the rapids beside the hospitals on Tiber Island. And yet nearly everyone we pass smiles at the twins. Grown men, in suits, stop and crouch over the stroller and croon. Older men in particular. *Che carini. Che belli.* What cuties. What beauties.

In the States, practically every time someone would stop us on the street or in the grocery store, they'd gesture at the stroller and say, "Twins? Bet you have your hands full." They'd mean well, of course, but to be reminded of something you can't forget is debilitating. I prefer the Italian mothers who lean over the stroller and whisper, "So beautiful," the smiles of passing children, the old Roman who stopped us today outside the cemetery and grinned at Henry and Owen before shaking my hand and saying, with a half bow, "*Complimenti*." My compliments.

4.

We take our sons to Sardinia for a week. Early May is early for tourists, and everything is closed and hardly anybody is on the beaches. The big resort hotel below our rented condominium is completely empty, just a lonely bartender named Claudio and a white stretch of beach and the wind blowing our footprints into dunes.

Henry and Owen are fourteen months old; they run laps in the sand, half-drunk with the pleasure of such a forgiving surface, tipping past us and cackling, "Go, go, go." Around and around they go, carrying their Legos or water bottles or balls, wiping out every twenty or thirty seconds. Shauna lifts them, kisses them, brushes them off. In a heartbeat they are running again.

Despite some telephone wires and the little hotel, this still seems like a place the first Sardinians would recognize: the flies, the thorns, the big granite hills crumbling and baking all day, the hours folding over the inlets like fog; the stars and sea, the caps of the rocks that show themselves at low tide before going under again—all of it has been here since before any of this had a name, and all of it will still be here after the names are forgotten.

Gulls soar hundreds of feet above us, like confetti. The sun swings over the hills in a low, smooth arch.

Inside, Claudio makes us caffè lattes, hot and foamy and perfect, and he wheels a little round table toward the boys with great ceremony and busies himself filling tiny coffee cups with foamed milk and sprinkling chocolate on top. The boys sit strapped into their backpack carriers and show varying degrees of interest. Mostly Henry just wants the spoon so he can drop it and hear it clink on the tile and then peer down at it and say, "Uh-oh."

In the evening we carry our boys up the hill to their port-a-cribs, and the maquis fills with night sounds: the wind, some insects, an owl. A herd of goats tramps along the cape road in the darkness, and their wooden-sounding bells clank softly.

After everyone is asleep, I hike back down to the abandoned hotel for a drink and tell Claudio that his resort is very beautiful. I am his only customer. He shows me a snapshot of his daughters, who live on the other side of the island, in Alghero, an hour and a half away. They are two and four years old, one blond, one dark.

We grapple forward in my sledgehammer Italian. Claudio's father was a fisherman. He does not like George W. Bush. He sees his wife and daughters one day a week.

"Is this common?" I ask.

"It is Sardinia," he says, and then says more, but I don't understand it. I nod anyway. Claudio chews his lip, and folds and refolds his bar towel into a perfect white square.

"Is it difficult?" I ask. "Not seeing your daughters?"

He nods, and I nod, both of us at the limits of our fluencies, and we look up at the TV, where two Indian men wrangle a cobra into a basket. When I look back at Claudio, tall and trim in his vest and collar, there are tears on his cheeks.

5.

We move back to the United States. Idaho. Suburbs, exurbs, brown foothills, and long-drawn skies. Welcome to America. In our first week back I drive to six ATMs, a bank, and a check-cashing agency; I spend an hour on hold with someone in a magazine subscription department; I wait two hours on the leather sofa in a car dealership to get a check engine light turned off in our car.

We buy a house with a slate stone fireplace. One crystalline, frosty night, when they are not quite two years old, Henry and Owen refuse to go bed; they sprint laps around the family room singing, "Chasing! Chasing!" and Owen chants, "Jump, jump!" and they grab opposite ends of a dog leash and perform short-lived matches of tug-of-war. It is after 8:00 p.m. when Owen jumps off the sofa, trips, and strikes his forehead hard enough against the fireplace that a piece of stone, the size of a dime, chips off. The sound is that of dropping a small block of wood onto a concrete floor.

Shauna has Owen in her arms in an instant. His screams are loud and edged with fear: a new kind of scream. The fireplace has gouged a hole in his forehead just below his hairline—it is the size of a paper clip and a quarter-inch deep. There is enough blood that by the time we have strapped Owen into his car seat every square inch of a dish towel we've clamped over the wound is wet.

We drop off Henry at his grandmother's. The examination room at the hospital is glaring, fluorescent. Owen is brave. A nurse numbs his forehead. Teletubbies wander across a television mounted in the corner. The doctor says it is good news that Owen did not get knocked out. He checks his eyes, his ears; he says our son is going to be fine.

There is dried blood on Shauna's hands, arms, and T-shirt. I'm thinking how lucky we are; I'm thinking about cholera, dysentery, fevers, oxcarts, and open wells—all of history's child destroyers. If you had a baby in Chicago in 1870, there was a 50 percent chance he'd die before he reached age five. If you had a baby in London in 1750, there was a 66 percent chance he wouldn't make it to five. For the entire history of humanity, except for the past, say, eighty years, parents were losing every other child. You get to keep Henry, but Owen's got to go. That's how things were for Phoenician dads, Babylonian dads, Aztec dads, Cherokee dads, for pioneer dads, and for caveman dads. The earth brims with the bones of children.

Just two days before this trip to the emergency room, Shauna was watching the boys play with ice in the backyard when she turned to me and said, "If we lost them now, after getting them this far . . ."

Instead of a needle and thread, the doctor uses superglue on Owen's forehead. One gloved hand pinches the wound, the other floods it with epoxy. Owen watches the Teletubbies, holding his mother's finger in his fist.

Afterward, we drive home in the frozen darkness and pet the dog and scrub the blood off the kitchen floor and put our son to sleep next to his brother.

6.

A brown disk of glue clings to Owen's forehead for months. When it finally peels off, the scar beneath is smooth and forked and pale. He and Henry turn two; they become muscular, long-haired, frighteningly smart. Their enthusiasm for the world astounds.

Everything warrants investigation: spiderwebs, thorn bushes, potato bugs. They crouch in our driveway, poking strips of sun-softened tar with their fingers.

"Boys," I say, "let's go. I've told you three times." I stand over them, clap my hands. "You guys need to learn how to pay attention."

They don't even bother to look up. Usually I would grab them, wrestle them into the car. But today I pause. Whoever says adults are better than children at paying attention is wrong; we adults are too busy filtering out the world, hurrying to some appointment or another, paying no attention. Our kids are the ones discovering new continents all day long. Sometimes, looking at them, I feel as if Henry and Owen live permanently in that resplendent state of awareness that grown-ups only reach when our cars are sliding on ice through a red light or our airplane is thudding through turbulence.

The boys drive their fingers deeper into the tar, then pull back and laugh as the tar rebounds to its original shape. They try jabbing sticks into it; they take off their shoes and press their toes into it. I try to imagine my great-great-grandfather at age two. Did he also think poking at tar—or squishing palmfuls of mud, or throwing pebbles into a creek—was the greatest pastime imaginable?

Eventually, I coax the boys into the car and drive them to a park and release them like hounds into the grass. They sprint toward the playground equipment and yell, "Running! Running!" As I watch them, the shadows of leaves flicker over the grass and the afternoon seems so precious that I wonder, only partly in jest, if I ought not to spend the rest of the week doing only this: watching my sons, watching the light falling through the trees. As if every minute spent doing something else would be a minute wasted.

7.

Soon Owen and Henry talk in complete sentences, carry back-packs to preschool, and want to know if the Elks Hospital is a hospital for elk or for "big people." And they have passions, hundreds of them: Tinkertoys, Gwen Stefani, puddle stomping, garden tomatoes, floor puzzles, ice cream, Elmer's glue. They find letters of the alphabet everywhere they look: Os in noodles, Ts in bathroom tiles, Xs in the poos our dog drops in the grass.

At work, as a kind of procrastination, I start reading Herodotus's *Histories*. Here he is on the Egyptians:

> When the rich give a party and the meal is finished, a man carries round amongst the guests a wooden image of a corpse in a coffin, carved and painted to look as much like the real thing as possible, and anything from eighteen inches to three feet long; he shows it to each guest in turn and says: "Look upon this body as you drink and enjoy yourself; for you will be just like it when you are dead."

An hour after I read that passage, I learn that Henry and Owen's great-great-aunt Dorothy has died. I spend the next few days thinking of Dorothy, who loved to sift through waist-high stacks of mail-order catalogs, who walked at the mall on winter mornings with her friends, who had a gold Saturn SL2 with six hundred miles on it. Who was childless but must have had some love stories folded tight inside her heart. What men loved Dorothy Lyskawa? Certainly some: She wore trim dresses and stylish skirts and crimson lipstick and worked as a secretary at Owens Corning and would pile onto the corporate plane and take notes at meetings and then rove New York City with her friends. And yet she stayed unmarried, lived in Toledo, Ohio, all her life, the gray Februaries and the big, brown Maumee sliding along beside the glass factories.

Again I wonder: Is there a heaven? Some place where our lost relatives peer down at us from the fleecy rims of clouds and know our hearts? And know one another's?

What's the alternative? That when we die all our stories disappear? Are our private lives so inconsequential?

Maybe consequence is something you have to create. Consequence is doing something like Aunt Dorothy did in the first years after my grandfather died, before I was born, when my mother and father lived in Mentor, Ohio, with two babies and one car and no money and Dad wore homemade suits to sales training sessions and Mom rode a bicycle with both kids to get groceries. Dorothy would slip Mom a twenty-dollar bill every time she visited. And twenty dollars, my mother says, "bought a lot of groceries back then."

Dorothy never got to see Henry and Owen.

8.

Shauna signs up our boys for Dance Camp. The evening after the first day, Henry breaks his arm in two places. Without his twin brother, facing down the enormity of Dance Camp by himself, Owen spends the entirety of Day Two with the front of his polo shirt clenched in his teeth. He hides on the outskirts of the activities, trying but failing to follow directions. He tiptoes through the songs, shy, afraid, the front of his little shirt dark with saliva and wrenched into wrinkles. Twice he is sent to the "growing line" for talking when he shouldn't.

Owen and Henry haven't spent a night apart since conception, and as I watch Owen chew his shirt to a pulp I wonder what his life would be like if his brother were permanently removed from it. Doesn't every little twin assume—wrongly!—that the world must naturally contain his twin? And on what awful day do they learn that the truth is the opposite?

"Even lovers," Annie Dillard writes, "even twins, are strangers who will love and die alone."

After snack time, with a half hour to go, the dance-campers take a walk around the block. And though there are probably twenty kids in the class, Jon Jon, one of the instructors, a kind-faced drummer with a beard and ponytail who already seems to know every child's name, makes a point of finding Owen and holding his hand.

Jon Jon and Owen start off at the back of the column of children, Jon Jon leaning over now and then to hear if Owen has anything to say.

When they come back, Owen hugs my leg. His shirtfront is twisted and wet, but it is no longer in his teeth. Jon Jon smiles. "He reminds me of my son," he says. "He notices everything."

9.

It's September. I'm sitting with the boys in loungers at the neighborhood pool. They are three and a half years old. We're eating Wheat Thins. Twenty hours ago their drum-playing dance-camp instructor, Jon Jon, had his whole, unknowable, interesting life abbreviated to two sentences:

Thirty-three-year-old Jon Stravers of Boise, Idaho, was driving the sedan. He and three-year-old Jonah Stravers were both killed.

Henry says, "You always say the pool is warm when it is cold, Daddy."

It's on my mind again, our ancestors, Mary Leakey's footprints, Keats's epitaph, Herodotus's Egyptians, the appalling brevity of our lives. We twist and swim and fold back into the invisible; our names are written in water.

How could the world possibly be better off without Jon Jon? How could anyone ever argue that his was a superfluous life? And what about Jonah's life, and shouldn't a prayer be sent up, too, for the now-ended twenty-six-year-old life of Bryant Hays of Sussex, Wisconsin, who (investigators suspect) had some alcohol or drugs in him and sent his pickup, grille-first, across the eastbound lane and into Jon Jon and Jonah's sedan?

There are so many lives that deserve prayers in this: Jonah's mother, Jon Jon's parents, Bryant Hays's parents, the woman who might have poured Bryant Hays his beer that night, who might have delayed his departure four or five seconds by dropping his change: a quarter and a nickel and a penny rolling down the wood floor behind some bar. "Sorry," she might have said, "Wait one second," she might have said, and that one second might have been enough—enough to set Bryant Hays on his ruinous trajectory: father and son, Jon Jon and Jonah, hurtling east along a mountain highway, Bryant Hays climbing into his truck, turning the key, starting west.

All those lives, all those people—each of us operates at a vertex of a vast, three-dimensional, crisscrossing network of relationships. Son, brother, husband, father, friend, teacher. No life is superfluous. And yet thousands go out the door every hour.

Look upon this body as you drink and enjoy yourself; for you will be just like it when you are dead.

There goes Mary Leakey's family of three; there goes John Keats; there goes Aunt Dorothy; there goes Jon Jon Stravers and poor, sweet, three-year-old Jonah. The great network vibrates and swings as lives are plucked out of it, one after another.

When you watch your kids begin to grow up, you cannot help but feel your impermanence more acutely; you cannot help but see how you are one link in a very long chain of parents and children, and that the best thing you have ever done and ever will do is to extend that chain, to be a part of something greater than yourself. That's really what it means to be a father—to be continually reminded that you are taking part in something much larger than your own terrifyingly short life.

A reef of clouds builds in the west, so gray they look almost black. Owen finishes his Wheat Thins and takes the pool key off our lounge chair and walks barefoot across to the gate and stands on his tiptoes while he tries to work the key into the lock.

Henry says, "I love Wheat Thins, Daddy," and crunches another one, spilling crumbs across his towel, and the wind blows into the valley and the sun slinks down into reds and purples and the sky takes on that deep, clarion blue of a September evening and we pack up our towels and swimsuits and walk home as the first cold air of the season slides down from the mountains.

You Can't Put Your Arms Around a Memory

BEN GREENMAN

1.

What is being a father? This is only the beginning. I remember thinking that when my wife had my first son, and then I thought it again when she had my second son. The first time it seemed unconditionally true. The second time it seemed strategically true. Whenever anything would happen with either of my sons—first word, first injury, first genuine insight, first legitimate dispute—I would think it again. This is only the beginning. It is rejuvenating to locate yourself near the start of things, whether a child's life or an essay. There is so much left to do. There are so many chances to get it right. The thought that you might also get it wrong flits across your mind for a moment at most, but it's gone before you can even shiver at its presence.

2.

What is being a father? Being a father is, at least in part, about beginning. But it's also about returning to that question repeatedly, asking it again and again, each time failing to acquire any additional insight. In that sense, being a father is being a question: discussion is opened, remains active, is filled in at the same rate that it's emptied out. Being a father is not a statement, at least not at first.

3.

"What is being a father?" isn't the same question as "What isn't being a father?" That's a statement, and a true statement. "What isn't being a father?" is a better question, perhaps, because it can be more readily answered. Being a father isn't indifference, certainly, but neither is it a steady stream of calm wisdom, or a place of consistent self-control, or a clearly delineated set of exercises engineered to help produce self-knowledge in offspring. Bridges are engineered. Children are worked toward, clumsily, imperfectly, with a deep and almost religious faith in trial and error. Children are refined over time with the assistance of many imperfect philosophies.

4.

Philosophies locate causes. Being a father is caused, at least initially, by that moment when the woman with whom you have shared some time comes to you with news. If you are especially lucky, she has already told you that what is about to happen is about to happen. Maybe she has invited you to go with her to the drugstore to purchase a small plastic device that can, when desecrated temporarily, detect the presence of new life. Maybe she has gone by herself. Whatever the case, that tiny round indicator indicates indisputably that a moment has occurred.

But a moment is not the moment after it. The tiny round indicator is a thing always in-between, not just an idea anymore but also not yet a fact. It is a piece of punctuation that operates both like a period and a comma: a full stop to one part of your life but also just a short pause before the rest rushes in. Many couples save that small plastic device. Ours is still in our medicine cabinet, oddly self-erasing, a reminder of something that we assumed, wrongly, would never need to be recalled to us. We thought we'd remember everything forever. I can't even remember why we thought that.

5.

Once my wife was reading a book. "Will I remember anything about this book?" she said to no one in particular. Her tone was airy and without judgment. It was simple curiosity on her part: would the book remain with her at all? A child, at least initially, seemed like it existed on the opposite side of the world from that question. How could you forget anything? You count fingers and toes. You run your fingers over the bottoms of feet thousands of times, just to remind yourself that they are there, and round, and soft like pads. You stare into eyes, beaming thoughts that you hope are received, translated, and appreciated. You stare into eyes, waiting for a beam to come back to you.

6.

Once, my wife was not reading a book. We were standing at the doorway to the room we had prepared for our first child. We had bought some furniture for the tiny bedroom located off of our kitchen and painted the walls white with blue trim since we knew it was a boy. He was due in late March, but as April rolled around, with nothing doing, she got angrier and angrier. She closed cabinets harder than was necessary. About two weeks after the official due date, my wife went into the hospital and came out a mother, which I remember thinking made me a father. Some late-night show was on television when my son was born. The host made a joke about the weather, and then a joke about how his joke about the weather was lame. A nurse handed me a baby. I went to get my wife some ice cream as a reward. This is like a scene in a book in the sense that I don't remember much more than that. It's a series of pictures, each held too long but not quite impressed upon the viewer, a movie run just fast enough so that the film does not melt against the projector bulb but not fast enough to seem like real motion.

A few years later, my second child opted in. He was even earlier than the other one was late. He was born small and squinted like he was angry. One of those things has persisted. When he came home after a week in the Neonatal Intensive Care Unit—they kept him until his lungs matured—my wife and I compared baby pictures of the two boys. "They look different," I said. She shook her head. "That's not why I'm looking at them," she said. "I want to remember this." I remember looking at the pictures with her only because she has told me about it. In my memory of it, I see myself from a short distance, sitting on the couch next to her. This is how I know it is not really my memory. On my desk at work I have those same pictures that she tells me we looked at, and I often challenge myself to see if I can locate the boys they have become in those smiling, round, unknowing faces.

7.

The other day, I was walking in Brooklyn, and I stopped on the sidewalk to let a baby pass. This happens more often than you would think. About fifteen seconds later, a man came rushing through, calling the baby's name, which I will not reveal so as to protect the very innocent. The baby turned, gave a half wave, and promptly sat down hard. He looked as though he might cry, but he did not even whimper. He waved again. The man, who I am guessing was the baby's father, turned to me before he went to collect his son. "You know how it is," he said. He was playing the odds, I guess—I didn't have either of my children with me, but I am a man of a certain age in a certain part of Brooklyn, so statistically speaking, I know how it is. The man picked up his baby, who was laughing a little now, and I continued down the street.

When I got home, I told my kids the story. My older son, who is twelve now, took it in stride. He's aware that there are babies walking around in the world, and that more often than not they fall down. My younger son is still more preoccupied with the idea of himself as manifested in others. He was in the other room but ran down the hall with a question burning in his mouth. "Dad," he said. "Dad. Dad. Do you remember when I was that size? When I was a baby? Did I ever do that?"

"Every baby does," I said. "I remember once you fell down the last step of our stoop. We thought you would be hurt, but you bounced right up like a rubber ball. I came to get you and you were brushing yourself off and you looked like you didn't need any help." My younger son laughed, sounding remarkably like the boy on the street.

"How old was I?" said my older son, sounding remarkably like my younger son.

"I don't remember that," my wife said.

"Sure you do," I said. But she was right and I was wrong. It may have happened, but I had no specific recollection of it. I had invented the memory because it plausibly resembles the experiences that fatherhood contains. "You remember," I said again, lowering my brow a little to suggest disfavor with the way she was forgetting.

8.

If, in part, fatherhood is remembering things that did not exactly happen, it is also forgetting things that did happen. Some of those things that happened are—or rather, were—transformative to a degree that I could not have imagined five seconds before they occurred. After they occurred, I knew I would never be the same again. But I was.

Children are not the same again. When you do not have babies any longer, you have boys and girls. That last sentence is among the most obvious that I have ever written, except that it is also filled with nuances that can barely be captured by language. When babies become boys or girls, they are exposed to the world in a new way, both more promising and more dangerous than before, and they have a greater need than before for both your intervention and your nonintervention. What is being a father? Whatever it is, it's something different than it was. Parenting boys instead of babies is already a grand departure from everything I have learned up until now, an island set off from all the expertise I idiotically imagine I have amassed. And I am just coming to see that it will be this way always, that parenting is an archipelago rather than a peninsula. I have a friend with a baby, and another friend with a grown son, and neither of them is doing anything even close to what I am doing. We give one another advice or support, but it is as if we are comparing warranties for entirely different products. The other day I was talking to the friend who has a baby, and in the course of talking to her, I was remembering again how little I remember about my years spent living the life she is now living. Of all those days spent lifting spoons to their mouths, of all the nights spent rubbing their heads until they fell asleep, of all the weekends spent holding them up to zoo cages or transporting the contents of stories from my brain to theirs, I remember only a few moments. When my older son was about two, I had him in a coffee shop, and he was playing with a machine that dispensed coffee beans. "Don't do that," I said. "Don't put that bean in your mouth." I turned away. When I turned back a second later, the bean was gone. "Come on," I said. "I thought I said not to put that in your mouth." He shook his head and pointed at his nose. Then he shrieked and cried the whole way home until I could grease the inside of his nose with Vaseline and squeeze the bean out from the top down. It fell on the counter and he was immediately fascinated with it again. When my younger son was just able to run, he ran full-speed into an iron ladder, smashing up his chin and putting a tooth cleanly through his lower lip. My wife was not there. I was having lunch with a friend of mine. My friend, who did not yet have children of her own, was greatly displeased by the brightness of the blood. My son cried until he heard me speaking calmly to my wife on the telephone, at which point he stopped. We got him some butterfly Band-Aids at the store, and I carried him home on my shoulders. I remember those things like photographs I am looking at now, but otherwise there is a large and unrecoverable set of joys and pains associated with that time that has gone by me like a purposeful vehicle on a narrow one-way street. I feel only the wind of the thing as it passes and soon enough I can't even feel that.

9.

I asked my sons about this recently. I was trying to figure out what fatherhood is. Someone had asked me to write an essay. I told them that I wasn't especially interested in the tasks associated with it, or for that matter the meaning of it. Those are things that we either do without thinking or that we think about forever. I was interested in that middle zone again, the place of change, when a man who is not a father becomes a man who is a father. "You know what's weird?" I said to my sons. "Even though I know it's changed me forever, I don't remember very much of it. I remember certain things that happened, but not as many as I would have thought." My older son had an explanation immediately. I saw it pop into his head. That's the way he is: thoughtful at a high velocity. "Maybe it's because you are thinking of us more than yourself. Maybe you want time to pass so we can get to the next thing in our lives." This was true, and not true. Or rather: it required some careful consideration. Was he saying that I didn't want to remember things because that fixed those scenes, and the people in them, in time? Was he saying that forgetting was a vital part of the process of moving forward? My younger son had been standing a short distance away, acting like he wasn't listening, but then he turned and meanly delivered a one-liner. That's the way he is: a sniper. "The problem is that you think it's parenting when really it's childing," he said. I laughed at the rhythm of the remark more than the sense of it, and only later really thought about what he had said. The sniper was right. What is being a father? It's letting someone else be a child. It's suffering through certain kinds of abstract pain so that they don't. It's bearing the brunt of disappointments so that they can go on feeling invincible. It's teaching how to forget as much as it is teaching how to remember. About a week after that discussion, the younger one came to me and said "Why were you asking us that yesterday?" I told him about the essay but also told him that it was not yesterday. "Sure it was," he said, smiling like he knew he was wrong and didn't care or knew I was wrong and did. The two of them went downstairs to play basketball. I watched out the window. The little one stumbled and fell. He came up smiling, under his own power, self-possessed but also still possessed by me. They were gone for what seemed like too long. Time passes happily for the young and somewhat less happily for the somewhat less young. Time accumulates as a mass inside the mind when you know how much it can weigh. Eventually the young will watch the less young pass into time. But this is still very near the beginning.

Empty Rooms

ANDRÉ ACIMAN

The doors to their bedrooms are always shut, their bathroom always empty. On weekends, when you wake up in the morning, the kitchen is as clean as you left it last night. No one touched anything; no one stumbled in after partying till the wee hours to heat up leftovers, or cook a frozen pizza, or leave a mess on the counter while improvising a sandwich. The boys are away now.

Two decades ago there were two of us in our Upper West Side home. Then we were many. Now, we're back to two again.

I knew it would happen this way. I kept joking about it. Everyone joked. Joking was my way of rehearsing their absence, of immunizing myself like King Mithridates VI, who feared being poisoned and learned to take a tiny dose of poison on the sly each day.

Even in my happiest moments I knew I was rehearsing. Waiting for my eldest son's school bus, standing on the corner of 110th Street and Broadway at 6:20 p.m. while leaning against the same mailbox with a warm cup of coffee each time—all this was rehearsal. Even straining to spot the yellow bus as far up as 116th Street and thinking it was there when in fact I hadn't seen it at all was part of rehearsing. Everything was being logged, nothing forgotten.

When the bus would finally appear, the driver, an impatient Vietnam veteran, would dash down Broadway, either squeaking to a halt if the light was red before 110th or hurtling across to 109th to let some of the students out. The bus, from Horace Mann, trailed the one from the Riverdale Country School by a few seconds every evening, with the suggestion that perhaps something like a reckless race along the Henry Hudson had taken place between the drivers. I'd remember that, just as I'd remember the reedy voice of the beggar squatting outside Starbucks, and my son's guarded squirm when I'd hug him in view of the schoolmates who watched from the school bus window.

By late November it was already dark at 6:00 p.m. As always, coffee, mailbox, traffic. Our ritual never changed, even in the cold. Together, we'd walk down 110th Street and talk. Sometimes we needed to buy something along the way, which made our time together last longer. Sometimes we made up errands to avoid reaching home too soon, especially after Thanksgiving, when all three sons and I would walk over to the Canadian Christmas tree vendors and chat them up about prices. And sometimes I'd tell my eldest that it helped to talk about the day when we wouldn't be able to take these walks together. Of course, he'd pooh-pooh me each time, as I would pooh-pooh his own anxieties about college. He liked rituals. I liked rehearsing. Rituals are when we wish to repeat what has already happened, rehearsals when we repeat what we fear might yet occur. Maybe the two are one and the same, our way to parley and haggle with time.

Sometimes, in late fall, these days, when it's not cold but already dark, and the feel, the lights, and the sound of the city can so easily remind me of the bus stop at 6:20 p.m., I'll still head out to 110th Street and stand there awhile and just think, hoping it might even hurt.

But it never hurts. Partly because I've rehearsed everything so thoroughly that scarcely an unchecked memory can slip through or catch me off guard, and partly because I've always suspected there was more sentiment than feeling in my errands to 110th Street.

Even with the eldest son just gone to college, email and cell phones kept him present at all times. Besides, while he was a freshman in college, his twin brothers still lived at home and would continue to do so for two more years, shielding me from his absence. Together the twins and I still walked by the tree vendors on 110th Street and still put off buying anything until it was almost Christmas Eve. Things hardly changed. We removed one leaf from the dining table, my eldest's dirty running shoes disappeared from our hallway, and his bedroom door remained shut, for days sometimes. Life had become quiet. Everyone had space. In the morning, in freezing weather and on his way to class in Chicago, he always managed to call. A new ritual had sprung.

Then one day, two years later in September, the twins left as well. Suddenly a half gallon of milk lasts eight days, not just one. We don't buy sausages or peanut butter or stock all manner of cereals that have more sugar than wheat. There is no one to rush home and cook for, or edit college applications for, or worry about when they're not back past 3:00 a.m. No sorting though dirty socks, no mediating the endless bickering about who owns which shirt, no setting my alarm clock to ungodly hours because someone can't hear his alarm clock in the morning, no making sure they have twelve No. 2 pencils and not just two.

All things slow down to what their pace had been two decades earlier. My wife and I are rediscovering things we didn't even know we missed. We can stay out as long as we wish, go away on weekends, travel abroad, have people over on Sunday night, even go to the movies when we feel like it, and never again worry about doing laundry after midnight because the boys refuse to wear the same jeans two days in a row. The gates are thrown open, the war is over, we're liberated.

Months after they'd left, I finally realized that the one relationship I had neglected for so many years was none other than my relationship with myself. I missed myself. I and me had stopped talking, stopped meeting, lost touch, drifted apart. Now, twenty years later, we were picking up where we'd left off and resuming unfinished conversations. I owned myself.

One evening, while preparing dinner with my wife, I went a step further and realized I had committed the unmentionable: I had stopped thinking of the three persons who are still dearer than life itself. I did not miss them and, stranger yet, hadn't thought of them all day. Is the human heart this callous? Can out of sight, out of mind apply to one's children as well? Really?

I was almost ready to pass the cruelest verdict on myself when I suddenly came across something I could never have foreseen, much less rehearsed. A young couple with twins in a stroller was crossing the street in a rush, precisely where the school bus used to stop after speeding to catch the green light on 110th. As I watched them chat with one of the Canadians at the Christmas tree stall, I suddenly wished I was in the young father's place with my own twins, ten years, five years ago, even last year. We'd buy something warm to drink across the street then rush to say hi to the tree vendors. Now it seemed I'd lost the right to walk up to them.

I envied the couple with the twins. And, as though to prod the knife deeper into the wound, for a moment I allowed myself to think that this is twenty years ago, I've just gotten married, my children are not born yet, and our new, three-bedroom apartment feels far too vacant for just the two of us. I stare at the couple and am thinking ahead for them, or ahead for myself, it's not clear which, picturing the good things that have yet to come, even telling myself that the time for the 6:20 bus lies so very, very far away that it's almost impudent to conjure it up just now.

And then I finally saw things for what they were: the time for rehearsing had already come and gone, just as the boys came and went this Christmas, as the tree vendors will indeed come and go each year—this is how it always is and has been: things come and then they go, and however we bicker with time and put up all manner of bulwarks to stop it from doing the one thing it knows, the best is learning how to give thanks for what we have. And at Christmas I was thankful; their bedroom doors were open again. But I knew, even as I welcomed the flurry of bags and boxes and hugs and yelps, that a small, sly corner of my mind was already dreading and rehearsing that morning in January when they'd all head back to the airport.

My Daughter and God

JUSTIN CRONIN

Four years ago, driving home from picking up our twelve-year-old daughter at summer camp, my wife reached into her purse for a tissue and lost control of her car. This occurred on an empty stretch of Interstate 10 between Houston and San Antonio, near the town of Gonzales. The accident occurred as many do: a moment of distraction, a small mistake, and suddenly everything is up for grabs. My wife and daughter were in the midst of a minor argument over my daughter's need to blow her nose. During high pollen season, she is a perennial sniffer, and the sound drives my wife crazy. *Get a Kleenex*, Leslie said, *for God's sake*, and when Iris, out of laziness or exhaustion or the mild, day-to-day defiance of all teenagers, refused to do so, my wife reached for her purse, inadvertently turning the wheel to the left.

In the case of some vehicles, the mistake might have been rectified, but not my wife's—a top-heavy SUV with jacked-up suspension. When she realized her error, she overcorrected to the right, then the left again, the car swerving violently. They were on a bridge that passed above a gully: on either side, nothing but gravity and forty vertical feet of air. That they would hit the guardrail was now inevitable. In moments of acute stress, time can seem to slow. The name for this is tachypsychia, from the Greek *tach*, meaning "speed," and *psych*, meaning "mind." Thus, despite the chaos and panic of these moments, my wife had time to form a thought: *I have killed my daughter.*

This didn't happen, although the accident was far from over. The car did not break through the guardrail but ricocheted back onto the highway, spinning in a one-eighty before flopping onto its side with a powdery explosion of airbags. It struck another vehicle, driven by a pastor and his wife on their way home from Sunday lunch, though my wife has no memory of this. For what seemed like hours the car traveled in this manner, then gravity took hold once more. Like a whale breaching the surface, it lifted off the roadway, turned belly-up, and crashed down on its roof. The back half of the car compacted like an accordion: steel crushing, glass bursting, my daughter's belongings—clothes, shoes, books, an expensive violin—exploding onto the highway. Other cars whizzed pass, narrowly missing them. A final jolt, the car rolled again, and it came to a halt, facing forward, resting on its wheels.

As my wife tells it, the next moment was very nearly comic. She and my daughter looked at each other. The car had been utterly obliterated, but there was no blood, no pain, no evidence of bodily injury to either of them. "We've been in an accident," my wife robotically observed.

My daughter looked down at her hand. "I am holding my phone," she said—as, indeed, she somehow still was. "Do you want me to call 911?"

There was no need. Though in the midst of things, the two of them had felt alone in the universe, the accident had been observed by a dozen other vehicles, all of which had now stopped and disgorged their occupants, who were racing to the scene. A semi moved in behind them to block the highway. By this time my wife's understanding of events had widened only to the extent that she was aware that she had created a great deal of inconvenience for other people. She was apologizing to everyone, mistaking their amazement for anger. Everybody had expected them to be dead, not sitting upright in their destroyed vehicle, neither with so much as a hair out of place. Some began to weep; others had the urge to touch them. The cops arrived, a fire truck, an ambulance. While my wife and daughter were checked out by an EMT, onlookers organized a posse to prowl the highway for my daughter's belongings. Because my wife and daughter no longer had a car to put them into, a woman offered to bring them to our house; she was headed for Houston to visit her son and was pulling a trailer of furniture. The EMT was as baffled as everybody else. "Nobody walks away from something like this," he said.

I was to learn of these events several hours later, when my wife phoned me. I was in the grocery store with our six-year-old son, and when I saw my wife's number, my first thought was that she was calling to tell me she was running late, because she always does.

"Okay," I said, not bothering to say hello, "where are you?"

Thus her first tender steps into explaining what had occurred. An accident, she said. A kind of a big fender bender, really. Nobody hurt, but the car was out of commission; I'd need to come get them.

I wasn't nice about this. Part of the dynamic in our marriage is the unstated fact that I am a better driver than my wife. I have never been in an accident; my one and only speeding ticket was issued when the first George Bush was president. About every two years, my wife does something careless in a parking lot that costs a lot of money, and she has received so many tickets that she has been forced to retake driver's education—and those are just the tickets that I know about. The rules of modern marriage do not include confiscating your wife's car keys, but more than once I have considered doing this.

"A fender bender," I repeated. *Christ almighty, this again.* "How bad is it?"

"Everybody's fine. You don't have to worry. No other cars were involved."

"I get that. You said that already." I was in the cereal aisle; my son was bugging me to buy a box of something much too sweet. I tossed it into the cart.

"What about the car?"

"Um, it kind of . . . rolled."

I imagined a Labrador retriever lazily rotating onto his back in front of the fireplace. "I don't understand what you're telling me."

"It's fine, really," my wife said.

"Do you mean it rolled *over*?"

"It happened kind of fast. Totally no big deal, though."

It sounded like a huge deal. "Let me see if I have this right. You were driving and the car rolled over."

"Iris wouldn't blow her nose. I was getting her a Kleenex. You know how she is. The doctors say she's absolutely fine."

"What doctors?" It was becoming clear that she was in a state of shock. "Where are you?"

"At the hospital. It's very small. I'm not even sure you'd call it a hospital. Everybody's been so nice."

And so on. By the time the call ended, I had some idea of the seriousness, though not completely. Gonzales was three hours away. I abandoned my grocery cart, raced home, got on the phone, found somebody to look after our son, and got in my car. Several more calls followed, each adding a piece to the puzzle, until I was able to conclude that my wife and daughter were alive but should be dead. I *knew* this, but I didn't *feel* it, not yet. For the moment I was locked into the project of retrieving them from the small town where they'd been stranded. It was after ten o'clock when I pulled into the driveway of Gonzales Memorial Hospital, a modern building the size of a suburban dental office. I did not see my wife, who was standing at the edge of the parking lot, looking out over the empty fields behind it. I raced inside and there was my daughter, Iris. She was slender and tan from a month in the Texas sunshine, and wearing a yellow T-shirt dress. She had never looked more beautiful, and it was this beauty that brought home the magnitude of events. I threw my arms around her, tears rising in my throat; I had never been so happy to see anybody in my life. When I asked her where her mother was, she said she didn't know; one of the nurses directed us outside. I found myself unable to take a hand off my daughter; some part of me needed constant reassurance of her existence. I saw my wife standing at the edge of the lot, facing away. I called her name, she turned, and the two of us headed toward her.

As my wife tells the story, this was the moment when, as the saying goes, she got God. Once the two of them had been discharged, my wife had stepped outside to call me with this news. But the signal quality was poor, and she abandoned the attempt. I'd be along soon enough.

She found herself, then, standing alone in the Texas night. I do not recall if the weather was clear, but I'd like to think it was, all those fat stars shining down. My wife had been raised Missouri Synod Lutheran, but a series of intertribal squabbles had soured her parents on the whole thing, and apart from weddings and funerals, she hadn't set foot in a church for years. Yet the outdoor cathedral of a starry Texas night is as good a place as any to communicate with the almighty, which she commenced to do. In the hours since the accident, as the adrenaline cleared, her recollection of events had led her to a calculus that rewrote everything she thought she knew about the world. Until that night, her vision of a universal deity had been basically impersonal. God, in her mind, was simply too busy to take interest in individual human affairs. The universe possessed a moral shape, but events were haphazard, unguided by providence. Now, as she contemplated the accident, mentally listing the many ways that she and our daughter should have died and yet did not, she decided she was wrong. Of course God paid attention. Only the intercession of a divine hand could explain such a colossal streak of luck. Likewise did the accident become in her mind a product of celestial design. It was a message; it meant something. She had been placed in a circumstance in which a mother's greatest fear was about to be realized, then yanked from the brink. Her future emerged in her mind as something given back to her—it was as if she and our daughter had been killed on the highway and then restored to life—and like all supplicants in the wilderness, she asked God what her purpose was, why He'd returned her to the world.

That was the moment when Iris and I emerged from the building and called her name, giving her the answer.

Until that night, we were a family that had lived an entirely secular existence. This wasn't planned; things simply happened that way. My religious background was different from my wife's, but only by degree. I was raised in the Catholic Church, but its messages were delivered to me in a lethargic and off-key manner that failed to gain much traction. My father did not attend mass—I was led to believe this had something to do with the trauma of his attending Catholic grade school—and my mother, who dutifully took my sister and me to church every Sunday, did not receive Communion. Why this should be so I never thought to ask. Always she met us at the rear of the church so that we could make a quick exit "to avoid the traffic." (There was no traffic.) We never attended a church picnic or drank coffee in the basement after mass or went to Bible study; we knew no other families in the parish. Religion was never discussed over the dinner table or anyplace else. I went to just enough Sunday school to meet the minimum requirements for First Communion, but because I went to a private school with afternoon activities, I could not attend confirmation class. My mother struck a deal with the priest. If I met with him for a couple of hours to discuss religious matters, I could be confirmed. I had no idea why I was doing any of this or what it meant, only that I needed to select a new name, taken from the saints. I chose Cornelius, not because I knew who he was but because that was the name of my favorite character in *Planet of the Apes*.

Within a couple of years I was off to boarding school, and my life as a Roman Catholic, nominal as it was, came to an end. During a difficult period in my mid-twenties, I briefly flirted with church attendance, thinking this might offer me some comfort and direction, but I found it just as stultifying and embarrassing as I always had, full of weird sexual obsessions, exclusionary politics, and a deep love of hocus-pocus, overlaid with a doctrine of obedience that was complete anathema to my newly independent self. If asked, I would have said that I believed in God—one never really loses those mental contours once they're established—but that organized religious practice struck me as completely infantile. When my wife and I were married, a set of odd circumstances led us to choose an Anglican priest to officiate, but this was a decision we regretted, and when our daughter was born, the subject of baptism never came up. Essentially, we viewed ourselves as too smart for religion. I'll put it another way. Religion was for people who wanted to stay children all their lives. We didn't. We were the grown-ups.

In the aftermath of the accident, and the event that I now think of as "the revelation of the parking lot," all of this went out the window. I was not half as sure as my wife that God had interceded; I'm a skeptic and always will be. But it was also the case that I was due for a course correction. In my mid-forties, I had yet to have anything truly bad happen to me. The opposite was true: I'd done tremendously well. At the university where I taught, I'd just been promoted to full professor. A trilogy of novels I had begun writing on a lark had been purchased for scads of money. We'd just bought a new house we loved, and my daughter had been admitted to a terrific school where she'd be starting in the fall. My children were happy and healthy, and my newfound financial success had allowed my wife to quit her stressful job as a

high school teacher to look after our family and pursue her interests. It had been a long, hard climb, but we'd made it—more than
made it—and I spent a great deal of time patting myself on the
back for this success. I'd gone out hunting and brought back a
mammoth. Everything was right as rain.

In hindsight, this self-congratulatory belief in my ability to
chart my own destiny was patently ridiculous. Worldly things are
worldly things; two bad seconds on the highway can take them all
away, and sooner or later, that's just what's going to happen.

Once you have it, this information is unignorable, and it seems
to me that you can do one of two things with it. You can decide
that life doesn't make sense, or you can decide that it does. In
version one, the universe is a stone-cold place. Life is a series of
accumulations—friends, lovers, children, memories, the contents
of your 401(k)—followed by a rapid casting off (i.e., you die). Your
wife is just somebody you met at a party; your children are biological accretions of yourself; your affection for them is nothing
more than a bit of well-engineered firmware to guarantee the per-
petuation of the species. All pleasures are sensory, since nothing
goes deeper than the senses, and pain, whether psychological or
physical, is meaningless bad news you can only endure till it's over.

Version two assumes that life, with all of its vicissitudes, pos-
sesses an organized pattern of meaning. Grief means something,
joy means something, love means something. This meaning isn't
always obvious and is sometimes maddeningly elusive; had my
wife and daughter been killed that afternoon on the highway, I
would have been hard-pressed to take solace in religion's custom-
ary clichés. (It is likely that the only thing that would have prevented me from committing suicide, apart from my own physical
cowardice, would have been my son, into whom I would have

poured all my love and sorrow.) But it's there if you look for it, and the willingness to search—whether this search finds expression in religious ritual, or attentive care for one's children, or a long run through falling autumn leaves—is what is meant, I think, by faith.

But herein lies the problem: We don't generally come to these things on our own. Somebody has to lay the groundwork, and the best way to accomplish this is with a story, since that's how children learn most things. My Catholic upbringing was halfhearted and unfocused, but it made an impression. At any time during my thirty-year exile from organized religion, I could have stepped into a Sunday mass and recited the entire liturgy by heart. For better or worse, my God was a Catholic God, the God of smells and bells and the BVM and the saints and all the rest, and I didn't have to build this symbolic narrative on my own. My wife is much the same; I have no doubt that the image of the merciful deity she addressed in the parking lot came straight off a stained-glass window, circa 1975. Yet out of arrogance, of laziness, or the shallow notion that modern, freethinking parents ought to allow children to decide these things for themselves, we'd given our daughter none of it. We'd left her in the dark forest of her own mind, and what she'd concluded was that there was no God at all.

This came about in the aftermath of our move to Texas—a very churchy place. My daughter was entering the first grade; my son was still being hauled around in a basket. Houston is a sophisticated and diverse city, with great food, interesting architecture, and a vivid cultural life, but the suburbs are the suburbs, and the neighborhood where we settled was straight out of Betty Friedan's famous complaint: horseshoe streets of more or less identical one-story, 2,500-square-foot houses, built on reclaimed ranchland in the 1960s. A neighborhood of 2.4 children per household, fathers who raced off to work each morning before the dew had dried, moms who pushed their kids around in strollers and passed out snacks at soccer games and volunteered at the local elementary school. We were, after ten years living in a dicey urban neighborhood in Philadelphia, eager for something a little calmer, more controlled, and we'd chosen the house in a hurry, not realizing what we were getting into. Among our first visitors was an older woman from down the block. She presented us with a plate of brownies and proceeded to list the denominational affiliations of each of our neighbors. I was, to put it mildly, pretty weirded out. I counted about a dozen churches within just a few miles of my house—Baptist, Methodist, Presbyterian, United Church of Christ—and all of them were *huge*. People talked about Jesus as if he were sitting in their living room, flipping through a magazine; nearly every day I saw a car with a bumper sticker that read, "Warning: In case of Rapture, this car will be unmanned." Stapled to the local religious culture was a socially conservative brand of politics I found abhorrent. To hear homosexuality described as "an abomination" felt like I'd parachuted into the Middle Ages. I couldn't argue with my neighbors' devotion to their offspring— the neighborhood revolved around children—but it seemed to me that Jesus Christ, whoever he was, had been pretty clear on the subject of loving everybody.

This was the current my daughter swam in every day at school. Not many months had passed before one of her friends, the daughter of evangelicals, expressed concern that Iris was going to hell. Those were the words she used: "I don't want you to go to hell, Iris." The girl in question was adorable, with ringlets of dark hair, perfect manners, and lovely, doting parents. No doubt she thought she was doing Iris a kindness when she urged her to attend church with her family to avoid this awful fate. But that wasn't how I saw the situation. I dropped to a defensive crouch and came out swinging. "Tell her that hell's a fairy tale," I said. "Tell her to leave you alone."

The better choice would have been to offer her a more positive, less punishing view of creation—less hell, more heaven—and over time, my wife and I tried to do just that. But telling your child to "love your neighbor as yourself" sounds a lot like "don't forget to brush your teeth" when you're seven years old—words to live by, but hardly a description of humanity's place in the cosmos. As the playground evangelism continued, so did my daughter's contempt, and why wouldn't it? She'd learned it from me. I don't recall when she announced she was an atheist. All I remember was that she did this from the backseat of the car, sitting in a booster chair.

After the accident, my daughter spent the better part of a week in her closet. From time to time I'd stop by and ask, "Are you still in there?" Or "Hey, it's Daddy, how's it going?" Or "Let me know if you need anything."

"All good!" she said. "Thanks!"

There were things to sort out: an insurance claim to file, a replacement vehicle to acquire, arrangements to make for our summer vacation, for which we'd be leaving in two weeks. My wife and I were badly shaken. We had entered a new state: we were a family that had nearly been annihilated. Every few hours, one of us would burst into tears. Genesis 2:24 speaks of spouses "cleaving" to each other, and that was what we did: we cleaved. We badly wanted to comfort our daughter, but she had made herself completely unreachable. Of course she'd be confused and angry; in a careless moment, her mother had nearly killed her. But when we probed her on the matter, she insisted this wasn't so. Everything was peachy, she said. She just liked it in the closet. No worries, she'd be along soon.

A day later we received a phone call from the pastor whose car my wife's had struck. At first I thought he was calling to get my insurance information, which I apologetically offered. He explained that the damage was minor, nothing even worth fixing, and that he had called to see if my wife and daughter were all right. Perfectly, I said, omitting my daughter's temporary residence among her shirts and pants, and thanked him profusely.

"It's a miracle," he said. "I saw the whole thing. Nobody should have survived."

He wasn't the first to say this. The M-word was bandied about freely by virtually everyone we knew. The following afternoon, we were visited by the woman who had collected Iris's belongings: two cardboard boxes of books and clothes covered with highway grime and shards of glass, a suitcase that looked like it had been run over, and her violin, which had escaped its launch into the gully unharmed. We chatted in the living room, replaying events. Like the pastor, she seemed a little dazed. When the conversation reached a resting place, she explained that she couldn't leave until she'd seen Iris.

"Give me just a sec," my wife said.

A minute later she appeared with our daughter. The woman rose from her chair, stepped toward Iris, and wrapped her with a hug. This display made my daughter visibly uncomfortable, as it would anyone. Why was this stranger hugging her? The woman's face was full of inexpressible emotion; her eyes filmed with tears. My daughter endured her embrace as long as she could, then backed away.

"God protected you. You know that, don't you?"

My daughter's eyes darted around warily. "I guess."

"You're going to have a wonderful life. I just know it."

We exchanged email addresses, knowing we would never use them, and said our goodbyes in the yard. When we returned to the house, Iris was still standing at the base of the stairs. I had never seen her look so freaked out.

"God had nothing to do with it," she said. "So don't ask me to say he did." And with that she headed back upstairs to her closet.

The psychologist, whom Iris nicknamed "Dr. Cuckoo," told us not to worry. Iris was a levelheaded girl; hiding in the closet was a perfectly natural response to such a trauma. The best thing, she said, was to give our daughter space. She'd talk about it when the time was right.

I doubted this. Levelheaded, yes, but that was the problem. Doing a double gainer with a twist at seventy miles per hour, without so much as dropping your iPhone, was nothing that the rational mind could parse on its own. The psychologist also didn't know my daughter like I did. Iris can be the most stubborn person on earth. This is one of her cardinal virtues when, for instance, she has a test and two papers due on the same day. She'll stay up till 3:00 a.m. no matter how many times we tell her to go to bed, and get A's on all three, proving herself right in the end. But she can also hold a grudge like nobody I've ever met, and a grudge with the cosmos is no simple matter. How do you forgive the world for being godless? When she declared her atheism from the booster seat, I'd thought two things. First, How cute! The world's only atheist who eats from the kids' menu! I couldn't have been more charmed if she'd said she'd been reading Schopenhauer. The second thing was: This can't last. How could a girl who still believed in the tooth fairy fail to come around to the idea of a cosmic protector? And yet she didn't. Her atheism had hardened to such a degree that any mention of spiritual matters made her snort milk out her nose. By inserting nothing in its stead, we had inadvertently given her the belief that she was the author of her own fate, and my wife's newfound faith in a God-watched universe was as much a betrayal as crashing their car into the guardrail over a minor argument. It was a philosophical reversal my daughter couldn't process, and it left her feeling utterly alone.

My wife and I felt perfectly awful. In due course our daughter emerged, with one condition: she didn't want to discuss the accident. Not then, not ever. This seemed unhealthy, but you can't make a twelve-year-old girl talk about something she doesn't want to. We left for Cape Cod, where we'd rented a house for the month of July. I'd just turned in a manuscript to my editor and under ordinary circumstances would have been looking forward to the time away, but it seemed like too much data. Everyone was antsy and out of sorts, and the weather was horrible. The only person who enjoyed himself was our son, who was too young to comprehend the scope of events and was happy drawing pictures all day.

The school year resumed, and with it life's ordinary rhythms. My wife began looking around for a church to attend. To say this was a sore spot with Iris would be a gross understatement. She hated the idea and said so. "Fine with me," she said, "if you want to get all Jesus-y. Just leave me out of it."

It didn't happen right away. God may have shown his face to my wife in the parking lot, but He'd failed to share his address. We were stymied by the things we always had been: our jaundiced view of organized religion, the conservative social politics of most mainline denominations, the discomfiting business of praying aloud in the presence of people we didn't know. And what, exactly, did we believe? Faith asks for a belief in God, which we had; religion asks for more, a great deal of it literal. Christian ritual was the most familiar, but neither of us believed that the Bible was the word of God or that Jesus Christ was a supernatural being who walked on water when he wasn't turning it into wine. Certainly somebody by that name had existed; he'd gotten a lot of ink. He'd done and said some remarkable stuff, scared the living shit out of an imperial authority, and given humanity two thousand years' worth of things to think about. But the son of God? Really? That Jesus was no more or less divine than the rest of us seemed to me the core of his message.

We wanted something, but we didn't know what. Something with a little grace, a bit of wonder, the feeling of taking a few minutes out of each week to acknowledge how fortunate we were. We decided to give Unitarianism a shot. From the website, it seemed safe enough. Over loud objections, we made Iris come with us. The service was overseen by two ministers, a married couple, who took turns speaking from the altar, which seemed as holy as the podium in a college classroom. After the hokey business of lighting the lamp, they droned on for half an hour about the importance of friendship. There were almost no kids in the congregation, or even anybody close to our age. It was a sea of white-haired heads. After the service, everyone lingered in the lobby over coffee and stale cookies, but we beat a hasty retreat.

"Well, that was awkward," Iris said.

It was. It had felt like sitting in the audience at a talk show. We tried a few more times, but our interest flagged. When, on the fourth Sunday, Iris found me making French toast in the kitchen in my bathrobe, and asked why we weren't going, I told her that I guessed church wasn't for us after all.

"Thank God," she said, and laughed.

In the end, as in the scriptures, it was a child who led us. To our surprise, our son, Tuck, had become a secret Episcopalian. His school is affiliated with an Episcopal parish, and students attend chapel once a week. We'd always assumed this was the sort of wishy-washy, nondenominational fare most places dish out, but we were wrong. One day, apropos of nothing, as I was driving him home from school, he announced that he believed in Jesus.

"Really?" I said. "When did that happen?"

"I don't know," he said, and shrugged. "It just makes sense to me. Pastor Lisa's nice. We should go sometime."

"To church you mean?"

"Sure," he said. "I think that would be great."

Just like that, the matter was settled. We now go every week— the three of us. St. Stephen's is located in a diverse neighborhood in Houston, and much of the congregation is gay or lesbian. There are protocols, but very loose ones, and the church has open Communion and a terrific choir. Pastor Lisa is a woman in her fifties with a gray pageboy, who wears blue jeans and Birkenstocks under her robe and gives a hug that feels like falling into bed. She knows I was raised Catholic, and she laughed when I told her that I didn't mind that she "got some of the words wrong." I have my doubts, as always, but it seems like a fine church to have them in. My son finds some of the service boring, as all children do, but he likes Communion, which he calls his "force field for the week." He has asked to be baptized next fall.

Will Iris be there? I hope so. But it's her choice. She has yet to go with us. I know this makes her sad, and it makes me sad, too. It's the first thing the three of us have ever done without her.

Three years after the accident, in spring 2012, I failed a blood test at my annual physical, then failed a biopsy, and found myself, two months shy of my fiftieth birthday, facing a surgery that would tell me if I was going to see my children grow up. Two of my doctors assured me this would happen; a third said maybe not. We were spending the summer on Cape Cod, where we'd bought a house, and in late July, my wife and I flew back to Texas for my operation. When I awoke in the recovery room, my wife was standing over me, smiling. I was so dopey with painkillers that focusing on her face felt like trying to carry a piano up the stairs. "It's over," she said. "The margins were clear. You're going to be okay."

Two days after my surgery, I was instructed to walk. This sounded impossible, but I was determined. With my wife holding my arm, I shuffled up and down the hall, gritting my teeth against the discomfort of the catheter, which was the weirdest thing I'd ever felt. The last two months had pummeled me to psychological pieces, but the worst was over. Once again, the car had rolled, and we had walked away.

From the far end of the hall, a woman was approaching. Like a pair of ocean liners, we headed toward each other in slow motion. She was very thin and wearing a silk robe; like me, she was pulling an IV stand. Some greeting was called for, and she was the first to speak.

"May I give you something?"

We were within just a few feet of each other, and I saw what the situation was. Her body was leaving her; death was in her face.

"Of course."

She gestured downward, indicating the pockets of her robe. "Pick one."

I chose the left. With a trembling hand she withdrew a wad of white cotton, tied with a bow. She placed it in my hand. I saw what it was: an angel, made from a dishtowel. To this she'd affixed a heart-shaped piece of laminated paper printed with these words from the Book of Numbers:

The Lord bless and keep you;
The Lord make his face shine upon you, And be gracious to
    you; May the Lord lift up His countenance upon you;
And give you peace.

When I first learned about my illness, a very smart man told me that I should select an object. It could be anything, he said. A piece of jewelry. A spoon. A rock. Since I was a writer, maybe something to do with writing, such as a pen. It didn't matter what it was. When I was afraid, he said, and thinking that I was going to die, I should take that object in my hand and put my fear inside it.

Wise as his counsel was, I'd never managed to do this. I'd tried one thing and then another. Nothing had felt right. This did. Not just right: miraculous.

"Bless you," I said.

Two weeks later I returned to the Cape to complete my recovery. There wasn't much I could do, but I was glad to be there. A few days before my diagnosis, I had bought a ten-year-old Audi convertible and shipped it north. Iris had just gotten her learner's permit, and after a week of lounging around the house, I asked her if she'd take me for a drive. The day was sunny and hot. We put the top down and sped north, bisecting the peninsula on a rolling, two-lane road. From the passenger seat, I watched my daughter drive. In the last year, a startling change had occurred. Iris wasn't a kid anymore. She was taller than my wife, with a full, womanly shape. Her facial features had organized into mature proportions. Her hair, a honeyed red, swept away from her face in a stylish arc. She could have been mistaken for a college student, and often was. But the difference was more than physical; to look at my daughter was to know that she was somebody with a private, inner existence. She was standing at the edge of life; everything was ahead of her. All she had to do was let it come.

"How's it feel?" I asked. She had perfect motorist's manners: hands at the ten and two, shoulders pressed back, eyes on the road. She was wearing large, tortoise-shell sunglasses that would have been perfectly at home on Audrey Hepburn's face.

"Okay."

"Not scary?"

She shrugged. "Maybe a little."

Our destination was a beach on the Cape's north side, called Sandy Neck. From there, on clear days, you can see all the way from Plymouth to Provincetown. We parked and got out of the car and walked to the little platform built to take in the view. I knew we couldn't stay long; even standing was an effort.

"I'm sorry if I scared you," I said.

Iris was looking away. "You didn't. Not really."

"Well I was scared. I'm glad you weren't."

She thought a moment. "That's the thing. I knew I should have been. But I wasn't. I actually feel kind of guilty."

"There's no reason you should."

"It's just . . ." She hunted for the words. "I don't know. You're *you*. I just can't imagine you not being okay."

She was wrong. Someday, I wouldn't be. But she didn't need to hear that from me on a sunny summer day.

"Do you remember the accident?" I asked.

She laughed, a little nervously. "Well, duh."

"I've always wondered. What were you doing in the closet?"

"Not much. Mostly watching *Project Runway* on my laptop."

"And being mad at us."

She shrugged. "That whole God thing really pissed me off. I mean, you guys can believe whatever you want. I just wanted Mom to feel the same way I did."

"How did you feel?"

She didn't answer right away. Boats were creeping across the horizon.

"Abandoned."

We were silent for a time. I had a sudden vision of myself as old—an old man, being taken to the beach by his grown daughter. The dunes, the ocean, the rocky shoreline where they met—all would be the same, unchanged since I was boy. It was a sad thought, but it also made me happy in a way that seemed new. These things were years away, and I would be around to see them.

"Are you doing all right? Do you need to go back?"

I nodded. "Probably I should get off my feet."

We returned to the car. Three steps ahead of me, Iris moved to the passenger side, opened the door and got in.

"What are you doing?" I asked.

She looked around. "Oh, right," she said, and laughed. "I'm the driver, aren't I?"

She was sixteen years old. I hoped someday she'd remember how it felt, how amazing, how alive. I'd heard it said that one-tenth of parenting is making mistakes; the other nine are prayer and letting go.

"Yes," I said. "You are."

As Long as He Knows You Love Him

STEPHEN O'CONNOR

I have always loved babies, and for most of my childhood and youth, I looked forward eagerly to the day I myself might be a father—so much so that, as a young man, I often felt ambivalent whenever a girlfriend would tell me her period was late. Yes, having a baby at seventeen or nineteen or twenty-two would have been a huge problem, but the idea of holding my own child in my arms had such a magical attraction that it was hard for me to summon up the necessary concern.

When I first met Helen, the woman who would become my wife, she told me that she wasn't especially interested in children, an admission that mildly unsettled me, even though I assumed (or hoped) that she would change her mind—as, indeed, she did, some three years later, when one of our best friends had her first child.

As Helen describes it, the desire to have a child seemed to come out of nowhere and completely take over her life. Far from being bored by our friend's baby, she delighted at his every wiggle and coo, and loved to hold him in her arms. A stroller couldn't pass on the sidewalk without drawing her gaze and, often, evoking a warm smile. We would linger beside playgrounds talking about which of the tiny people toddling across the rubber matting was cutest, smartest, funniest. And, inevitably, we would talk late into the night about how we might be able to afford a baby and when we should start trying.

I ought to have been filled with happy excitement at this turn of events, and, indeed, I was happy—but not only happy. I was also afraid. And the nearer we drew to actually trying to conceive, the more frightened I became. I would get dull headaches; my fingertips would turn sweaty and cold. Helen, too, had her anxious moments, but none as intense as mine.

There were many practical reasons for being afraid. As freelance journalists, we had no health insurance, almost nothing in the bank, and we sometimes ran up Visa debt that took months to retire. And then there was the fact that both of us were working on novels. As much as we wanted children, neither of us could stand the idea of forgoing careers as fiction writers. One of the main topics of our late night discussions was how we would block out and pay for fiction writing time, but the truth was we had no idea how our plans might fare once we actually had to contend with the costs and needs of a growing child.

Legitimate as such practical concerns were, I am not sure that they were the primary source of my anxiety. When I think back on my state of mind during that period, it seems to me that the fear I was experiencing was much more primal, vast and mysterious—which, perhaps, was why it so troubled me, and why I sometimes felt I was turning into someone I had never imagined I could be.

. . .

So we bought health insurance and a basal thermometer. And then, after a couple of months, and one really wonderful New Year's Eve party, Helen brought a pregnancy test home from the pharmacy and, in a matter of minutes, showed me that pale but very significant blue X.

From that morning on, we dutifully abided by the wisdom of our generation. We bought all the right baby accoutrements and compendiums of child-rearing advice, and spent countless hours poring over a book that made miscarried embryos and fetuses look like the star child at the end of *2001*. We also took a months-long Lamaze class in which Helen was told she could transcend the pain of childbirth by puffing through her loosely pursed lips, and I was informed that, as her "labor coach," I could help her dispense our child with maximum efficiency by timing her contractions and counting out her puff rhythm like the coxswain in a crew boat.

Wouldn't that have been nice?

When Helen's contractions finally started in earnest, they were brutal and fast. She vomited before we even arrived at the hospital, and once we were there, her contractions came every minute or two for hour upon hour, then for a day, and then for more than a day. A cardinal tenet of our generation's parenting credo was that children should be born "naturally." Thus we had told our obstetrician that we didn't want any anesthetics that might diminish Helen's ability to push during labor, and that every possible step should be taken to avoid a C-section. What this meant was that Helen had to endure thirty-six hours of relentless agony, during which all of my supposed "coaching" was revealed as a pointless charade. More than once, when I tried to lift her out of her pain by getting her to "breathe," she would fix me with a stare halfway between incredulity and contempt. In the end, I resorted to more traditional comforts: I held her hand, kissed her forehead, and massaged her lower back. But most of the time, I felt entirely powerless: a mere spectator at the crucifixion of the woman I loved.

We arrived at the hospital around midnight, and Helen's cervix had already dilated to four centimeters. But by midnight of the following day, despite all of her effort and pain, and all of the contraction-inducing hormones that had been pumped into her veins, her dilation had not increased by even a quarter centimeter.

I don't think we slept at all our first night. By the evening of our second, we were utterly exhausted, but could only catch micro-naps between each of Helen's relentless contractions. The world began to go surreal. Sounds turned tinny, and the light went yellowish-gray. Nothing was fully real for us except the relentless NOW of pain, dread, hope and love—so much so that, to this day, although I know that our son, Simon, was born around six o'clock, I have no idea whether that was in the morning or evening. I do remember, though, that when the baby monitor showed Simon's heart in distress, and our obstetrician told us she would have to perform an emergency C-section, Helen and I cast each other glances that expressed far more relief than disappointment or fear.

As Helen was being wheeled into the delivery room, our obstetrician offered me a surgical gown, cap and mask. I shook my head. I was too exhausted, physically and emotionally, to watch my wife's belly being cut open by a scalpel. Instead, I paced the hallway outside the delivery room, a cliché of the expectant father. After what seemed hours, but was probably only minutes, I heard an oddly duck-like wail, and then, after another surrealistically elongated stretch of time, a nurse arrived with a bundled swirl of cotton blankets, at the center of which was a tiny, pink face.

Simon was still crying when the nurse put him into my arms, but as soon as I spoke, he went silent. His eyes lolled and he squinted against the fluorescent ceiling lights, but he seemed to be listening as I told him his name and welcomed him into the world.

Yet again I was existing exclusively within an overwhelming now. I was still exhausted, still afraid for Helen, who was being stitched up on the other side of the delivery room door, but these were mere shadows on the outskirts of the huge joy that had filled my whole body. This was my baby. My firstborn. I was a father and this tiny, warm, gently wriggling bundle was my son. Every one of my realizations at that moment was entirely banal, and every one of them made me feel in the presence of something miraculous, something so utterly unlikely and wonderful that it could not possibly be true. And yet it was.

The nurse returned. She had to clean Simon up, she said, and take him for tests. He had been silent the whole time I had been holding him, but as soon as he left my arms, he started to cry again. Could it be that he had actually recognized my voice? Was it possible that, in some inchoate way, he had known, even before coming into the world, that I was his father? Could I already be so important to this tiny, helpless human being?

Now I must talk of things that shame me. The source of my shame is in other banalities: that the human heart is not pure, that the reality of parenthood is incomprehensible in advance, and that we must live with the consequences of our own actions.

I don't think that we had been home from the hospital for

more than two or three days before I was humbled by my realization of the extraordinary amount of work and self-sacrifice my parents had put into keeping me healthy and happy. Not only had I taken their labors for granted my entire life, I had grown irritated whenever they had suggested that attending to my needs had entailed the tiniest modicum of hardship. In my sudden remorse, I called them each to say thank you and apologize. They insisted, of course, that raising me and my siblings had, in fact, been an unmitigated joy, but I could tell from their slight hesitations that, even now, they were not telling me the whole story.

Newborns don't give a lot back. There must be a dozen pictures of Helen and me staring enraptured into little Simon's face, while his expression alternates between blank and suspicious. The main thing newborns do is eat voraciously from breast and bottle, and then they fill their diapers. Sometimes they more than fill their diapers, and so a change of clothing or bedding will be required, and maybe also a bath. They cry a lot. They sleep much of the time, but never for very long, and they make no distinction between daylight and darkness. And when they wake three, four, or five times during the night, they cry, and they won't stop crying until you have heaved yourself groggily out of your own bed and attended to them. Sometimes, of course, your attentions are not enough. You may fill your baby's belly, change his diapers and, in guilt and desperation, stick a pacifier into his mouth, but still he keeps crying.

Although Helen and I were resolved to split child care fifty-fifty, breast-feeding alone ensured that she bore most of the burden during Simon's earliest weeks—a period when she was also still exhausted from her thirty-six-hour labor and incapacitated by the lingering pain of the C-section. This meant that the bulk of the middle-of-the-night care fell to me. I was the one to get up and bring Simon to Helen for a feeding. And then I was the one to change his diapers and put him back to bed—and, on those occasions when food and clean diapers were not enough, I was the one to pace from one end of our street-lit apartment to the other, my wailing baby on my shoulder. I remember staggering with exhaustion as I paced. Once I actually fell asleep on my feet, and woke only as my shoulder struck the wall.

Exhaustion took its toll. During these early weeks I was dim-witted and quasi-demented a lot of the time—states of mind that did nothing to quell my anxiety that Simon's bouts of crying might be a sign of some life-threatening disorder, or that I was just exactly as incompetent a parent as I often seemed to myself.

Exhaustion made one other aspect of parenthood harder to bear. While there are ways in which having a baby is a narcissist's holiday—the fulfillment of one's fondest desires and the ultimate expression of self, both existentially and genetically—it also entails a significant negation of self. Your life is not your own once you have a child. Everything you do must accommodate this very small, demanding and helpless person who has come to live with you. Long accustomed freedoms become mere memories. Spontaneity is confined to the trivial: Shall we order pizza or Chinese food tonight? Should I put on Bach while I do the dishes, or the Talking Heads? And as for those extemporaneous rambles from apartment to café to park to museum to movie to bar—that's over! Don't even think about it! Dancing till dawn? Give me a break! . . . Alas, the dark side of the eternal bond between parent and child is that, especially during moments of extreme sleep-deprivation, it can feel like penal servitude.

So there I was: a weak and impure being, filled with love, wanting to do the best for my baby, but also exhausted, worried, overwhelmed and, secretly, shamefully resentful.

And then I made a big mistake.

Our pediatrician insisted that we give Simon a dropperful of vitamins twice daily. They were a sour-smelling, bitter-tasting brew that the little boy clearly detested and that, with great efficiency, he would spit, bubble and tongue out of his mouth. I hated giving them to him, and wasn't sure they were necessary, considering the fact that he was being breast-fed. But I respected our pediatrician and wanted Simon to thrive, so I gave him his vitamins—or attempted to—every day.

The scene is vivid in my memory: It was Sunday morning, and Simon was lying in my lap. There was a hot ache at the center of my skull, and my vision was constricted by tiredness. He had already extruded my first dose of vitamins as a stream of frothy brown drool, and I had refilled the dropper, on the idea that if I gave him a second dose, maybe enough would leak down his throat to keep him healthy. Just as I lifted the dropper out of the bottle, Simon opened his mouth wide. While I was sure he had not done this because of a sudden eagerness for the disgusting substance, I decided to seize the opportunity. To this very minute, I am haunted by the fact that even as I aimed the dropper at Simon's tongue, I wondered if what I was about to do was wise. I didn't care. I just wanted to get the fucking business over with.

Nothing would have happened if it hadn't turned out that exactly as the vitamins splattered out of the dropper, Simon took a deep breath—probably in preparation for a cry. The brown fluid swerved, midair, away from his tongue and down his throat. His eyes went wide; he gagged and fell silent. After a few seconds I realized he wasn't breathing, and that his lips were turning blue.

I flipped him onto his belly and patted him between his shoulder blades. When he started to make small, cry-like noises, I turned him over and saw—to my immense relief—that his lips were no longer blue, and that he seemed to be breathing normally. But when I lifted him head-upward, to give him some comforting pats against my shoulder, he gagged again. Once more his eyes and mouth were wide open, and he couldn't breathe. I placed him belly-down on my knees again, patted his back, and soon his lips returned to normal and he seemed able to breathe—but not, it now seemed, with perfect ease. And when I held him head-upward a second time, his breathing stopped and the blueness returned. I had already shouted to Helen, and she was in the room with me. We put Simon belly-down in his crib, and once again, he seemed fine, although streams of saliva bubbles swelled and burst on his lips with every exhalation. Helen watched him while I ran to the phone.

We didn't like or trust the doctor who covered for our pediatrician on weekends, so I called one of my best friends, who was not only a pediatrician, but a lung specialist. By the time he picked up the phone, Simon had fallen asleep, pink-cheeked and, apparently, breathing normally. I asked my friend if we should go to the hospital just in case, and he said that as long as Simon didn't seem in distress, we should let him sleep. Everything would probably be okay.

So Simon slept. One hour. Two hours. Maybe three. His breathing seemed fine, except for the strange bubbling on his lips, but he had never slept so long before. I called my friend again, just to make sure there was nothing to be concerned about. He said that Simon had probably only been worn out by his ordeal, but that we should try waking him and see what happened when we held him upright. Helen did exactly as my friend suggested, and as soon as Simon was vertical, he gagged again, and started to turn blue.

"Take him to the emergency room immediately," my friend told me. "Make sure you keep him flat on his belly the whole way."

We carried Simon to the hospital in a shopping bag–style portable crib that we laid across our knees in the cab. Utterly terrified, hardly able to believe any of this was actually happening, Helen and I kept trading dread-filled glances as we tried to comfort each other. Hearing our distress, the driver told us, "Just keep talking to him. As long as he knows you love him, everything will be okay." We did exactly as the driver instructed, hoping against hope that our love might actually prevail against the worst we could imagine.

When the cab pulled up outside the emergency room, I hurried ahead with Simon while Helen paid the driver. She caught up with me, and as soon as we walked through the double doors and said that our baby was having trouble breathing, people started running toward us. Within seconds Simon was on an examining table, and a doctor had inserted a slender plastic tube down his throat. There was a sucking noise, and a small amount of saliva shot backwards through the tube, but nothing brown. "It doesn't look like there's anything in his lungs at all," the doctor said. We told her about how he had turned blue when we held him upright, but when the doctor lifted him to her own chest, there was no gagging, and his lips remained their usual healthy red.

I could tell from her expression that she thought we were just typically hysterical new parents, but I didn't care. Simon was okay, his lungs were clear—that was all that mattered.

Only once Helen and I had had time to absorb this very good news did she notice that her wallet was gone. She must have left it in the cab. But just then, I glanced over her shoulder and saw our cabdriver in the middle of the emergency room, clutching her wallet.

We both ran over and thanked him. When we informed him that our baby was all right, he smiled and said, "See, that's what I told you. All you had to do was let him know you loved him."

At that particular moment, this grizzled, Russian cabdriver seemed bathed in saintly radiance. I thanked him again and again.

Although further tests had revealed nothing in Simon's lungs, and he was breathing normally, the doctors wanted to keep him overnight for observation. Helen and I went to the pediatric ward with him, and I hung around as long as I was allowed. Only Helen could stay the night.

She called me near bedtime to tell me that Simon was still fine, and that he would be sleeping right next to the nurse's station so that there would always be someone watching him, even when she could no longer keep awake. She promised to call me again in the morning, as soon as she knew when Simon would be discharged.

It has always seemed strange to me that an emotion as important as love should be substantially inaccessible to consciousness most of the time. We might fill with warmth, joy and, sometimes, of course, desire whenever we look at someone we love, but as powerful as such feelings may be, the true intensity of our attachment to that person only becomes fully conscious when we think we are going to lose him or her.

I had loved Simon from the instant I first held him in my arms.

Many times daily during his first two weeks of life, I would look at him, and my heart would swell with an affection that was almost more than I could bear. But it wasn't until I hung up the phone after talking to Helen that the full extent of my love became available to me, and I began to sob. As I thought, again and again, of what had nearly happened as a result of my single instant of mindless, irritable selfishness, it seemed to me that I loved Simon more than my own life, and that I would not have been able to go on living had he been taken from me.

I have often told people that I didn't really become an adult until I became a father. But what I have told almost no one is that I didn't really become a father until that night I sobbed all by myself in my living room. Until then, I had seen my happiness as primarily a matter of the satisfaction of my own desires, but from that moment on, I knew that every aspect of my life was permanently and inextricably intertwined with Simon's, just as one day it would also be with his sister Emma's. In a completely matter-of-fact way, I was no longer only myself.

In all of the years since, I have never been truly happy if my children are not also happy, and when things are going well for them, everything in my own life seems brighter too. I can't claim that I have had much success at transcending the weaknesses of my character, or that parenthood doesn't have its downsides (by far the worst being my massively amplified vulnerability to loss), but I can say with complete certainty that absolutely nothing in life has made me happier than my two children. They are, by far, my greatest joy.

Father's Prayer

CHRIS BACHELDER

At night, before sleep, I occasionally forget to floss, to set the alarm, to start the dishwasher, to transfer clothes to the dryer, to take out the trash, to turn off all the lights, to change the batteries or bulbs I promised to change, or to ask my wife about her day, but I never forget to check on my sleeping daughters. Every night I enter the dark chapel of their bedroom to see the girls in their twin beds—A., age seven, decorous and contained, her body long and straight beneath perfectly oriented sheet and quilt, her bed in essence *still made* while inhabited, her cheek actually resting on her palm as in some Pre-Raphaelite vision, her perimeter established with a meticulously arranged gallery of stuffed animals, and, across the room, her sister C., age five, more in the style of her father, sweating, drooling, wheezing, her sheet discarded, her pillow disdained, her blanket cockeyed, her animals free-range, her limbs scattered and splayed as if she plummeted to the mattress from some great height. Like other parents I say I am "checking on" my children, or "looking in on" them, as one would look in on an elderly neighbor during a snowstorm, as if these visits have anything at all to do with the health, safety, or well-being of the girls. The girls are fine—they have divergent nocturnal techniques, but they know how to be unconscious, how to breathe deeply, how to dream, how to grow. If this were indeed my duty, my responsibility, I would most certainly not be so reliable, so attentive. But I never forget, just as I never forget there are distilled spirits in the cabinet, sports on television.

The girls are fine, the girls are thriving. The girls, in fact, are remarkable. The purpose of the visit is to witness them, to receive a form of spiritual nourishment. These daughters . . . knob-kneed, gap-toothed, long-lashed. Healthy, hearty, reasonably hygienic. They follow rules, they tell the truth, they don't cause property damage, they are not unduly fascinated with fire. They are not, as they very well could have been, boys. In the near dark I watch for their breathing, for the pulse in their necks. I smooth hair from their faces. I attend to wayward animals. In the stillness I move between the two beds, stepping over a cash register, a coloring book. I lean down to study their faces in this profoundly quiet room. The silence of the room is like the silence of a photograph. Here the girls are fixed, they lie quietly outside of time. In this silence I can *see* my daughters. I can feel tender gratitude, I can tally my immense good fortune, appreciate the privilege of stewardship. The girls might stir or murmur, but they do not say a word. Not one word. I lean down toward each girl in turn to listen to what she does not say. How conspicuous, how marvelous is their silence! Because during the daylight hours, while awake and in our house or cars or backyard, these extraordinary girls, these two sources of wonder and light, *almost never shut their mouths*.

. . .

The urgent beeping of my daughters' Hello Kitty alarm clock each morning at 7:03 functions less as a signal to wake than as a signal to begin the day's talking. There is no clearing of the throat, no testing of the cords, no groggy and gradual passage into spoken language. The girls' mouths are fully and instantaneously engaged, and each has achieved an impressive word count before her feet even touch the floor. One girl reports a weird dream, and the other, not to be outdone, concocts her own weird dream. Look out the window, down there at the ground; it either rained during the night or it did not rain—in either case, it should be announced loudly. They narrate their clothing selections, and it probably goes without saying that each girl can deliver a lively discourse on underpants. They narrate their dental care, bickering violently over the bathroom footstool. Toothpaste ends up on the floor, and that is both grave and very funny, but most of all it serves to stimulate discussion. For breakfast they audibly cannot decide if they want cereal or toast or muffins or oatmeal or waffles or just nothing. In the half hour before they catch their bus, they have easily surpassed my speech output for the day, perhaps the week. After the girls leave for school—where, their teachers tell us, they are pleasant, though a bit reserved—the house feels like a flattened cornfield. If I stand still in the eerie quiet, I can hear a bird, a dog, a siren. I can hear the shouts of the roofers across the street. I can hear the jolly and determined tumbling of the rock polisher in our basement.

This placidity is short-lived, because C., the youngest daughter, is in a half-time pre-kindergarten program that ends at noon. At *noon*. Two or three days a week, I pick her up and take her home, and it is my privilege to steward her solo until we gather A. at the bus stop at 3:35. With big sister out of the picture, C. has no verbal competition. She knows full well that this is her precious opportunity to palaver without cease, to create hours of uninterrupted oral noise. Dear God, she takes full advantage. And while I am occasionally prone to embellishment, I offer here not an exaggeration but pretty much a straight transcription of a recent lunchtime moment with C.:

Dad.

Hm?

Dad.

Yeah.

Actually, Dad?

What is it?

The small guys that broke R2D2? Those guys aren't bad. They're not like Darth Vader or the Empire. But they're not like Luke and Leia, either. They're in the middle. The sand people are bad, though. They knocked out Luke.

Do you mean Jawas?

I always forget their names. I've got my robe on and my jammies and my slippers. These slippers are kind of like pop-up slippers. Dad?

Yes.

Vivian Whaley has pop-up slippers, and when you step kind of hard like this, a unicorn horn pops up.

Neat.

Actually, it's kind of warm in here so I'm going to take this all off.

Go ahead.

Dad, what is this for?

What?

Dad?

Please put that down.

Dad, did you have a bathrobe when you were a kid?

I can't remember.

Were bathrobes even invented?

Bathrobes have been around—

Dad? Oh, yeah, they were probably made out of quilts and stuff.
Are these your silver dollars? Look, I made a sandwich.

You did.

Actually, Dad? You know how I like to sleep with things that
are not stuffed animals? That's what I'm going to do with
my backpack. Dad?

[. . .]

I don't. I don't. I can't remember what I was going to say. Oh,
man. Well. Actually, Dad? I want to get my own hula hoop.
Can I get my own hula hoop?

Maybe.

Look, Dad. Dad, look. I'm hula hooping.

Whoa.

Dad, I'll wash my hands anyway because I have to go pee. Dad?

Go ahead and pee, honey.

Dad? Where does the pee go when you flush it?

It goes through—

I'm hula hooping like this.

You should pee if you have to.

Where does the pee go?

It goes—

Actually?

Through—

Through the ground?

No, through pipes and into a big tank.

Are there lobsters in there?

What?

Oh, Dad! Speaking of lobsters, we made octopuses today at school. Here's what we did. First, we took a bag. Then—well this is not an important part, though—we wrote our names. Then we kind of crumpled it up. Like crumpling? Dad? . . .

Prolixity is no sin, I realize. You should not, I know, reprimand a child simply for talking. I fight the urge, I do, to ask my daughter to "keep it down," to "take a breath," to "put a sock in it." I resist the temptation to wince, to flinch, to put my finger to my lips like a joyless substitute teacher. I try not to fall on the floor. I know she's not bad, I know she's not bad, I know she's not bad. Deep within my heart I understand there is a difference between being wicked and being loud. But here's the thing: C. is our *quiet* daughter. It's true. She is our reticent and keenly observant second child. She is the *watcher*. She has grown up in a windy valley of verbiage, in the fallout zone below her older sister's oral cavity. She has known nothing else. . . .

Whereas I, on the other hand, hail from a distant land of silence. I grew up in quiet houses. My sister, my only sibling, is eight years older. We obviously didn't have the same interests as children, and we were not in quarrelsome competition for games, toys, books, friends, clothes, or pastel jaguars. She moved out of the house when I was still young. We had wall-to-wall carpeting. The fibers absorbed sound. You could not slam a door even if you wanted to (and who would want to?). The doors slid across the carpet with a gentle aquatic murmur. People in my house did not raise voices; people rarely even used voices. I am not suggesting that we got along well, but the ways in which we did not get along were very, very quiet. Talk was trouble. We were an epistolary household. Letters beneath doors, sticky notes on bathroom mirrors. We liked televised baseball. We liked jigsaw puzzles, which are also quiet, unless you do them with your mouth, as my daughters do. You would not believe how quiet I could be as a child, even a big kid like me. Heel toe, heel toe. Before my parents' divorce, there was no arguing, no broken glass. There was just a silent cot in the basement.

At 3:35, C. and I walk down the street to pick up A. at the bus stop. As we walk, C. can sense a disturbance in the Force. She knows that A. is nearly home, and therefore she increases her words per minute to a nearly anaerobic rate. It is said that Anton Chekhov, having once been asked how he arrived at the subjects of his stories, shrugged, picked up an ashtray, and said, "Tomorrow I shall write a story called 'The Ashtray,'" and for C., as well, the acquisition of material is seemingly effortless. With disquisitional intensity she treats squirrel, chimney, pothole, litter, hydrant, speed bump, trash can, weather, neighbor. She marks the neighborhood in words as a dog marks it in urine. Here is a rock, indistinct in size, shape, and color. It actually kind of looks like a stone. It kind of looks like a bigger rock she saw once. Did it come from the sky? It just moved on its own. Actually, can a rock move on its own? Does it grow? Can you eat it? Can a squirrel eat it? Actually, a boy at school drank from the hamster's water bottle.

And then here is A., emerging from the school bus. She walks down the steps, looking taller, looking beautiful, looking almost shy. She has been polite and studious most of the school day, and now one senses her verbal fullness, her ripeness. Her head almost seems to be humming with language. She gives us a nice smile, she hands me her pony backpack, and then she commences. Her own loose teeth are interesting, she says, but other people's loose teeth are gross. Why did we send that different kind of plain tortilla in her lunch? They played crab soccer in gym class and she found a key chain. This is a girl who can talk while eating, while drinking, while brushing teeth, while swimming under water, while doing headstands. Though she is entirely fluent in narrative forms, her preferred mode is the oral report. My wife and I call her Wikipedia, though rarely to her face. She wants me to know that dive sticks are not really sticks. Like from trees. Sticks from trees float. Dive sticks are plastical and they are filled with something heavy to make them sink. Often, her entries are taken verbatim from me or my wife, and she repeats them fervently, as if we are amnesiacs she is attempting to rehabilitate. We own a house now, she frequently tells me. The house belongs to us. Last year we rented a house, but now we own a house. When you rent a house, it doesn't belong to you. You have to take care of it. But when you own a house, you still have to pay the bank every month. That's right, honey, I say, but would you please please please please please please please put your socks and shoes on?

If A. is not talking, then she is singing. Some of these songs are recognizable, but many are improvised, invented on the spot, using a kind of Feisty Princess song generator implanted in her brain by the Walt Disney Company, with the final words of each line extended loudly while she tries to invent a rhyme. In terms of lyrical content, the songs are typically about resolutely living a life that she was destined to live, or resolutely refusing to live a life she was destined to live. Destiny, at any rate, is crucial, as is the wind.

When the girls are together in the afternoons and evenings, they set about demolishing tranquility with a high-decibel gale-force assault. Yes, there is typically some thumpy gymnastic activity, some clog-on-pine track-and-field, some standard door-slamming and bed-vaulting. But primarily and relentlessly their collaborative project is mouth-based—arguing, compromising, boasting, planning, role-playing, screaming, threatening to tattletale, tattletaling, crying, fake crying, singing, talking, baby talking, animal talking, robot talking, concurrent talking, synchronized talking, laughing, teasing, taunting, coughing, accusing, cajoling, bartering, bellowing for medical aid, requesting permission for unsafe acts, announcing excretory intentions. (And squealing, too. I am just an imperfect clay-footed dad, and thus I can never hope to understand why God, in His infinite wisdom, created the horrid and contagious squeal of girls.) With each boisterous syllable, I can feel them gaining strength, while I am reduced to a wincing invalid, yearning for a sturdy cane with which to strike the ceiling or floor. I allow the translucent glaze to settle over my eyes like the nictitating membrane of some birds and reptiles. I ignore what is ignorable, and some of what is not. I recall with grim amusement how assiduously I myself once beckoned these children into the kingdom of language ("Who says Moo?!"). And I try my best—I confess that I occasionally fail—not to scold my daughters, not to request a cessation or reduction of words, and not, worst of all, to make a terrible father face that is no doubt the emotional equivalent of corporal punishment.

At dinnertime, we generally all sit down together. It's a nice opportunity for the girls to tell us about their day.

When I visit the girls' room each night, I have occasion to notice that their pajamas are defective. They used to fit, but they do not fit anymore. "They've gotten too small," we parents say of our children's clothes, because it is less painful than the truth, and because we do not want to admit to ourselves that we stand in such stark opposition to the right and natural order of the universe. When I visit their dark and silent room, I receive the spiritual nourishment and etc., but I also feel the regret and sorrow that I must in some sense require. I look forward to the morning, to the beeping of the alarm clock, when I will be given another chance. Tomorrow I might be more patient and engaged, tomorrow I might cherish the uninhibited noise that emanates from their faces. Because I know well that there might come a day, and it won't be long, when they will not be so eager to talk to me, their father. It is difficult to imagine now, but there will be a day when they have thoughts that they will not automatically convert to sound. They will become more interior, less transparent, their voices diminished by adolescence, by the virulent social forces that strike at the mouths of girls. They will not live so garrulously in the waves of the air. It's a terrible thing, an inexcusable thing, really, to wish a young girl to be quiet. Even a squealing girl. So I hope that tomorrow I may not regard gift as tribulation. I ask that tomorrow I have the strength not merely to withstand those voices but to encourage them. May I have the fortitude to inquire about Maleficent, the chicken dance, Swiper. The pre-K curriculum. The benefits of home ownership.

I don't pray, but I pray every night in the dark silence of my daughters' bedroom. There, beneath spiritual icons such as Tennis Ball Snowman and that salacious Princess Leia decal I have modified with a construction paper cloak, I arrive at the same old prayer. Not a prayer for a silent house but for comfort in the din. Oh Lord, shut me up. Shut me down. Open me up.

Taking Her Measure

KARL TARO GREENFELD

We tell ourselves we are doing this for our children: the early mornings, the cold walk to the costly rental car, the long drive through predawn murk to a distant suburb where we wait, huddled against the glass doors to a not-yet-set-up-for-competition gymnasium, parents bundled in parkas and hoods, daughters wearing down coats and sweats over sparkly leotards while their mothers do a last-minute hair touch-up, securing bow, sprinkling pixie dust, and applying eyeliner. The six-year olds, in dawn's first light, faces bright with artificial blush and lip gloss, stand with their teammates, the girls from NYC Elite here, the girls from Long Island Athletic Club there, while the parents, yawning, sipping coffee, freezing, check their watches and wonder when this damn gym is going to open.

It has become a dreaded ritual in our family, the predawn Saturday patrol, the loading of girls into car and then the long drive with its inevitable argument and dispute about which turnoff and exit—we don't have a GPS—while the kids slept in the back. I wonder how did an innocent, three-hour-a-week after school activity evolve into a team membership, many thousands in annual fees, more spent on private training and another couple hundred on leotards and uniforms and sweats and, don't forget, the competition fees and, oh yeah, my favorite, the $20 they charge you, as the parent, to go and watch your precious little flower in this competition? When did a little healthy fun turn into a grueling parental obligation, every bit as ghastly in its early rising and road tripping as being a hockey mom, the same planning, mapping, spending, and cheering—ultimately, for what? So little Lola can be judged—oh no, she only got an 8.2 on beam!—and so take home a "Participant" trophy? Why, my wife and I begin to wonder, are we doing this?

When I ask my daughter, Lola, if she enjoys being on the team, she says yes, "but I hate practice."

Ah! "So you don't like the team."

She shakes her head. "I love the competition."

Eye of the tiger, that little lover of American Girl dolls has, the eye of the tiger.

At one point, my wife Silka considers offering Lola her pick of American Girl doll paraphernalia—canopy bed, roll-top desk, baby carriage, anything—if she would quit the team, before deciding that would send the wrong message (the message that if you think of ways to wake your parents up early, then they will give you money to stop). Like sports parents everywhere, we are, for better or for worse, committed to doing everything we can so our little Lola can march onto the mat, to the accompanying "Axel F" routine music, with her mincing, toes-pointed walk, and attempt to dazzle with forward roll and back bend kickover. She is, at six, more of a competitive athlete than I ever was.

And mornings like this, I curse that fact.

I sometimes wonder as I watch the girls and their feckless attempts to vault and execute on the beam, what is the end game? Say Lola continues, despite her Iversonian approach to practice, to excel and somehow, after another ten years of even earlier mornings and, I presume, plane trips to even more distant cities, wherever larger numbers of even more coordinated and competitive little girls will aggregate in an even larger sparkly human caravan of cuteness, say she reaches that upper echelon of girls who might someday win a scholarship. These girls are—how can I say this and remain politically correct? Fuck it, I can't. Have you ever seen Shawn Johnson or Nastia Liukin? They are cute, adorable, and built like hobbits on HGH. Silka, Lola's mother, is the same height as me, five-eleven, and she's the shortest person in her family. What are the odds that our little Lola is going to stay little throughout her gymnastics career? And do we really want her to end up a female Super Mario with taped up ankles and multiple knee surgeries by the time she's sixteen?

But if she's really great at this—and the kid clearly has some chops—then shouldn't we push her as far as her talent will take her? Or, even better, what if there were some way to *know* if Lola may have a future at this? What if there were a test, a genetic screening of some kind, to see if she, you know, has a disposition for this?

When it comes to youth sports, we have always been armchair geneticists. When we see a promising Little League pitcher, don't we always wonder if his father played high school ball, Legion ball or maybe even college or lower minors, and then we extrapolate from there? Don't we discreetly take the measure of a promising basketball player's mother and father to divine how tall this talented fifth grader might yet grow? What is that but genetics of the most basic, Mendelian kind, the assumption that athleticism is passed down from father and mother to son and daughter, like the pigment in green or albino pea pods? But despite our careful scrutiny, it is still a genetic lottery. Why isn't Michael Jordan's son more like Mike? Why wasn't Jose Canseco's identical twin brother good enough to stick in the major leagues? Obviously, our genomic inheritance does not entirely define us and our athletic prowess. But we know it plays a part, a big part.

That is where my experiment with Atlas Genetics comes in. Atlas, a Boulder, Colorado–based company that previously specialized in growth supplements, recently introduced a take-at-home test that detects the presence of a variant of the ACTN3 gene that blocks the expression of the alpha-actinin-3 protein. This protein, expressed in both copies of the gene, one from each parent, is associated with fast-twitch muscle movements and is present in a high percentage of elite athletes. As many as 50 percent of a pool of 107 athletes tested by geneticists in 2003 had at least one copy of the variant; the fifty Olympians included in the pool all did. In results published by that team in the *American Journal of Human Genetics*, only 6 percent of the elite athletes had this protein blocked in both copies of their genes. What this means, according to Atlas founder Kevin Reilly, a fifty-five-year-old former football player and power lifter who competed in both sports at the University of Northern Colorado, and who is also a manufacturer of weight lifting equipment and the owner of a string of health clubs, is that this test can help to determine how likely you or your offspring are to become elite, "sprint, power and strength" athletes.

In other words, the best athletes among us, to a higher degree, lack this gene variant and so express this protein and, possibly, are therefore faster and stronger.

What Atlas seems to be offering, in other words, is the possibility that you can ascertain the likelihood that junior-with-the-good-jump-shot is nine years old going on LeBron. With college as expensive as it is and youth sports leagues as sophisticated as they are, why wouldn't you want to know if your little tiger has the game to, say, become Tiger, or at least win a college scholarship? Though Mr. Reilly is very quick to stress that this test should be a part of a complete evaluation process—vertical leap, ten-yard dash, a lateral side-to-side speed drill—he says that it is very hard to do those evaluations on an eight-year-old because kids that age just don't have the motor skills yet, while his test requires nothing more than a saliva swab. Mr. Reilly believes that his test should not be taken as the sole criteria in assessing a child's likely athletic success: "If the only thing you use is the genetic marker and forget about the other tests, then you're going to get it wrong." But, he adds, for a parent who is "wondering if the $10,000 a year spent on hockey programs, travel and equipment for their nine-year-old is a good investment," wouldn't that nine-year-old "be better to get into a sport where they might excel when they are eighteen?" And his tests help to identify those tendencies.

The implications, of course, are disturbing. Do we want to know this much about our children? Do we want to think, while we watch our son or daughter walk a half-dozen consecutive batters, "Of course this is happening! What do you expect if you have the ACTN3 gene variant?" Extrapolate further. As we bring to bear ever greater levels of resolution on the genome, locating and identifying the proteins and amino acids that make for beauty or intelligence, do we really want to be able to test our children for each of those traits? This debate rages beyond the confines of sport, yet it seems that here in our Little Leagues and gyms is where the first real-world application is happening. "We're not saying, 'let's test a one-year-old and see if they have the genetic potential to be the next superstar,'" cautions Reilly. Yet that is exactly what will happen, as some parents decide they want to know if this is time and money well spent. Where does this end?

Boyd Epley, the founder of the University of Nebraska strength training program and a consultant for Atlas, admits to worrying about the potential misunderstanding. "One guy wrote in and asked if the kid didn't have the correct gene, should you euthanize him?" Mr. Epley believes that the test provides information, nothing more. "What you do with it is up to you." Other countries, notably China, are starting to take these tests even more seriously than the U.S., and may soon begin applying the results as part of their athletic screening processes. "This is the future of sports, this will be part of the talent evaluation process going forward," says Mr. Epley.

But some specialists in the field describe the process as being more primitive and less conclusive. "I think the bottom line is that there is no single gene that is the gene for athletic capability," says Theodore Friedman, the director of the University of California's San Diego Medical Center's gene therapy program. "And there will be no such gene. There are some correlations but these are absolutely not predictive values."

When I asked Mr. Friedman, who has two grown-up sons, if he would have given them an ACTN3 test if it had been available, he pauses and then says, "I don't think I would have my children tested. I think I learned far more about my sons' interest in sport by watching them do sport. We learned who our children were at a very early age without genetic testing."

I have to admit to a certain ambivalence when a colleague of mine suggested I have myself and my daughter undergo this test, to determine her proclivity for "strength, power sports" like gymnastics. To call my own athletic career disappointing would be an overstatement. It was a non-career—feckless in Little League, a few seasons of disappointing flag football, years of goal-less soccer capped by a completely undistinguished run of coeducational college soccer. I have continued playing soccer into my forties, and for a few years in my thirties I was a serviceable though unspectacular midfielder. My wife was a more promising genetic package: tall, muscular and strong, a physical specimen, a talented child athlete, an accomplished equestrian. Who did my daughter take after?

But was this information I even wanted? Perhaps, before those early winter mornings of wiping ice from windshields and huddling in cold Long Island parking lots, I would have declined. Let little girls be little girls. Let Lola pursue gymnastics as far as her talent would take her, even if she ended up like one of those squat little homunculi who performed in the upper age groups, as long as she was happy. But then, one hungover morning, squinting into the blinding sun rising into our faces on the Long Island Expressway—I had forgotten my sunglasses—I reconsidered. Lola didn't love this sport *that* much. She hated practice. She complained when the coaches made them do sit-up drills—and why should six-year-olds be doing sit-ups anyway? Who does sit-ups when they're six? Shouldn't they be playing with My Little Pony or some shit like that instead of going through pint-sized basic training?

Maybe it would be nice to know if she really does have a future at this. Say the 577R allele, the variation of the ACTN3 gene that allows for full expression of the alpha-actinin-3, is in full effect. How would that change my feelings about early rising and unpleasant, distant gymnasiums and moms in loose-fitting denim cheering for their daughters and tinny-sounding routine muzak played over and over and over again?

The test was easy enough—a mail order kit, a swab inserted into Lola's mouth and then sealed in a little plastic pack, and then all of it sent back to Colorado. A few weeks later, the results came in.

As you watch the little girls lined up before their floor routine or their tentative first forays on the beam, you can't help but gasp at how adorable the whole production is. The tiny little legs and arms, no thicker than celery stalks, the sparkled and shimmering leotards, the hair pulled back into tight buns—you almost wonder at how these good-natured little darlings don't all just sit down to throw a big tea party. It is hard to remember that these little girls are competing against one another and the other far-flung teams, from Rye and Port Chester and Staten Island, girls as eager and enthusiastic as our New York City kids, parents who seem more driven, coaches who seem more focused. As a father, you can't help but get caught up in the competition. I look at those other little girls in their blue and gold or pink and silver leotards and find myself silently scoring their floor routines—*Look, she didn't land that kickover!*—and thinking, *Come on, Lola, nail it. Nail it!* The team is invitation-only, the practices three days a week, three hours a day, the routines judged and scored so that your little girl's disappointing 7.9 is on display for all the parents to see. So much *seems* to be at stake—the judges, the officials holding up the scores, the parents leaning forward, silent and tense—that it is hard to remember that absolutely nothing is at stake. We forget, in the midst of our national orgy of sports celebration, as we slide back and forth on that vast continuum between Olympic Games and this little, cold gymnasium, that for the kids, for Lola, this is supposed to be fun. Nothing else. She's not thinking of how good she'll be at fourteen or even how good she'll be next week. She likes dressing up in a leotard and doing cartwheels.

So it was a little bit of a surprise when she told me, just a day after her last meet, that she wanted to quit the team, citing, once again, her dislike of practice. My wife and I asked the dutiful questions: Was she sure? Did she want to give it one more try? And then my wife called the gym to tell them Lola was out.

A few days later, we receive the results from Atlas. I have the variation in one set of genes; as I already well know, I am an unlikely elite athlete. My daughter, Lola, however, lacks the variation of the ACTN3 gene on both sides; in other words, she is a fast-twitch, strength-power genetic type all the way, a potential elite gymnast in the making.

But I'm never going to show her those results. Let her find her own way.

Dinosaur

PETER HO DAVIES

My son has known that I'm a writer since he could read. One of the first places he recognized his own name in print was on the dedication page of my last novel. In subsequent years he's often asked me to write a book for him, and I've tried gamely enough a couple of times. For a while I fooled around with a picture book, a surreal riff on the famous Dylan Thomas story that I planned to call *A Child's Christmas in Whales*. There was a lobster called "Santa Claws" counseling the castaway not to be "shellfish" and a "tree," a shipwreck's mast and rigging, decorated with puffer-fish and sea stars and an eclectic eel. Another time I spun a little tale around the stuffed panda my son sleeps with, Nightbear, whose job is to ward off bad dreams from the waking world. But he grew out of these stories before they could be properly finished, and lately, now that he's graduated from picture books to chapter books, he's been asking me to write a book not for him, but *about* him. And I find myself mumbling excuses, changing the subject.

This hesitancy, I should say, isn't anything new. Long before he started asking, I'd considered writing about him (I'm a fiction writer, but most of my stories spring from some autobiographical source), and yet always with this same strange flicker of hesitation. Strange, because parent-child relationships are a recurring theme in my fiction, most notably in my story collection, *Equal Love*, which takes its title (and epigraph) from E. M. Forster's *Where Angels Fear to Tread*: "For a wonderful physical tie binds the parents to the children; and—by some sad, strange irony—it does not bind us children to our parents. For if it did, if we could answer their love not with gratitude but with equal love, life would lose much of its pathos and much of its squalor, and we might be wonderfully happy." But I wrote those stories years before my son's birth. If they're about him, even obliquely (and the book is at least as much about being a child as it is about being a parent), they're about my anxious anticipation of parenthood.

My hesitancy also seems strange in light of the preoccupation with parent-child relationships in much contemporary fiction, where it has arguably supplanted the venerable "marriage plot"—think Jane Austen—and what we might call the "adultery plot"—think John Updike—that subverted it in the second half of the twentieth century. The traditional marriage plot itself often encloses a secondary parent-child plot. Marriage, after all, is a decisive moment in our separation from our parents. But as marriage has receded as the defining choice in our lives (it's at once less essential—socially or economically—and less permanent), we're presented with other choices, notably to have a child or not, a choice previously subsumed/assumed within the marriage plot but no longer, thanks to scientific and social transformations in the availability of contraception, abortion, fertility treatments, and adoption.

At the same time our relationships with our parents and children have come to last longer than in previous generations by virtue of increased life spans. The parent-child bond is no longer "merely" formative, but is likely to outlast our marital relationships, and over that period to present us with evolving challenges unfamiliar to our forebears. We can see some of these anxieties reflected, albeit grotesquely and often cynically, in political discourse over abortion and "death panels." Issues from the deficit to the environment are commonly framed as questions of generational indebtedness. Americans are perhaps particularly inclined to these obsessions. The U.S. is, after all, a nation established by founding *fathers*, a nation presided over by a first *family* (and several such families have dynastic aspirations), a nation of immigrants and their offspring (who often feel alienated from each other), and a nation obsessed, for several generations now, with youth (and thus equally with the denial of aging and death). And American writers, who from the start have defined themselves in opposition to a parent culture, an established tradition of British literature—there's that marriage plot again—have a long-standing awareness of forebears that precedes even our current phase of postmodernity.

So what is holding me back?

What I usually say when asked this by friends and readers who know *Equal Love*, and share my own expectation that I'll write about parenthood, is that I did write about my son once . . . and it didn't go well.

I'd been invited to pick a favorite word for World Book Day, a whimsical request, but one for a worthy cause that seemed churlish to decline. I chose "fountain" because, as I explained, fountains were one of my toddler son's favorite things and because he'd just used the word in his first simile, pointing out that a tree in our local park was like a fountain.

So far so cute. Calendar pages fall from the wall. I publish a novel, it gets long-listed in the UK for the Booker Prize, a prize which in addition to being an honor akin to the Pulitzer or the National Book Award in the U.S. is, largely unlike those other awards, the subject of some frenzied cultural commentary. It's possible, say, to wager on the winner with British bookies. I should say at once I didn't win, didn't even make the cut from the long list of thirteen (the "Booker's dozen") to the short list of six. Fine. It's an honor to be nominated and all that (and at least I got to place a bet on myself). In those few heady weeks of possibility, though, vanity did lead me to Google myself quite a bit, and one morning a hit caught my eye: "Another Smug Parent." The blogger in question—I won't identify him though you can be sure I made it my business to find out his name, and where he worked and his address (hi there!)—was referring to my post for World Book Day, added a few disparaging comments about my book, and ended with the line "Which reminds me of my favorite word: cunt."

I did not take this well. "This guy's calling me a cunt," I raged to my wife, who very sensibly advised me to drop it. "But he's calling me a cunt!" And so on and so forth for several fuming minutes . . . (while I have occasionally claimed that my outrage was on behalf of my child, my real anger was, of course, at the insult to me) . . . until my son, on the living room rug looked over from his construction paper and scissors and called, "Look, Daddy, I'm cunting. I'm cunting!"

What are you going to do? Kids say the darnedest fucking things. To this day, and for my sins, I'm very precise in enunciating the glottal "t" in the word cutting. At the very least, I have a new word if the World Book Day people ask again.

While this makes for a good story, it's less a reason than a comic excuse for not writing about my son. Over the years I've offered others—whether reasons or excuses—mostly to myself. In his first eighteen months of life, between sleep deprivation and the steep learning curve of parenthood, I didn't have the time or the energy to write much of anything. I suspect, too, that some part of my reluctance to write about my son—and he's nine this summer, I should say, so I've had plenty of time—is because the reality has proven "a kind of embarrassment to [my] own meager imagination" (to borrow Philip Roth's famous lament).

None of this is to say I've not *tried* to write about my son, about fatherhood. I've had the time, and the inclination, but the results have been dissatisfying. Distasteful, I might even say. There's a selfishness to writing, I think, emblematized in the time this solitary activity takes away from our loved ones, but also inherent in the act itself. My writing at heart (this essay included) is about me—if not myself per se, then my obsessions, my satisfactions, my ego—not about him, a selfishness fundamental to the idea of self-expression, and at odds with what we think of as good parenting.

This suspicion of selfishness underlies my sense that it would be unfair, a usurpation, to tell *his* stories. The "right to write" is something that writers—especially the young writers I teach—struggle with. Are we allowed to tell the stories of others—those of another gender, or sexuality, another race or ethnicity, another class? As a writer, I resist these barriers. They seek to limit our imaginations, even our empathy. And as a teacher, I encourage my students to write through this (mostly) self-censorship. Their doubts shouldn't *stop* them from trying, I say; instead those very doubts, their recognition of the difficulties involved, will help them overcome the challenges. And yet all these perceived transgressions are about power relations—male students worry much more, say, about writing from a female point of view than female students worry about writing from a male point of view—and ultimately I can't help feeling that writing about my son risks taking something from him.

Finally, I've always been a writer who needed distance to write. I was able to write about my native Britain from the U.S., about my own childhood from a remove of years. More generally, something, an event, a period, needs to be *over* for me to address it in fiction. Narrative, after all, is typically retrospective; writers like to know where they're going, how it ends. My son, though, remains in constant flux, changing—albeit a little more slowly now than in his first couple of years of life—growing month by month, a pace which my slow process of writing can't match. I can't get the necessary distance from him, nor would I wish to. It is every parent's most fervent wish not to see the end of his or her child's story. (Children, by contrast, are less squeamish in their anticipation of our deaths. Their fascination with dinosaurs—towering, massive, and extinct—is surely some imaginative, albeit indirect, version of our end.)

My son, as I noted at the start, is the one now who most often encourages me to write about him. He's a keen young reader with a lively sense of narrative. (I read to him now less than when he was younger, and one thing I miss is his habit of shouting, "Dun . . . dun . . . dun!" at cliffhanger chapter breaks.) These reasons, this essay, as you might have already guessed, are for him, even if he might not be able to appreciate them yet. And perhaps that "yet" is the key here, it's anticipation of who he'll become. He takes some satisfaction in that novel of mine that's dedicated to him, something I can only hope will continue, since he—or at least his future self—has become my ideal reader, the one I'm writing for. He's become, in that sense, my posterity. Writing in part surely springs from an apprehension of our own mortality. We write to live on after our deaths, and we have children out of the same imperative. In some basic way I need to write less now that I'm a father. I am already—in some incomplete, hapless, and collaborative way—in the process of authoring my son. He is already in the process of reading me. But ultimately (*Dun . . . dun . . . dun!*) it's his job to write my story, not mine to write his. Another inequality in our love to add to Forster's list.

To put it another way, I learned the news that I hadn't made the short list for the Booker Prize at a rest stop in Ohio on a cross-country drive; to be precise, in a family bathroom, while changing my son's diaper. That one failed (and likely chimerical) bid for immortality was placed in perspective by the squirming, squalling, stinking embodiment of another before me. But whether that's smugness or humility, I'm not sure.

A World in Which We Refuse to Play

BRUCE MACHART

One cauldron-hot Houston Saturday in 1977, my older brother Chris and I told my father we wanted to fly a kite. The wind was playing hell with the leaves of the live oak across the street, and the flickering old black-and-white television set had, for once, lost some of its allure. There was a good kite-flying wind worked up out there. We could hear it funneling loudly between the neighborhood houses, hurling itself against the corrugations of the red cedar siding. We could see it whipping the white undershirts on Mrs. Baker's clothesline next door. The whole planet, it seemed, had come thrillingly, somewhat violently alive, and there was only one apparent problem in the whole beautifully animated world. No kite.

No kite, and no sweat. Not for my father anyway, he of the swollen biceps and tree-trunk legs, he of the quick temper and quicker smile, he of the perennial desire to foster and amplify the delight of his children. No, sir. My father was a player, and not the gold chain, leisure suit sort. What I mean is, my father liked to *play*. A lot.

For three hours, we built the mother of all box kites. We used newspaper, glue, string, dowels, fabric, numerous gauges of wire. We measured and nipped and scissored and folded and taped. I think we may have even soldered. Who solders a fucking kite? My father, that's who. You know why? It's fun. Soldering is fun, and so is building a kite, and we were doing both. Plus, it was going to work. This kite was going to fly.

Our labors complete and our various adhesives cured and dry, and our mother shaking her head in the kitchen, we took our creation outside. In the vacant lot across the street, well out of the live oak's greedy reach, Chris stood holding the kite while I, with some twenty-five feet of kite string unspooled between us, spat between my teeth—a new, as yet unrefined talent—and steadied myself for some kick-ass kite piloting. A promising hot gust rippled my *Star Trek* T-shirt and set my father's comb-over to flapping. Then came the countdown, the launch, the skyward and hopeful faces. And the thing flew! It flew straight up and into a kazillion little fluttering pieces.

My father couldn't stop smiling. This was fun, by damn! *Wasn't that fun?* Hadn't it been fun? I can hear him now. He loved every blessed second of it. The smell of glue and the bickering fraternal negotiations and the fateful, short-lived, unraveling flight. My father loved to play. He *still* loves to play. How lucky are the children whose fathers genuinely love playing with them! I have been one of those children, and so it saddens me greatly that I have never been, and likely will never be, one of those fathers.

Confucius once said that it is better to play than to do nothing. Ain't that just a rousing endorsement? If you ask me, the big Conman was perhaps a bit too enthusiastic. I find doing nothing *largely* preferable to playing. I find ingrown toenail surgery at least *slightly* preferable to playing. Get this: I would rather *work* than play. So let's get real, Confucius. Let's tell it like it is: Playing blows.

There, I said it. I hate playing.

But wait, you say. Hold it right there, mister. I've seen you at all those sweltering, down-home south Texas family reunions, throwing washers with your brothers and cousins and uncles. I've seen you play forty-two and spades with such demonstrative vigor that your knuckles blossom most bloodily from thumping trumps down onto the hard, resoundingly oaken table. I've seen the old photographs, the ones of you in the regrettably short shorts of your 1970s youth basketball league, the ones from your numerous baseball and football teams. I've seen you throw the pigskin around the yard, shoot pool with friends, play Golden Tee video-for-godsakes-*golf* with the regulars at the local bar.

Well, fine. Make me invoke the caveat. I hate playing with children. Even with *my* kids. And most especially with *your* kids.

Oh, sure, you say. But didn't I see you with your two young eventual stepchildren nearly a decade back, one hanging from each of your legs in a game they for some unintelligible reason called "Monkey"? Wasn't that you missing-linking it across the family room to their dangling, delirious, and discombobulated delight?

Yep.

And wasn't that you with your mucus-glazed and toddling nephew, tying oh-so-vibrantly appointed squares of fabric to your balding head, playing something called "Rainbow Pirate"?

Aye, me hearties!

Uh, and weren't you, just last month, when you flew back to Texas for a weekend with your son at your parents' house . . .

weren't you planted at the computer, breaking only for the occasional bowlful of chips, teaming with your beloved boy, Dalton, to defeat some arrestingly flatulent monsters in a marathon of Wizard101?

Yes, that was me, too. But listen, I said that I hated playing, not that I didn't do it. Not too long ago, I removed the drain plate from the upstairs bathtub, and, with an ingeniously repurposed and most expertly manipulated coat hanger, I tugged a slimy, soap-slicked, long-since-exfoliated-skin-encrusted rope of hair from the drainpipe. This bad boy was a thing of wonder, at least four years' worth of showering in the making, nearly a foot long, and I extricated it with my bare hands (and the aforementioned coat hanger). As a chore, this was pretty high up on the old disgusting scale. But it was better, far better, than playing. In short, I do things I don't like doing, and I do them all the time. We all do. Yet there's an important distinction to be made. When you unclog a pipe, something tangible is accomplished, and there's no pretense. No one stands over you, smiling at what a marvelous unclogger you've become, asking you how much fun you're having. No one expects you to enjoy it, and no one judges you if you admit to hating and resenting every second of it.

It might hearten you to remember that I am a genetic aberration. I come from a long line of dedicated playtime enthusiasts, my father foremost among them. But he is not alone. If you gave my two grown brothers (both fathers now themselves) the privacy necessary to avoid self-consciousness and a dozen or so vintage *Star Wars* action figures, they would play their asses off. Given two hours together in a bedroom turned galactic battleground, they would emerge, glowing with the triumphant goodness of Jedis and the knowing, noble nods of those who had driven the Empire asunder. These are two proverbial nuts who fell right damned next to the proverbial tree, and it's a beautiful thing if you ask me.

As I've mentioned, my father freaking *loves* to play, and his dedication to this, the selfless art, grows disproportionately to the age of the playmate. Just as this rare trait once launched kites destined for ecstatic failure, it nowadays makes his grandchildren, my son Dalton the oldest among them, some exceedingly lucky little farts. By contrast, it makes me feel like a simultaneously lethargic and egocentric turd.

Perhaps some exposition would be handy. More than a decade ago, when my son Dalton was a fetus, I fell in love with a woman who was not the woman in whose womb said Dalton was happily and umbilically tethered, floating as he was with all the worries of the world as yet unknown to him—floating and bobbing and biding his miraculous, fetal time until his 0th birthday. I am a lifelong Catholic, and I'm a self-centered novelist who eschews quality family time in favor of time spent not quite writing in a room all alone, and I now live eighteen hundred miles from my only biological child, all of which means that I don't much need a reason to feel *more* guilty, but there you have it. I have few regrets, but I am good at guilt. It's got a look and a feel that never goes out of fashion.

By the time Dalton was six months old, I was broke, in the midst of a contentious divorce (see broke), living back home with my parents (see broke), and, because I taught at the local community college only on Mondays, Wednesdays, and Fridays (see broke), while waiting tables at night and on weekends (yep, again), I had my lawyer demand that I get "visitation" with my son every

Tuesday and Thursday in addition to the normally decreed every other weekend.

And so it was written. The custody decree, that is. In hindsight, other than my subsequent marriage, this was perhaps the most beautiful and rewarding commitment I've ever made. For two and a half years, until Dalton reached the age of three, I would drive thirty miles into Houston, pick my son up from his mother's house, and drive back to my parents' home in the suburbs. In the evening, I would make the trip again to drop him off. At this time, my mother was still working as an RN at a local clinic, but my father had already retired from his lifelong career as a letter carrier. In this way, Tuesdays and Thursdays were three-generational carnivals of playtime, and it was during these many hours that I first recognized my deficiencies in this unhappy realm of obligatory parental participation.

In those two and a half years, we spent 260 weekdays together, just the three of us—Dalton, Daddy, and PawPaw, as he has come to be cleped. A triumvirate of Machart masculinity. And while I will take credit for the diaper changing, for the bottle feeding and then the strained-pea spooning, for the tantrum wrangling, for the slow, sweet, naptime routine of swaying with my son in my arms to the same worn track of a Townes Van Zandt record, for many of the "chores" of parenthood, I would be lying if I told you I did any playing that I truly enjoyed. From the start, that was PawPaw's territory, and he cultivated it both figuratively and literally.

In the backyard, he kept a densely wooded green space meticulously cleared of briars and other prickly pitfalls. This was Dalton's "jungle," and by the time he could walk, he spent hours in that imaginary wonderland of trees and pine straw and sticks and pinecones and (thanks to PawPaw's narrative constructions and penchant for realistically rendered animal sounds) wild, wild beasts roaring and screeching and tickling toddler funny bones.

One afternoon, when a municipal landscaping crew that had been charged with mowing the banks of the nearby bayou left a tractor sitting idle, it was my father who took two-year-old Dalton to "ride" the tractor, a ride that turned into rather a long one, maybe a hundred imaginary miles of lip-sputtering engine sounds and expert steering-wheel work, the whole world gone ripe with the diesel-rich redolence of one wondrously combustible imagination. This was some serious work, after all, some serious play.

Where was I? Sitting on the back porch, just in view, smoking a cigarette, waving periodically and feigning a big, happy, *Daddy-is-having-fun-too* smile.

So what exactly is my problem? My aversion to play might be more palatable (for me and for others) if, for instance, my child was an entitled pain in the ass, or horrifically ugly, or mean-spirited. But he's just not. He's a joy. He's beautiful. He's empathetic. On his fifth Christmas morning, he descended the stairs, looked at all his gifts under the tree, and, without investigating further, pulled a package from the pile and brought it to me where I sat sipping coffee on the couch. "Open it, Daddy," he said. "I got it just for you!"

What kind of five-year-old doesn't think first of himself on Christmas? What kind of daddy doesn't want to play with that kind of child? And then there's this: Just imagining the premature seriousness of his dark, dark eyes pulls the musty drapes back on my big, bruised heart. Here's a boy who feels the world so deeply

I would swear that each time he sees birds aloft there's a feathery fluttering in his very marrow. I simply adore him, and he's so beautiful that it hurts me to love him so. It is, in the watery wisdom of Marlin from *Finding Nemo*, a "complicated emotion." Surely, somewhere in the deep grain of the heartwood of my love for him worms the guilt of having moved, two years ago, across the country to get married and start a new job. And maybe there, too, lies the guilt of having "wasted" so much of my time with him over the years, but the simple fact remains—I don't like playing now any more than I liked it when I saw him every Tuesday and Thursday. Which is to say, I don't like it at all.

For several years, until recently, I had a theory. I imagined that only "imaginative" play repulsed me. I considered the likelihood that my work as a writer demanded that I reserve my imaginative energies for the page. After some reflection, though, I'm not sure this logic holds. For me, it's all really just a matter of remorse. I can think about clog-removal at great length without ever once feeling guilty about it, without the kind of self-flagellation so often reserved for my fellow Catholic reprobates. Ask me to play cards, and I'll usually take you up on it, even if you aren't yet old enough to have mastered, say, washing your own hair or cutting your own steak. Card games, board games, even the oft-maligned video games— these things have trajectories, timelines, endpoints. Ask me to "go outside and play jungle because the animals are afraid because there's a new mean lion and he lives in Africa and he's going to bite the other animals especially the monkeys and I love monkeys and then he will kill them and eat all their Cheerios" (or some such other enticing narrative), and I will begin a panicked perusal of the house to find out just where the hell PawPaw is. Once PawPaw is on the job, however, I'll sit steeping in my own shame.

Were this all as cut-and-dried as I might like, my stance here might be defensible. Instead of turning the paternal reins over to PawPaw, I could say, "Son, I love you more than lions love bloody, gamey slabs of monkey meat, but I just don't like playing pretend. Want to play Hungry Hungry Hippos?"

The trouble, of course, is that "playing pretend" is widely considered so very, very important—vital, even. Ask kids. Ask grown-ups. Ask pediatricians. Ask child psychiatrists. Hell, ask the good scientists who keep deepening our understanding of neuroscience and brain function.

Ultimately, though, I have to confess that even games with time limits and rules kind of stink when you are playing them with your own progeny. In these moments (or long, long hours . . . the game depending), you can't *just* play. You have to instruct, to psychoanalyze, to anticipate, to correct, to encourage and reward, to preempt and redirect, to engage and distract. In short, you have to *parent*, and parenting is a fun-suck, plain and simple, no matter how hungry your hippos are for those pure and little and elusive white marbles of quality time.

I suspect that I'm not alone. A couple of years back, I was visiting my dear friend Matt in the Twin Cities. Before we found ourselves on our own for the day, we had to engage in the ritualized driving of Emory, his precocious and towheaded son (and my enchanting godson), to his Montessori school. Let me just say this: If I could go back in time and meet Maria Montessori, I would wash her feet and kiss her ring and extricate the filthy hair-snake from her bathtub drainpipe. Here was a woman who found a way to employ most of the adults in the world who actually do like playing with children, and a way that is somehow good for everybody involved, all the while making use of whacked-out but ingenious implements like deci-pockets and Moonjar banks. Show me a Montessori-educated four-year-old, and I'll show you a kid who is full of well-mannered wonder. Moreover, I'll show you a kid who knows how to roll up his or her own work rug and put it exactly where the fuck it goes. It's a glorious thing, but I digress.

So Matt and Emory and I are in the car, Montessori bound, and I am stricken all of a sudden by high-frequency waves of panic. Matt drives carefully, his cargo precious, but before I know what's happening, I have to roll down the window. We are driving though an industrial enclave of St. Paul, and the whole neighborhood smells of axle grease and ozone, but it's better than the rank fumes of "make believe" in the car. This, apparently, is a ritual, a way to pass the thirty-minute drive. My perfectly sensible and intellectual friend (he's a tenured professor, after all) is speaking in the voice of a "good dragon," and the good dragon sounds a lot like the curious lovechild of Grover and a castrato who smokes a pack a day. Matt's son is the prince or some such, and there's traffic rushing by like mad, and I'm horrified. Because of this, for a long while, I have worried about Matt. Turns out, though, that he hates this kind of play just as surely as I do. Why, then, does he degrade himself by impersonating the fire-breathing bastard child of a puppet and a gelding?

Guilt. If he didn't do it, what do you suppose he'd be? He'd be something far worse than a nutless Muppet; he'd be a bad father. And isn't this what we all fear, the damnation of a world in which we refuse to play?

Still, I'm not really talking about Matt, about his guilt, about the condemnation of some world-at-large. I'm talking about me, about a father who has failed to meet his son's every need, about a father who has failed to afford his child the delights that he himself was so generously afforded as a child, about a father who has moved nearly two thousand miles away from his son only to end up here, speaking about himself in this pathetically guised third person.

And why? Because I am ashamed, because I am remorseful, and because this self-awareness has triggered no real change. I can sit here now, having loads of playful fun with these words on this page, but I can't find a way to enjoy playing with my own flesh and blood. Today, as I worry about the self-consciousness of this paragraph, I am back in Houston to see Dalton. It's a trip I make, airfares be damned, at least once per month, and it's a lovely, warm spring day. It would be a great time to go outside and play with my son, wouldn't it?

I have only ever had one dream about my son, though I have had it many times. He is two. The sun is out in earnest, blazing and yellow, and we are at a playground, bathed in jaundiced light. We are alone, just the two of us, and the playground has one of those elaborate and expensive wooden structures, an elevated platform of slides and fireman poles and such, but in the dream it is so, so very high, and there's no railing.

Dalton is always two, and I am always sweating beneath the yellow sun, following him around as he navigates the elevated platform. He is going to fall. That's the cruelty of dreamworlds. He is going to fall, and I know it, and I follow him as he teeters

on the brink, his little blue-and-white Stride Rite sneakers slipping as he goes. In the dream the sun makes the platform slippery,
and this makes perfect sense to me. Overhead, the loud protesta-
tions of three circling crows. When I look up at them, Dalton slips
and falls, and for a long while he hangs suspended, clinging to my
outstretched hand, his little fingernails biting into the skin of my
thumb.

The sound he makes is the same sound he makes when the
nurse at the pediatrician's office gives him an injection, the sound
he makes when his perfect olive skin yields to the needle, a gasp
of surprise, then a breathless cry of disbelief. And I would know
how to comfort him if we were in the doctor's office, but we're not,
and now the ground begins to pull back, to recede such that I'm
holding my son over an abyss, and my boots are sliding on the
sun-slick wood and he's dangling, slipping from my grasp, crying,
and the crows throw their mad, circling shadows around the perimeter of the hole that is widening forever beneath us.

And then my two-year-old son, my darling Dalton, has the
voice of a much older child. His face drains of its terror and innocence, and he's calm, mature, serene. "It's okay, Dad," he says.

And then he falls.

Several years ago, after waking from this dream, I went downstairs to find Dalton on the sofa, safe and munching dry cereal and
watching some vaguely inappropriate television. I poured coffee,
sloshing it into the cup with an unsteady hand, then I walked
outside and smoked a cigarette and made a promise to myself.

It was a futile promise but one that made sense at the time.
I would play with my boy, I would help him grow into a man, I

would teach him how to flourish in a world overrun by horror and violence and injustice, and I would do it all in an encouraging, playful way. This, I see now, is preposterous, a promise born of my own unsettling inability to do just the things I was promising to teach my son to do. I might as well build a kite out of newspaper and expect it to hold its own against the indifferent and tireless forces of nature. I might as well teach my son to be small and vulnerable and afraid, as we ever are, and to find some way to turn it all into some fun little game.

Back inside, I sat beside Dalton on the couch, rubbing his back through the thin, flame-resistant fabric of his *Clone Wars* pajamas. On the television, some kid pressed a glowing wristwatch-like device and morphed into a yellow, slithering alien creature with a considerable flair for the dramatic. Overhead, the ceiling fan turned slow, deliberate circles.

"Do you want to go outside?" I asked.

"Why?" he said.

"I don't know. We could play."

He shot me a funny, knowing look, his dark, dark eyes glimmering with the light of all they knew. "It's okay, Dad," he said, and he put his tanned little hand on my knee. His nails needed trimming. For a while then, we just sat there together, watching the make-believe monster on the television.

Our Birds

MATTHEW SPECKTOR

Elizabeth told me she was pregnant in November. We were sitting in a parking lot in northern New Hampshire, where we had just pulled in to buy groceries. I'd killed the ignition, and was folding my way toward the door of an unheated Subaru when she said it. *I'm pregnant.* I was staring at a dirty snowbank, a landscape all grim and gray and crappy, and the moment that ought to have been poetry was as prosaic as you can imagine. It was fourteen degrees outside. The sky was a wall of colorless frost. I was from California, where I was used to seeing living things even in winter, to a sky filled with sunlight and birdsong. Her words fell into a mortuarial silence. I tried to process them. My hands were cold and my blood ran colder.

"Really?" My voice sounded tremulous, thin.

Elizabeth and I were three years away from a divorce when she told me, and at least two from a recognition that either of us would ever want one. Still, we'd decided to try to have a baby. Her pregnancy was certainly no accident. Yet only at the moment that she proclaimed it to me did I realize—if not yet articulate to myself in any way that could be considered conscious—that I was having a child, perhaps, with the wrong person.

Such a stark, and monstrous, realization. I write with the panicked sense that our daughter, who is now eight, will read this someday and be hurt, imagining that what I'm saying here is that *she* is, or was, the wrong person. Nothing could be further from the truth. Virginia is what all children are, unmistakably the right person, born to human beings who need to catch up and become fit parents themselves. We have—my ex is a splendid mother—but our union was fucked, somehow, from the beginning.

Imperceptibly so, as we could not have enjoyed each other's company more, but perhaps we were not, in the most adherent sense, "in love." Whatever glue there is that makes two people tolerate each other once there is a child in the picture, once there is a focus on somebody other than themselves, we lacked. And so it was Vivi (we agreed on almost everything, to that point: even Virginia's nickname) who shone the light, exposing the crack that had been there all along, and which we'd been too at ease to see.

She was nearly two and a half when her mother and I split up, and *then*—only after Lizzie had left me and it became plain that every last moment I would be spending with Vivi, at least for the foreseeable future, was going to be mine alone—only then did I become a dad. A sentence that still gives me pause, because "dads" do all kinds of things—they grill meat and drive minivans, are sexually mute as they wander through a suburban fog—I do not, and did not. I identify more, perhaps, as a "father." I realize I'm stereotyping here, but these words carry contrails of overt and covert suggestion. With the divorce, however reluctantly, I became a dad: that guy you see battling valiantly with an unruly toddler on an airplane, the one you see prowling the margins of athletic fields squinting lustily (or, alas, not so lustily, but tiredly or foolishly) at the women, wondering if they are having affairs or would like to. I became, in other words, responsible at the expense of my own dignity, not just a spiritual overseer ("father"), but a material problem solver ("dad").

To this point, I'd been able to shirk the latter, if not in literal fact—of course I was a material problem solver, from the very first diaper full of tar onward, every day—then in spirit. My ex was the one with the baby; I was the guy who stepped in for the photograph. I should clarify: I was Vivi's primary caregiver, at least during the week, when my ex went to work at 5:00 a.m. for an investment bank, but I was still, in my mind, outside it. Until I was pushing forty and alone and the sole proprietor of all my time with Vivi; then, truly, she became my child and I became, irrevocably, her dad.

Her single dad.

Vivi's been such a citizen since, such a pure and lovely emanation of everything I could ever bring myself to call beauty. Fair of heart, as well as fair of feature: I know it sounds like I'm describing something out of a Disney movie, but Vivi *is* like something out of a Disney movie, one of those fucking princesses (excuse me) surrounded by twittering birds as they sing. Vivi loves to sing, she belts out songs by Adele and Taylor Swift, and even when she's alone in her room I hear her chiming softly to herself, and if she's not surrounded by birds when she does, if she's merely human, she's still the girliest human I've ever met, prone to wearing a costume wedding dress to school for picture day (no, really), prone to fretting about her hair and asking me at least three times a week just when she'll be permitted to pierce her ears. I know, I know: I'm gendertyping again, but really all I mean is that Vivi is this way, just like every three-year-old boy I've ever met is fascinated by trucks, and it's nothing *I* ever showed her. I'm a man, and my limited understanding of women is indicated by the number of times I've had my heart broken by one and vice versa. She likes these things, and has always liked them: at two, she refused to wear pants, even soft ones, because they were uncomfortable; now, her funky and elaborate fashion sense is such that she struts around with bags and boots and sunglasses and hair clips and *Cat in the Hat* or *Jawbreaker* or John Cassavetes T-shirts, a riot of influences coordinated into something ineffable, one part teenager to one (much smaller) part toddler, talking about God and Santa Claus and Katy Perry and record players and earrings (again, with the earrings) and meteorology and books and *Adventure Time.* You know. And you know if you've ever held an eight-year-old's hand— an eight-year-old girl's hand, at least, or maybe just *my* eight-year-old girl's—you don't care if you never get to hold any other.

Or not. Because one thing about being a single father? It's lonely. I would imagine for most parents, if not all, there are moments of scorching weariness and isolation, those feelings infants can wail about and adults are meant to tolerate. (Why? It's not like those feelings don't grow worse.) Yet there is something marginal about being a single dad, and equally so about being a writer, and also so, in an undiscussable way, about being relatively poor—I'm not talking about *actual* poverty, of course, just the relative kind that you become aware of when you are living in an affluent urban center, so that as one attends the soccer games and the gymnastics classes and the birthday parties it becomes noticeable, or at least it becomes *felt*, that you do not belong there. The other people are all married, the grown-ups, and the children are used to having their parents in one place. Elizabeth and I get along well, or at least we have, ever since we divorced, and so the question is less *How does this affect our child?* and more, well, *Does everyone else feel this lonely?* Am I alone in not so much loving the accoutrements of parenting, the competition and the solitude and the strangeness and the accidental socializing? Grateful as I am for all the parents with whom I feel an affinity (Matt and Kelly! Jonathan and Amy!), I am so often alienated when I am with people whose only connection to me is the fact that our kids appear to be enjoying one another's company.

Perhaps everyone feels this—I can't imagine that most people do not, at least some of the time—but since there is no one with whom I can peel the husk of my alienation, I am always conscious of it. Except when I am alone with Vivi. Then, now that she is old enough to share a non-knock-knock joke or watch a non-hackneyed movie or read a non-predictable narrative, we are as one, or as two but each breathing and delighting in the other's company as one. The other day I was carrying her up the street—she's so long and tall now, but I can still do it—and I heard her mumbling in my ear.

"What's that, Vivi?" I said.

"I was just saying, *My strong, beautiful, handsome daddy*," she said.

I don't know that I can convey, quite, the degree to which I felt mocked, adored and condescended to in equal measure, but I did. And because this is not a million miles from my attitude to myself—because my narcissism is pretty steadily undercut by a sense of my own preposterousness—I feel, in such moments, like my daughter understands me. Which is amazing.

The thing is, though, it matters not at all whether Vivi understands me. (It may matter to her in later life, but it doesn't matter *now*.) It matters if I understand her, or if her needs are legible to me. They may not be. What do I know of such an urgent need for pierced ears, or to recount, in great detail, the plot of an episode of *Victorious*? More than I should, probably. But she is a mystery to me, and I, in my rattling solitude, with no one to ask but the occasional teacher or pediatrician—relationships where I again feel oddly marginal, with a slight sense of beside-the-pointness—with no woman to look at and say, *What's going on here?*, am thrown back infinitely upon my own limitation. What do I know? Am I a decent parent? I have no idea—despite being deeply involved in my daughter's life, attentive to her needs, awake to her conversation and affectionate for all I know to a fault, despite, even, Vivi's quite unmistakable delight in *me*, I still have no idea. And no sense of when, if ever, I might.

Nor do I necessarily care, so long as I have a happy child, who is safe from as much horror as I can possibly screen, who absorbs only minimal scarring. This simply isn't about *me*, which is why those thoughts I had in the parking lot feel as jejune and useless as any I've ever had, and why whatever things I felt or failed to feel with regard to my ex don't matter either. "Poetry?" For God's sake. There was no Vivi, and now there is. Things don't get more poetic than that.

Once upon a time, I met my ex-wife and I married her. This feels so far away now, that "once upon a time" seems appropriate. It was—and I don't think this is nostalgia speaking—an exceptionally lighthearted and joyful period. We were in Manhattan, I was finishing a novel for which I had only the brightest hopes, and we were in love. How easy it is to forget this. I recall walking along the Bowery one night and discussing a pair of birds, Pickle and Freckle, who were never to actually materialize as pets. Nevertheless we spoke of them often, our birds, as we did our future, our careers, our child or children—all things that stretched out in front of us, pure potential, as things we hadn't polluted yet, or fucked up, things that were sure to bring us as much joy as the present.

Only they didn't. *I* fucked up, and maybe Elizabeth did too—I can't speak for her—but I ruined this future with inattention and poor execution and bad luck, the same things that ruin so many possible futures (but not all of them!), and which are simply the forces with which the world curbs us, when it does.

Except for you, V. You are the one thing I did not fuck up, and will not fuck up, except in the routine ways a parent can mar his or her children (like by using profanity in your presence, which I know you happen to hate). I will not fuck you up, Philip Larkin's famous adage notwithstanding, because no matter how many mistakes I make, and have made, *you* will never be one. Your mistakes, whatever they are, have already been forgiven, however many years in advance we are of their commission. I may never forgive myself a thing, but your sins will always be pardoned. And whenever I am with you, whenever I hold your hand or carry you in my arms—for however much longer I am permitted to do either—I feel almost pardoned too.

I realize the flaw was never in the world, the coldness was never New Hampshire's, but only my own. The world with you in it will never look that way again, because where I sit now there is sunlight splashing the edge of my desk, I see greenery and vegetation everywhere, and just above the sound of your singing I hear on loop in my head, I hear something else too. I hear birds. And if they are real or merely imaginary, just cartoons or actual dreams come true, I hope you can hear them also, and that you always will.

Your Own Worst Enemy

BENJAMIN PERCY

My newborn son would not latch on to my wife's breast. Weight dripped off him like candle wax. The nurses handed us nipple guards, sighed whenever I mentioned formula, rattled off statistics about allergies, health problems later in life. A mother's milk is what an infant needs, they said. But he would not drink. His skin yellowed. His face sank into shadows. A few days later, one of our uncles held him a moment, then handed him back and gave us a thin-lipped expression and said, "I hope things work out."

This was supposed to be the beginning, but I was already bracing myself for the end.

We developed a routine. Every few hours, day and night, our son would cry and my wife would pump and I would bottle-feed, and in this way the months progressed, both of our eyes glazed with exhaustion. He plumped up. His belly swelled and his cheeks wobbled. His arms looked like skewered marshmallows.

And then, just when I was beginning to feel good again, to feel rested and secure, he came down with croup. That is the sound he made—croup, *croup*—when he coughed, like a shark-bit seal. The doctor said it would pass. She said not to worry. But his throat continued to close, even when I ran the shower until the bathroom ghosted with steam, even when I mummied him in a blanket and carried him around in the winter cold. Nothing helped. His lips turned blue. When we brought him back to the clinic, they said, "Oh my god," and called an ambulance.

That might qualify as the worst moment of my life, when I watched my nine-month-old son gurneyed into an ambulance, when I followed it desperately through a snowstorm. At the ICU, they shot him full of steroids and debated a tracheotomy while he, in a hospital gown patterned with tiny balloons, twisted and wept and croup-croup-crouped.

Seven years later, and I still have not recovered from that time. Becoming a parent fundamentally changed my vision. I cannot help but see the world in sharp angles. I walk into a room and itemize the woodstove, the electrical socket, the scissors, the open window, the bottle of bleach—whatever can hurt. Everything is a hazard.

The other day, I gave my son an old key I found in a junk drawer. I told him it was the key to Neverland. That it would open a door and he would step through it and into another world. For some time he carried it around in his pocket. And then, in the other room, I heard him whispering to himself. There I found him knifing the key into an outlet. When I cried out, "No!" he flinched backward so suddenly I thought he had been shocked.

But he had not. I crouched beside him and grabbed him by the shoulders and asked him what the hell he was thinking. With tears in his eyes and a trembling voice he said, "I was trying to find the way to Neverland."

I can't stop running. I run on treadmills and I run on forest paths and I run on county highways with grain trucks blasting by, knocking me onto the shoulder with the big balls of air that come rolling off them. Sometimes people wave and sometimes people throw things at me. Sometimes I run so far I can't feel my feet and it is as though I am clopping along on my anklebones. My throat goes raw and my breath tastes like blood. My eyes burn with sweat and the world goes blurry.

I am running because my cholesterol is dangerously high. In the red zone, my doctor says. I cannot stop eating and I cannot stop drinking. I have tried, and then decided life isn't worth living without a bacon double cheeseburger washed down with a beer and a bourbon sidecar. So I run instead, my only antidote.

I am running because I am training for a marathon, and I am training for a marathon because I am thirty-three. The Jesus year. The year of reckoning, when I look back and see the time that has slipped away, when I look forward and guess how many years I have left. Already I am considering the grave. I have created a bucket list. The marathon is on it. My heart may very well explode before I finish the race.

The other day, for the first time, someone called me middle-aged. At first I thought it a joke, then a curse, then a reality. We loudly celebrate eighteen as the gateway to adulthood—you can gamble, enlist, vote, buy porn—but we only quietly, shamefully acknowledge thirty-three, the door to middle-age. My hair is threaded with gray. I drink too much coffee to stay awake and too much bourbon to fall asleep. I get fat when I don't exercise.

There is something wrong with my back, an old injury returned to haunt me. It could have been the time I was T-boned at 45 mph or it could have been the time I tried to do a backflip off a ski jump and landed on my head or it could have been the time I deadlifted two hundred pounds and felt something burst inside me. An X-ray reveals the disc, directly between my shoulder blades, has almost dissolved. A horn of bone reaches from one vertebrae to the next. They are fusing, calcifying. Without a chiropractor I suffer from chronic headaches, an electric spike of pain that rises from my back, up my neck, into my left temple, and hooks my eye. The other day it felt as though the disc were a jellyfish bulging from my spine, sizzling me with its tendrils.

Nothing says middle-aged like a bad back. I try to ignore the pain. My feet pound asphalt. I glance at my ticking watch. I am running away. I am running to my own Neverland, a place where I will never grow up.

My neighbor, Dave Tapper, is the kind of guy who builds his own ice rink, who quotes *Consumer Reports*, who gets red-cheeked with excitement when advising me on dishwashers, flat-screen televisions. With his short blond broom of hair and shoulders rounded with muscle, he could pass for a California surfer if not for his thick Minnesota accent. He recently helped me break down and fit back together a floor-model treadmill I couldn't shove through my patio door. Soon we will wire my living room for surround sound.

He understands how things work, how to put them together and pull them apart, in a way that I do not. Maybe this has something to do with his job as a family physician at the Allina Medical Clinic in Faribault, Minnesota. The body is just another machine to him. Blood replaces oil, wires replace tendons, gears replace joints. He buys the best brands—and maintains them—because he wants them to last. He eats the best food—and exercises religiously—because he sees every day what happens to people who don't take care of themselves.

Dave says there are two types of aging: physical and psychological. Physical aging is what we see, but psychological aging is what we feel. They don't always advance together. Often the mind gives in before the body. Once the indestructibility of youth is gone, people start to feel *old* even though their body remains quite capable. "Often this happens to people in their late twenties and early thirties," Dave says, giving me an appraising look, like I'm suddenly his patient, not his friend, with some awful fungus dribbling out of my eyeball. "Like you."

And that, he says, is the beginning of the end. People gain weight. They stop conditioning. They prepare their body for the chronic disease that will knock them out years later.

"You are," he says, "your own worst enemy."

My grandfather—my father's father—did not expect to live past thirty. Throughout his childhood, he experienced severe abdominal pain, constant diarrhea, and at sixteen, his colon was removed. For the rest of his life he wore a colostomy bag that looked like some kind of medieval girdle. He couldn't run. He couldn't play football or basketball. He couldn't go swimming, couldn't even take his shirt off at the beach. From the time he was a teenager, he lived a life as sedentary as a seventy-year-old's.

When he ate celery or turkey or roast beef—anything rough—
he would chew the taste off it and then spit it delicately onto the
tines of his fork so that by the end of every meal his plate was
wreathed with chewed balls of green, yellow, brown.

He was tall and broad enough to fill doorways. He spoke at a
near yell. He was rarely seen without a vest, bolo tie, and newsboy
cap. When he spoke to women, he said, "Listen here, Dixie." He
drove a Lincoln Town Car as big as a sperm whale, and even in
the summer, he wore driving gloves. He referred to the Beatles as
"noise." He had inside shoes and outside shoes. He labeled everything he owned—his books, his tools, even his car—with his ini-
tials, HLP, as if afraid they might vanish.

This same compulsion made him drive by the buildings he
designed as an architect. "I made that one," he'd say and a point a
finger cubed with arthritis. "That one too." It must have been a
good feeling—like that of a writer who sneaks through a book-
store to find his novels on their shelves—seeing your work, your
physical tether to the world.

Once, when I was a boy, when my grandfather walked away from
our house, when he climbed into his Town Car, when he tooted the
horn and started down the long gravel driveway, my mother said,
"Take a long look. This might be the last time you see him."

I felt then as fearful and bewildered as he must have when he
drove me to a Portland address and found not the high-rise he'd
promised me but a work site jammed with bulldozers and cranes
and men in hard hats and steel-toed boots. "I'll be damned," he
said. "It's gone. It's vanished."

So did he a few months later. He ended up living until he was
ninety-three, but it was as though he had been ninety-three forever. He spent his whole life as an old man.

. . .

My father—who is in his mid-sixties—says he doesn't feel old. Not anymore. He says he once did, when he turned thirty, forty, but after that, age ceased to affect him. He says his mind feels the same as it did when he was twenty. "You're only aware of growing older when you're younger. It's like some sort of inverse ratio. The younger you are, the more fascinated and anxious you are by aging."

He won't accept senior citizen discounts. He tosses out the AARP magazine that magically began appearing in the mail one day. He dyes his hair a charcoal black. He turns his head when a pretty woman swishes past.

I'm not sure I believe him. I feel old after all. I feel like as soon as we finish growing we begin falling apart.

He and I recently got into a wrestling match. Over the years physical violence has been our standard. He cannot shake without trying to crush my knuckles with his grip. He cannot hug without slamming a palm against my back, knocking the air from my lungs. Once, when I was a teenager and we were shopping at a department store, he called out my name and I turned to face him, and he sprayed my eyes with a sample bottle of cologne as if it were mace. I collapsed to the floor, howling in pain, blind for the next few minutes. This is as close as we will ever get to *I love you.*

In the past he always won. He was always bigger, the standard of strength and manhood. He once snapped a wrench in half when working on a rusted bolt. He once stacked two rowboats on top of each other and heaved them into the back of our truck. From high in the mountains, miles from any road, he packed out the elk he hunted. When he was a kid, playing baseball, the catcher dropped his mitt and took the bench, complaining that my father's fastballs hurt too much. No matter how many hours I put in at the gym, he would always overpower me when we were grappling, crushing me to the floor, hurling me onto the couch so severely the frame broke.

But this time was different. This time I was stronger. It was difficult for me to recognize at first. Even as I strangled him into a headlock—even as I dropped him to his knees—I kept expecting him to rally, to twist an arm behind my back and smash my face into carpet. But he didn't. I pinned him, smashing my knee into his spine, and he stopped struggling, and then we shoved away from each other and fell back against couches on opposite sides of the room and gasped for breath and didn't look at each other.

My father does not want to discuss getting older. This is his nature. He prefers silence. He mutes commercials. He writes single-sentence emails. Every road trip I took as a kid—to Yellowstone, to Yosemite, to Puget Sound, to the scablands of Eastern Oregon—the radio remained off. My childhood was muted of music except when I drove alone with my mother and she tuned in to KICE 100, the local country station. "*Quiet*," might have been the word my father said most often.

I remember stepping into the garage and finding him next to the carcass of a deer. He had gutted it and strung it from the rafters by its hind leg. A big silver bowl sat on the floor beneath it, and the only noise was the drip-drip-drip of blood.

His silence is more layered and complicated now. There is the silence between us in the bathroom, where I have stood by him at a bank of urinals and heard the stop-and-go progress of his urine. There is the silence in the kitchen, where he stirs medicated powders into his drinks to battle his high blood pressure. There is the silence in the bedroom, where he sleeps late every morning and takes a long nap every afternoon. And there is the long silence that gets closer every year. The silence I can sometimes taste in my own mouth, that of cinders and sulfur, of blood in a bowl.

Sometimes people ask me why I work so hard. Because that's all I do, I work. I wake up early and go to bed late, without so much as a fifteen-minute slot unaccounted for. I wash the car and pound out push-ups and install a new light fixture and critique a student manuscript and review a book and blueprint a novel and revise a short story and put together a puzzle with my daughter and read with my son and shove my mouth full of dinner and soap through the dishes and teach a night class and then return to the keyboard and hammer some more.

I don't tell them the real answer. That I think I am going to die. I *am* going to die, of course, but most people don't really consider their mortality until their car flips or the X-ray reveals a tumor or they hit their seventies and start showing up to church every Sunday. I don't know when this began, maybe when I was a teenager and skied into a spruce and crashed into a sudden darkness and woke up an hour later alone in a tree well with frostbite. But it seems like I have always felt the specter of death nearby, like a shadow a lamp won't bully from the room.

I often wonder how it will happen. Will a cancerous cauliflower bloom in my colon? Will a grain truck smear me across a country road? Will I collapse on a long run or stroke out on the chiropractor's table or perish quietly in my sleep? I do not mind the idea of dying violently, and if I do manage to survive into my seventies, I joke about ending my life cleanly—avoiding the slow, crippling descent—plastering myself with T-bone steaks and wandering off into grizzly country. However it happens, whenever it happens, when the grave widens its jaws, will I feel I have lived too long or not long enough?

Kwame Dawes—a writer, a fellow teacher—once told me a story. He said he saw a man being wheeled on a gurney, surrounded by EMTs, and felt a pang of jealousy. Because that man could rest, that man had an excuse to neglect his emails, to skip work, to ignore office hours, to stare at the wall and think *nothing*. We both laughed, but the laughter was cut short. Because he was telling the truth, and I could relate. I am terrified of getting old, but I am unafraid of dying. Because then I can rest, can pause the urgency that otherwise infects me.

I drink every night. I don't think that makes me an alcoholic, but I'm sure some would say different. I need it, just like I need the gallons of coffee to jump-start and settle and cure a mind and body that sometimes feels so stimulated that thousands of centipedes might be twisting inside of me.

I told my grandfather about the pregnancy over the phone. He was weak and addled at the time, on his way back from a visit to the doctor. There was a benign growth in his stomach, the size of a football, and it was interfering with digestion. A surgery had been scheduled, the surgery that would kill him.

"It's a boy," I said. "We're having a boy."

"Well, that's fine," he said. "That's *good*. That's what we do. We have children. And you'll have your boy and you'll keep him in line, won't you?"

"I will," I said.

"Be firm. Set rules. Give him love but not too much." He sounded very far away. "He'll be fine. You'll be fine."

"Yes," I said.

My grandfather was more demonstrative with me than he ever was with my father. And that tradition carries over to my father and my son, his grandson. There is a video on my phone. My son likes to watch it. In it, my father holds him by the hands and spins him in circles until his body lifts off the ground, faster and faster still, until his body flattens and twirls like a compass held over a magnet. They are in a bark-chipped playground. They both say, "Whoa, whoa, whoa," with every turn and laugh maniacally. And then they stop and stumble away from each other. My son falls and lies facedown. My father braces himself against a swing set. They convulse, laughing in a gasping, choking way.

Sometimes my son talks about death. He says, "If your hair is gray, that means you're going to die soon," and I say, "Not necessarily. You could die at any time," and he says, "Do you mean I could die?" and I say, "Not for a long time. As long as you stay safe," and he says, "Do you mean you could die?" and I pause for a moment before saying, "Hopefully not. Not for a long time."

The other day, when I was lacing up my shoes, my son asked if he could join me. I didn't think he would do very well, but he did, following me through the woods for a good half mile, then a mile, and I imagined his legs growing longer, his torso more muscular, his face bonier, one day passing me, my only company the shadows on the trail. But for now we ran alongside each other. "Are we racing?" he asked.

"No. Just running."

The smile slid off his face. "Why?"

I didn't say because I eat too much—because I drink too much—because I feel poisoned and furious if I don't exercise—because I'm my own worst enemy. "To be healthy," that's what I said.

"So that you'll live a long time?"

"Yeah."

His words came out in little puffs. "Well, it isn't very fun."

"You're right. It's not."

"Are we even going anywhere?"

I almost said no, but then my speed surged and I said over my shoulder, "To Neverland."

Arcadia

FREDERICK REIKEN

I am looking at my daughter, Arcadia. She is four. It is winter of 2013. She is making valentines. She has construction paper, stickers, Magic Markers, glitter glue, and other art supplies. I suspect she is the only person in her preschool class who will deliver handmade valentines to all her classmates. She did this last year too.

She is beautiful beyond comprehension, beautiful in her perfect four-year-old wit and innocence, beautiful in her prolonged flights of imagination, even when it drives my wife and me a little crazy. Three days ago, while home from preschool with a cold, she banged her eye into the corner of a cabinet door, and because it hurt, she decided to keep her eyes closed. She announced that she would have to keep them closed for a long time. I assumed that this would get old after fifteen minutes. Thinking it would lure her out of the game, we let her watch a video, but she listened to it with her eyes closed. So, not a game exactly. I had to beg her to open up the injured eye for a few seconds so I could see if there was anything really wrong with it. There wasn't. The next morning she was still at it, playing with Play-Doh with her eyes closed. Then she started walking around, eyes closed, and bumping into things. A debate ensued, which included my attempts to get her to open her eyes because, rationally speaking, if a girl doesn't open her eyes for two days, then probably we need to take her to the doctor. With eyes still closed, she almost kicked her baby sister, who is six months old. I suggested a time-out in her bedroom. She went up the stairs, eyes closed, lay down, and fell asleep. She awoke later, opened her eyes, and as quickly as that, she was no longer concerned about the injury. I stood by feeling relief and wondering if there was a lesson here, something I needed to learn about raising a precocious, wildly creative little girl. The lesson seems to have been: Give up the illusion of control.

Her full name is Arcadia Vivian Miranda Reiken. My wife, Cailin, was sure she was going to be a boy, because she dreamt it. We had the name all set. Jacob. I was surprised that my wife would go that biblical—not to mention that Jacob has been the most popular boy name in the United States for the last decade— but the name was set because she had dreamt that too.

In the last few months before the birth, I began to suspect—for equally unsubstantiated reasons, as we had not determined the sex with an ultrasound—that we were going to have a girl. I put forward Alexandra, as well as Abigail. Neither was compelling to my wife, but she was sure we had a boy, so it didn't matter. She was speaking to Jacob by name already. She said I should feel free to choose the girl name, because she knew we wouldn't have to use it.

Just a few days before Cailin went into labor, I came up with the name Arcadia. It was the heat of a fruitful summer, a forty-year boom for high-bush blueberries, and we picked literally gallons along the paths around Ames Pond. Nature teemed in our little Arcadia in western Massachusetts. I wrote about frogs, turtles, dragonflies, katydids, butterflies, blueberries, and birdsong in a long letter to my unborn child.

My wife immediately loved the name Arcadia, and the plan, if by some fluke of the great wheel we had a girl, was to call her Katie for short, a decision that seemed to be reinforced by the katydids, which were mating at that time and which would infiltrate our house nightly, waking us with their strange clicking sounds and their other noise—the alien noise, we called it—which sounds like radio static. Then she was born. A girl. Born at home in a tub in the exact spot where her bed is now. Arcadia in Arcadia. Katie became Cady. Vivian was my recently deceased grandmother. We both liked Miranda as a middle name. After debating whether to honor the deceased or to go Shakespearean, we chose both.

I sent out a birth announcement email to many people. Most wrote back with congratulations. A few complimented the name, which I was nervous about. A few asked what the name meant, and I found myself explaining that Arcadia is a mythologized rural paradise in ancient Greece, safe haven for the eponymous child Arcas (son of Zeus and the nymph Callisto, who was turned into a bear and placed in the night sky as Ursa Major, bear mother of the Arcadians; Arcas eventually became Ursa Minor), that it was also the home of Pan, etc. I was thinking I should have pushed harder for Alexandra or that we should have gone with Miranda as her first name.

A playwright I have known since childhood responded that he loved the name Arcadia and that it was also the title of his favorite Tom Stoppard play. At that time, I'd never heard of Stoppard or the play. Another person, a magazine editor, wrote that I must be getting a lot of *Et in Arcadia ego* references. I looked up the Latin phrase, learned about the epitaph on the tombstone being observed by Arcadian shepherds in two famous paintings by Nicolas Poussin. I also learned that the epitaph had been featured in *The Da Vinci Code*, a book I tried to read in the height of its popularity but could never get past the first few pages. I wrote back to the magazine editor and told her that so far she was the only one who'd made the reference.

Et in Arcadia ego. It means "And I am also in Arcadia" or "Even in Arcadia, there I am" or "I too am in Arcadia" or "Also in Arcadia am I." There are essays written about the epitaph's double meaning, the most famous of these being German art historian Erwin Panofsky's "*Et in Arcadia Ego*: On the Conception of Transience in Poussin and Watteau." As Panofsky notes, the phrase inscribed on the tombstone may be interpreted as a *memento mori*—something like "Even in Arcadia (paradise), I (death) am present." Or it may be more of a consolation regarding the eternal—"In death I know paradise for I have once lived in Arcadia." In other theories, the grave is possibly that of Christ. At least, this is the fuzzy, far-fetched hypothesis—involving an omitted Latin word and an anagram—that has been tossed around by conspiracy theorists and which was co-opted as part of *The Da Vinci Code*. But that hypothesis has mostly been debunked. What we are left with is the implication of a binary. Life and death. Presence and absence. Light and dark.

Arcadia. I am trying to say something about being her father. It occurs to me that I have not given the whole matter of parenthood much reflection. My excuse is that I'm too busy trying to manage it.

I am relatively old to be a father of young children. I'm forty-six, with a four-year-old and a six-month-old baby. I'll be sixty when my older daughter goes to college, sixty-eight when my younger daughter graduates. According to my plan, I will have paid off my home mortgage just in time to start paying back student loans. Up until this past year, when I had shoulder surgery and then got a concussion, I played on a competitive men's ice hockey team. But I think my hockey playing days may be over. I have back issues, neck issues, and more shoulder issues, despite the surgery. Most notably, I'm still post-concussive after banging my head on a playground structure while lifting my daughter up at a birthday party last summer. It was the second time I'd done that, on two different playgrounds. Same exact spot on my head. This after forty years of contact sports without any head issues. My daughter has watched me play organized hockey once—or maybe twice, if I count a time she does not remember—and what she knows is that I skated fast and wore a yellow jersey. She knows I took a shot that the goalie saved with his glove. She knows she drank hot chocolate and sat with Mom under a blanket. But the fact that I've played in something like two thousand hockey games, that there is probably nothing in my life that, for flat-out excitement and exaltation and intensity, can compare to certain hockey-related moments that replay in my mind, involuntarily, on a very regular basis—all this, for her, is insubstantial; for me, it's history.

How many other facets of my life will she know nothing about, save what I tell her? Is it important that she know about the dog and cat who were my closest companions for ten years, or the falling-down farmhouse that, throughout most of my twenties and thirties, I inhabited in the town of Cummington, thirty miles west of here? Is it important that she know about her great-grandmother and namesake, Vivian, who was a showgirl and later ran a dance school in North Arlington, New Jersey? Is it important for her to know that on December 20, 1995, while I was working as a journalist for a daily newspaper, I wrote an article about a winter solstice celebration at the Arcadia Wildlife Sanctuary in Easthampton, Massachusetts, on what was probably the day (or night) that I first registered the meaning (at least one of them) of Arcadia? Is it important that she be able to imagine me living in that falling-down farmhouse, dog and cat at my side, space heater blasting during the winter, box fan running in the summer, sheep in the pasture outside, mice scurrying in the attic overhead, actual rats one year, the same year that a family of skunks spent the winter in the crawl space under the kitchen tiles, which was also the year I wrote my first novel, which she will perhaps read when she's eighteen or so? Or is everything still here anyway, recognized in some nonverbal way, in some empathically intuited glimpse of me that cuts beyond the frame of this time and place we are cohabiting, this room, where she is happily making valentines?

Staring at Arcadia, I have questions. Not about her. She is perfect. The questions, the anxieties, the uncertainties all pertain to the vague sense that I'm in deep. Possibly in over my head. That other clichés pertaining to water may be appropriate. I have the sense that any father, regardless of income level, has a moment in which he looks at his first child and thinks, My God. I need more money! And while I do—I certainly need more money—I know enough to understand that what is deep and altogether new about the context has very little to do with my annual income or the life insurance policy I recently purchased. It has to do with the feeling that I have changed forever, that I am qualitatively different from the non-father—pre-father?—I was five years ago, or ten or fifteen or twenty. I seem to have little in common with that solitary journalist-writer who lived with a dog and cat for more than a decade in an old, falling-down farmhouse. Who the hell was that person, anyway?

So much was pulling me back then, one way and then another. I often received calls from the newspaper at six, would be out reporting on some accident or arrest from the night before, and then filing a story before the final morning deadline. Then I would go back to sleep. Later, I'd get up and walk my dog, and then spend three or four hours working on my novel. Then I'd dash out to cover another story for the paper. What was the point? Honestly, I have no idea. This is not to say that my life is calm and simple now, or that I've figured out the answers. But there's a force that pulls with quiet, steady gravity. A single force that doesn't go away, no matter where I am or what I'm doing. It seems primordial. I suspect that it has something to do with love. Or that it is, precisely, love. Whatever name one wants to give it, it is the force that trumps all else, the force that causes me to wish to be right here, just as I am, forever, watching my daughter as she makes another valentine.

This one has cats on it. And plastic jewels.

Last week I picked Cady up at school and took her to a small library in North Amherst, where they happened to have a book I wanted to read as part of my ongoing research for a novel I have been working on, in one form or another, since 1992. I have joked with myself that in giving Cady the middle name Miranda, I must have been deciding that, like Prospero does in *The Tempest*, it was time to drown my book. Then my wife and I, after prolonged postpartum deliberations, went and named our second child Miranda, although by then I was lobbying for Eliza, which became one of her two middle names. Miranda Eliza Lily Reiken. All that I'm contemplating here is, of course, equally applicable to Miranda. It's just that she is not yet talking—not yet asking things like, "Why do you stay up writing every night? Are you nocturnal?"

In the library in North Amherst, while I was checking out the book, I noticed the audio recording of a full cast production of Tom Stoppard's *Arcadia*, written in 1993. I grabbed it. I drive to Boston and back to teach, an hour and forty minutes each way, so I listen to a lot of recorded books.

Stoppard's *Arcadia*, it turns out, is all about the intersection of art and science, of present and past, of the impossibility of ever knowing anything for certain. It is a play of ideas but also an entertaining drama. It is a mystery, a comedy, a tragedy. It talks a lot about iterated algorithms, which is probably my favorite part. Stoppard's original working title was, incidentally, *Et in Arcadia ego*.

There are themes within themes, and mysteries within the mysteries, but top dog, as far as the play's thematic focus goes, seems to be the weighing of Newtonian determinism against chaos theory and random chance. Of the many epigrammatic lines in the play, several resonated enough for me to write them down. I offer this quote for consideration: "The unpredictable and the predetermined unfold together to make everything the way it is."

In theory, the imperative to reproduce is encoded in our DNA. Biologists have argued that, from an evolutionary standpoint, the sole purpose for our individual existence is the maximization of the number of our own genes that we can pass on to the next generation. As the biologist Richard Dawkins, author of *The Selfish Gene*, has famously suggested, we are, in a sense, merely the survival machinery for our genes.

And still we try to get the upper hand. Our lives get messy. We do things early, late, or not at all. We write poems, plays, novels. We travel to far off places for different purposes, some of them noble, some instructive, and some pleasurable. We go here and there because we're trying to work it out, a life, a way to have a few of the things we want. My latest plans include a research trip to Greenland, a fellowship in the Netherlands, and maybe—just maybe—I will complete the book I'm working on. One never knows. And as a father, this never-knowing, when it comes to career endeavors, grows more acute.

I listened to *Arcadia* three times over a period of weeks. It's fairly short, only three CDs. When it concluded the second time, I wept profusely in my car while I was driving on Route 2 somewhere in central Massachusetts. As it concluded the third time, I pulled over so that I could avoid becoming a road hazard. I wept for the unknown nineteenth-century genius Thomasina Coverly, who dies in a fire in 1809 on the eve of her seventeenth birthday, having foretold a mathematics of irregular forms nearly two centuries before anyone would begin to understand it. I wept for her tutor, Septimus Hodge, who devotes his life, after Thomasina's death, to the mad task of computing iterated algorithms for the purpose of elucidating Thomasina's theory. I wept because the play is so astoundingly perfect in its depiction of the relative scale of things, of how the tiniest of moments may be remarkable, though usually in hindsight. I wept because the play, however briefly, took me out of my time, into other times, and into other small paradises of wonder. Later I left the CD case on the kitchen table. When my observant daughter noticed it, she yelled, "Hey, Arcadia!" and pointed happily to the letters of her name.

She cuts out another heart for another valentine. She says she's feeling inspired to make a few more. She says she's dying for a glass of water. She picks up colloquial phrases like no four-year-old I've ever known, though in truth I have not known many, except perhaps when I was four. She is wiggling in her chair. I point this out. She says she's probably having one of her growing days, a term my wife uses to explain why on certain days Cady gets extraordinarily hungry, thirsty, and wiggly. Everything she does, right at this moment, is predictable, except that nothing about it is predictable. Nor is what the future holds predictable. I am the father of two girls whom I love so much that it is frightening. I am often literally frightened. Not only of fevers and coughs and cabinet corners that might blind them, but of everything that may or may not happen in the chaos that will unfold and will make their lives exactly what they are.

My daughter is making valentines. She is also in Arcadia. We are also in Arcadia. She is Arcadia. I am looking at her on a Wednesday morning in January, with snow falling outside. Her baby sister squawks and belly crawls. Her mother is making soup and talking. Even after I stop writing, I am looking at Arcadia.

I will sit next to her and make valentines. She has given me three so far. This year she has learned to make snowflakes out of construction paper and can also count to fifty. She can write her name, both as Arcadia and Cady. She can write *I love you.* Her *y*'s are usually backward. She likes coconut juice and fish sticks and homemade popsicles and Nori seaweed snacks and pretzels. She likes music. Her favorite Daddy songs (the ones I sing at bedtime) are the Beatles' "Blackbird" and James Taylor's "You Can Close Your Eyes." The final lines of the JT song are *But I can sing this song / And you can sing this song / When I'm gone.* She sometimes laughs at this and says, "But you're right here."

Arcadia is making valentines, and her sister rolls over, something the baby has learned to do only this week. Cady and Miranda are now looking at each other, and I am looking at them looking at each other. And I am saying things, of course. I'm saying many, many things.

I am talking to my daughter about her valentines. And about chickens and ducks and turtles. I am playing a game in which she has us pretend that we are eagles and that we have to fly down to the eagle store and that Miranda is a baby eagle and that my wife's Honda CR-V is our eagle's nest. I am hearing about Cady's friend Evie's upcoming birthday party, at which apparently they are going to make tiaras. I ask her if she knows what a tiara is. She does. All of this happened a few minutes ago or hours ago or days ago or years ago. I have the valentines to prove it.

I am old and I am young. (Isn't this always the case?) I am right here, in the paradise of this room, and long beyond it.

I am looking at Arcadia, who sits by the glass door and squeezes more pink glitter glue onto red construction paper while the snow collects in our front yard and on our cars and the world seems slower than it really is.

Or else it's faster, if I am trying to record every last instant, as they race by at intractable speeds, since there is no methodology for quantifying what takes place on a quiet, snowy morning in which there is no particular reason to take note of it all anyway. Nothing is happening and everything is happening. I don't dare ruffle it. For now, I don't dare move.

On Fatherhood and Separation

RICK MOODY

1. I almost always feel like a failure as a father. Is it possible that feeling like a failure as a father is an attempt to protect myself from this very failure? Through repetition of certain key phrases? Would repeating the phrase "I almost always feel like a failure as a father" somehow indemnify me? Or would this phrase at least indicate that I am reasonably concerned with parental failure and thus am willing to entertain the notion in order to prevent it? During the time when I am thinking all of this stuff—about how I probably *am* a failure as a father—I should really be interacting with my daughter, who is often right here on the couch next to me asking if I will play with her. She is holding up a Barbie doll— about which I feel like a failure because I have dubious feelings about Barbie dolls though not to the point of preventing Barbie ownership in all cases.

WHEREAS, _____ and _____ were married on
May 10, 20__, in a religious ceremony, in the Borough of
Manhattan, the City of New York, the County of New York,
and the State of New York; and

2. Did my own father feel like a failure? I used to feel that there
were certain ways that my father was *definitely* a failure. For example, after my own parents were divorced, he had a number of
girlfriends for a few years, and all of their names started with *S*.
Or, let's say, a *number* of these names started with *S*. This is an
oversimplification for the sake of a story, but not much of an
oversimplification. It was hard to keep track of *who was who*, or
perhaps I was simply looking for a way to torture my father—out
of my own discomfort at the advent of a broken home. Confusing
the names of his girlfriends, whether consciously or uncon-
sciously, was one way to torture him. When I was younger I felt
like this period constituted a failure on my father's part, even
though I have now done so many worse things, been inconstant,
impatient, disengaged. The alleged failure of my father was probably more mine than his. I would put this even more strongly,
actually: I feel like I have failed in ways far worse than my father
failed. I'm betting he never really thought of his failure (nor mine)
at all.

WHEREAS, in consequence of irreconcilable differences,
_____ and _____ have separated; and

3. I almost always feel like a failure as a father. My father was a
yeller, at least when I was very young, and for most of my four years
as a father, I have striven not to be a yeller, and while my daughter

and I have strenuously disagreed (last week it was over whether or not she was allowed to have a second helping of dried cherries right before sleep), I have not so far yelled at her. But maybe the desire to avoid yelling at her constitutes a paradoxical difficulty. Maybe I *should* be yelling at her, because that would be honest, and a reflection, on occasion, of my exasperation. Or: maybe my yelling would cause some other harm. I took the getting-yelled-at thing very hard when I was a child, and I don't want to visit this syndrome on my own daughter. However, sometimes I am so firm on this point that I can't even express sharp disappointment without feeling like I've failed in a new way.

> WHEREAS, ____ and ____ desire fully
> and finally to settle all issues arising out of their marriage,
> including the care of their child, their domestic affairs
> and property rights; and

4. I almost always feel like a failure as a father. The other night, I was in the bathroom while my daughter was taking a bath, and she remarked that she had asked her mother, with whom I am no longer living, if she (her mom) wanted to have a slumber party in this apartment where I am living now with my fiancée. My daughter had an explanation for why this was impossible, and she seemed to be wanting to rehearse that explanation with me. She had a stricken expression as she explained, and I was about to embark on some attempt to soothe when it turned out she was really stricken by something she had seen in the Winnie the Pooh movie we had just watched. And so: Winnie the Pooh, it seemed, was the transition through which feelings about separation might begin to take place. Tigger, lost in the woods.

WHEREAS, ____ and ____ know that
they have the right to have the issues which
they have resolved through collaborative negotiation,
and which are reflected in this Agreement,
resolved instead through adversarial legal proceedings
in which they would each be represented by separate independent
counsel,

5. The separation of my parents, which took place, I think, in 1970 (or somewhere right at the juncture of 1970 and 1971), was also hard on me. Harder on me than on my brother, at least as he recounts it. I cannot ask my sister about it because she is no longer living. Still, I found it especially hard, harder than anything I had experienced to that time. I suppose I had normative ideas about family, and these normative ideas were normative because there was no other family on our street that was separated. (Within a few years there were several.) I remember, for example, my mother sleeping on the couch downstairs while my parents were separating, and how embarrassed and ashamed I felt about the fact that she slept on the couch. My father made jokes about the sofa in the years after, and we can only assume that he made jokes about the sofa and my mother's having slept on it because he was embarrassed and ashamed of my mother having slept on it. In the last years of my marriage, I too slept on the couch for a while. That I am repeating the circumstances of my childhood in my daughter's childhood makes me feel like a failure indeed.

____ and ____ acknowledge that it was
and is their desire to avoid the delay, expense, stress
and uncertainty of adversarial legal proceedings.

_____ and _____ believe that no expert knows them
and their family as well as they do, and that the needs
and interests of their family will be better served
by their having concluded these matters

6. I almost always feel like a failure as a father. My daughter likes to watch television, like many four-year-olds. I like to watch television with her, and I have an appetite for things I would never put up with otherwise, if it were not for the fact of my daughter's interest. *Curious George*, for example. My daughter really loves *Curious George*, as of this writing. I understand the hatred of television among the attachment-parenting parents, or even the parents who are mildly culturally sensitive. I understand. Television is a force for evil. It's an ideological tool. But it is also true that I regularly logged from four to six hours a day in front of it when I was young. Which reminds me of that story that Harold Brodkey used to tell, and that I'm recreating here from memory: "I was in a period when I was especially afraid of death. I called my friend Don DeLillo and asked him what I should do. He said, 'Watch more television.' So I did. And it worked!" Anyway, I should not allow my daughter to watch television at all, according to the Waldorf School, et al. And yet I do let her watch, and I often watch it with her. It's one way we spend time together, and that is good, and yet the feelings of enjoyment are circumscribed by the feelings of failure.

in collaborative negotiations rather than
through adversarial proceedings. Finally, _____ and _____
acknowledge that they are aware that this
Agreement may be materially different from an agreement

resulting from adversarial proceedings, or a decision which
might have been rendered by a Court of Law in
the State of New York;

7. My daughter's mother is an especially good cook, and very mindful about nutrition and such things, and I can barely heat a microwave-only item, and normally shrink from doing much more out of fear, and so when I feed my daughter, I rely on her obsession with eating the same things over and over again. Thank god for string cheese, this month, or thank god for dried mango. I think the obsession with eating the same things over and over is a stabilizing force, and maybe it is a stabilizing force in the midst of her parents separating, and I am all for any kind of stability she can manage. Here are some other things she is willing to eat right now: pears, apples, bananas, chicken nuggets. I should learn to cook, yes, but the best I can give my daughter is the dad she *actually has*, not the dad she should have.

NOW THEREFORE, in consideration of
the foregoing and the mutual promises, agreements, covenants
and provisions of this Agreement, ____ and ____ agree as
follows:

8. I almost always feel like a failure as a father, because I imagine that fathers should be sterner, more uncompromising, that they should be law-givers, and rule-deployers; indeed, I recall from my period of reading about psychoanalysis that at some point in the literature of poststructuralism, there is this characterization: that fathers are meant to be construed as *law-givers*. I am an ineffective law-giver. I try to do it sometimes, but I feel that laws are relative,

and should be applied only for the greatest possible good, and not simply because there is *the law* and you have to obey it. I am not a father like Antonin Scalia. I would hate it if Antonin Scalia were my father. Maybe some of this uncertainty, this shortage of paternal certainty, comes from the fact of my separation from my wife, or maybe it just comes from my having endured my parents' separation.

> ___ and ___ shall continue to live separate
> and apart, each free from the interference, authority
> or control, direct or indirect, of the other, as fully as though
> unmarried.

9. I almost always feel like a failure as a father. For example, tonight we were walking from my apartment to my ex-wife's apartment (and I feel like a failure a bit because she is not quite my ex-wife, but neither is she my wife, and so I use the "ex-" prefix because, grammatically speaking, there is no clear cut guidance on how to speak of her) for the drop-off, and my daughter fell while we were walking, and she fell because for a split second I let go of her hand to put my phone in my pocket, and in that brief interval she tripped on a cobblestone-ish bit of sidewalk—and face-planted. I felt, naturally, like I could have done better here, and the sad part (her scrapes were not so bad) was that she kept saying, *It still hurts, it still hurts*, to keep me up-to-date.

> Neither ___ nor ___ shall in any way disturb,
> trouble or seek to compel the other to associate,
> cohabit or dwell with her or him, or seek
> the restoration of conjugal rights. ___ and ___

both agree to respect each other's privacy,
to regard each other as separate individuals,

10. I feel like a failure also because I believe most fathers are failures, and that fatherhood, in a way, is a construct that invites
failure, because the system of expectations, these days, that the
father, by definition, should be masculine, and the father should
"provide," and the father should hand down the law, and the father
should be a coparent and fill in around the mother, and the
father should be a diaper-changer, and a feeder of children, and
the father should avoid the excessive trappings of masculinity, and
the father should be loving, and available, and not miss stuff, the
father should show up for the child's life, and not be an absentee
father (I remember, for example, that while my parents were still
married, the time that I generally saw my father was while he was
watching the TV news, and that when the TV news was done, my
bedtime came around, and so if I did not watch the TV news
with my father, I did not see him at all), and some of the items in
this catalog contradict other items, and I, for one, do not know
how to be a father exactly, and I especially do not know how to be
a father in the midst of separation, because my preference would
be to protect my daughter from all possible sources of pain, but in
this case I am myself a *cause* for some of the pain, and if the pain
is not apparent yet, I assume that the pain will at some point manifest itself, and that it will be clear, at that time, that I was the
cause of some of this pain (whether I am causing merely 50 percent, or *more*, I do not know), and this constitutes a kind of failure
for me, one that is *more* acute as the weeks pass and I am not fully
divorced.

And yet:

1. It is also true that I view my self-consciousness as a father, my uncertainty, which I mostly keep to myself (though I am announcing it to the world right now), as a generational improvement on a kind of fathership that had no convictions about parenting whatsoever, and simply blundered on, smacking the kids around on occasion (I, for one, was smacked around a couple of times), not bothering to *aspire* to fatherhood, but rather just *falling into* fatherhood, which I myself would have done on multiple occasions if this were not an enlightened period. I believe that my self-consciousness as a father constitutes an improvement, and in this period of separation I would like to make use of a generationally permitted reboot, if at all possible, to make life better for my daughter, to be a *father of intention*, a delighted, aspiring, ambitious father.

> The Parents agree to have joint custody of ____,
> in all spirits of the words. The need to ascribe
> one Parent as "custodial" and the other as "non-custodial"
> is a requirement of the NY courts, and is used
> in this document only because required to be.

2. Parenting is what happens while you are too busy to read up about parenting, and there is a danger, too, in being theoretical, at the expense of actually doing stuff with your kid. I try to do stuff with my kid to the best of my ability. Recently my child has outgrown my ability to carry her on my shoulders without

bodily aches of various kinds (the knee I had surgery on does not favor this, nor does my back, and then there is the whole problem of my shoulders, etc.), and so we have evolved a new plan. If she is certain at a given juncture that I should be carrying her on my shoulders, I will, for a brief moment lift her up into my arms and give her a hug and a kiss, and then place her back down on the ground so that she can walk some more. Walking is good, and is especially good for my daughter, who was born with a congenital skeletal defect. Walking is a use-it-or-lose-it proposition. It would be possible to think this through to an alarming degree, as in: (1) the child has a skeletal defect, so she should not be forced to do physical things that she's not ready for, or (2) the child has a skeletal defect, so she should walk, so as to develop her musculature to compensate for her skeletal defect, or (3) I have to be on the alert for making incorrect decisions about her and her skeletal defect, or (4) I have to be on the alert for her mother's feelings about my decisions about her skeletal defect, or (5) I have to be able to make compromises about my inability to carry my daughter and the toll this is taking on my own body in order to be mindful about her skeletal defect. And so on. But at a certain point the considerations of this stuff become overwhelming, and one simply has *to act*, because otherwise the relationship and its implications are more discussed than acted upon, and a relationship is something (father and daughter) that happens together, in space and time, not in the waiting room of parental theorizing, and so where possible give the hug and kiss and abjure theorizing.

The Parents agree that they will periodically discuss
the schedule, and how well or not well it is working

for the Child and for the Parents. They shall take into account,
among other things, how the Child is dealing with the
transitions,

3. The theory should be simple, and despite my feelings of failure it is simple, because the theory should be that at all times in all places I am motivated simply by love. This is idealistic, which means, I guess, that I am a father who is idealistic, but it is also a *reasonable* theory, love above all things, and it is easier when you consider that, in fact, I feel great surgings of love and esteem and adoration in dealing with my child; I feel these feelings and mostly do not discuss them with my child, only occasionally, but rather I savor them as the inevitable by-product of being a father, and in this case a father who waited a long, long time to have a child (I was forty-eight at the time of my daughter's birth), and who was not always certain that he was going to have a child, and who therefore became a father at a moment in life when he absolutely fervently believed in the necessity of becoming a father, and who did so with some foreknowledge that younger fathers might be more physically fit and less prone to physical difficulty, but there was no way that younger fathers could have had more emotional experience (I am an uncle five times over), or be more patient, or more thorough in preparation as calculated in life experiences. I am in no way ambivalent about being a father. The worst that I feel, as a father, is exhausted and uncertain. Never ambivalent.

_____ and _____ agree that they will both
use their best efforts to shield and protect _____
from members of their extended family who might
make disparaging remarks about either _____ or _____.

> Each will advise extended family members about
> the stresses and risks to _____'s self-esteem which
> would arise out of such comments.

4. I aspire to resolution and determination through this period, this bad period, this period of separation, because there is no cessation in the surgings of love and esteem for my daughter, despite all the difficulty; on the contrary, and this is perhaps how the generations grow and change, I look at her for some lessons that she doesn't even know she's giving me—concentration on particular tasks, the value of repetition, the involvement in this twenty-four-hour period to the exclusion of others, faith in others, the ability to express emotion without shame and without self-consciousness, the love of community, the total enthusiasm for today's new discovery. Despite feelings of failure, there is so much to learn, and even the hardest patches can be negotiated. Seems so easy, right?

To Tell a Happy Story

STEVE EDWARDS

Early on there were nights I thought my son might die, and I thought it might be better for us all if he did. If on those nights his crying ebbed and his breathing stilled, I would lie in bed waiting, listening, the way you lie and wait and listen if you suspect an intruder in the home. I imagined Rebecca at the funeral, out of her mind with grief, and how in the days that followed sorrow would be all we knew, until one day—years later, perhaps—we would have made our peace with what had been taken from us.

Had he been born with some physical problem? Some incurable disease? No. Aside from mild jaundice and a hemangioma, the doctors pronounced him perfectly fit and we brought him home to begin the life we had been imagining for so long. The life of a happy, healthy, and loving family.

The trouble started that first week when Rebecca's milk didn't come in. We bought the special nursing pillow, the pumps and bottles. We went to a lactation consultant. Maybe our son wasn't sucking right, getting a good seal. Or maybe Rebecca needed to pump more often. Or maybe, the consultant finally suggested, Rebecca was suffering postpartum depression and wasn't trying hard enough. Not ten days before, Rebecca had had a completely natural childbirth—not so much as an aspirin crossed her lips during labor or delivery—and it wasn't painful, she assured me, but joyful, full of love. And even that first night in the hospital, when our son couldn't stop crying and we didn't have a pacifier: I stood by his crib and let him suck the tip of my thumb for over an hour because somewhere in our copious preparations we had read that this might comfort an infant. My wife and I are people who try our hearts out. But you can't *try* to make milk come in. It comes or it doesn't.

When our son began experiencing colic-like symptoms—"inconsolable crying, distress, irritability, sleeplessness"—our pediatrician told us we had gotten unlucky but that it would pass. We tried to laugh it off. We smiled through our tiredness and the well-meaning comments and teases from family, friends, elderly checkers at the grocery store: about how hard it is, how it would get better with time. We looked forward to when he would surprise us by sleeping the night.

As the first wearying, wondrous days of his life turned into weeks and months, an edge crept into his voice. He started screaming. He screamed every day, *screamed*, at such a high pitch and volume that if he screamed as I held him on my shoulder after a feeding, my ears would ring for hours. He was a shrill, writhing knot of muscle. Still too young to lift himself up on his arms, he somehow found the strength to buck his entire body away from us.

We laid him on the changing table, on a blanket on the floor, on a couch cushion, on a chair, and we turned on ceiling fans, radio static, music soft and loud, and always—his face puckered and red, his tiny hands curled into fists—he wailed. Often without shedding tears. During the first snowstorm of his life, I rushed him outside thinking the dizzying zigzag of snowflakes might calm him down. It didn't work. Nothing worked. In our exhaustion and fear, Rebecca and I argued bitterly until we lost even the words to say why we were mad or what was happening to us. Or to him. Or what we should do now. We were attached parents—devoted, gentle—and we never once touched our son in a way that wasn't loving. But as three months turned to six, nine, and twelve, an instinctual, insuppressible rage sometimes welled up in me, and I slammed doors, kicked over chairs. On bad nights it took everything I had not to bend down and scream *shut up* into his little face. Not to fling him across the room.

At the doctor's office we put on a brave front and did not complain. Down deep, of course, we were incredibly scared. After having dragged ourselves in multiple times for vaccinations and well-checks that provided no remedy or respite, we debated: *Should we go again? Will they be able to tell us anything this time? Are we going too often?* Finally, we brought in a cell-phone video of his screaming, evidence that to us clearly meant something was wrong. *Nonsense,* our pediatrician said. *He's going through a "screechy" phase. Stretching out his vocal cords.* The footage of his full-body convulsions on our changing table at home didn't alarm her in the least. She prescribed an antacid and said we could try to make him "a little happier." He was still steadily gaining weight after all. And after doling out a few final pieces of advice, she quickly excused herself.

On our way home that day, Rebecca wept in the car and said she felt like an abuser. We could not save him.

For our own survival, we fell into shifts. Since Rebecca took care of so much during the day (feedings, laundry, dishes, bills, her own work as an editor) while I taught my writing classes at the University of Nebraska, I picked up the slack at night. When his crying started at one, two, three in the morning, I rose and went to him. I changed his diaper. I tightened his swaddle blankets. I rubbed his little back. If he had spit out his pacifier, I put it back in his mouth. I held him in my arms and sang in a whisper. And always my mind went down the ever-growing checklist of what could be wrong. Was he hungry? Thirsty? Was he too cold? Too hot? Did we need a white-noise machine to imitate the sound inside the womb? Did we need to let him cry it out? Was he napping too much during the day? Was he overstimulated? Was he just fussy? Spoiled? Trying to manipulate us? In those moments in the darkness, alone with my son, I blamed myself for never having an answer that helped him.

Other men pulled off fatherhood with such grace and humor, and with multiple kids: the difference, I thought, had to be me. Our son's crying was a problem because I wasn't patient enough. Because I wasn't man enough. The thought that he might die, that it might be better for us all if he died: I saw it as a personal flaw, and the night shifts were my penance. Sometimes he slept for an hour or two between crying jags. Other times it was only ten minutes. Rebecca would roll over, drowsily ask if I needed help. But if the two of us got involved, half-asleep and tense, it could lead to a fight, and that was the last thing we needed. I would tell her I was already up, that everything was fine, that she should rest. To keep myself awake I shouted into my pillow, punched myself in the thigh. Whatever it took. Again and again, over weeks and months that slowly turned into a year, then two, I rose in the night and went to our son.

Through it all we were compulsive about documenting his good times. We kept a camera with us and were ready at a moment's notice when any smile, like a ray of sunlight, passed over his face. To tell a happy story about our child, even if slightly fictional: we needed that. For all of his desperation and pain, he was still an incredibly beautiful boy. Dark blue eyes and soft honey-blond curls. Chubby dumpling cheeks inherited from Rebecca's Polish family. He was the baby strangers at the grocery store, men and women alike, stopped in their tracks to coo over, who people called a little doll. Rebecca organized our pictures of him on Facebook to share with friends and family, and in any spare moment of downtime she and I found ourselves scrolling through them, hungry for the lives of wonder and enchantment the pictures suggested.

And, yes, there were the rare good days: the times we put him in the stroller and, one foot in front of the other, walked the neighborhood. There were the days we stopped to chat with friends down the street about Nebraska football or the weather. He would sleep a bit, then wake and keenly take in the world, and even play peekaboo and giggle a little. We began to wonder if it were all in our heads.

I remember one day we came home at dusk to the sound of a robin chirping in the maple tree in our yard, and that sound—those gurgling chirps—lifted me out of myself, out of my pain, out of despair.

Other days I managed to write for an hour or two, or garden in the backyard, or cook Rebecca a nice meal and chat with her in the evening as we watched television. For those few hours his screaming and screeching, his terrible sleep, as well as his new symptoms—the eczema scarring both his cheeks and forehead, his distended belly and disgusting bowel movements—belonged to a distant, harmless past. On the good days we were as optimistic as we had been on the night he was born.

Unfortunately, there was no method for inducing one of those infrequent good days. What calmed him on one occasion could provoke him on the next. If one thing went wrong—if none of our bottles were clean and we had to wash one before feeding him, and if in the time it took us to wash the bottle he started to cry— nothing brought him back. Theories about his pain dominated our talk. We got different brands of diapers. We changed formulas. Changed detergents. We got him softer sheets and an organic mattress pad. We put him to sleep in his crib in his room, in a swing, in a co-sleeper by our bed. We put him to bed early, kept him up late. Fed him vitamins, a probiotic. Every minute of every day was consumed by the most basic of necessities: getting him to eat, getting him to sleep, getting him to *stop crying*. Like wild animals—like wolves frantic over a wounded body in the pack, faced with blood, raw bone—we circled and paced around our helpless child. We kept a vigilant watch for clues, for answers that never came.

In the meantime, in our hour of need, Rebecca's job—our main source of income while I was in grad school, and which allowed her to work from home and be with the baby full-time— was slashed by two-thirds. Friends fell away. Certain academic mentors shunned, admonished, or ignored us. Only a chosen few understood our predicament: we were not *sleeping*; we had no *money*. Then after my graduation and a year spent working as a lecturer, my job, too, was cut. We were grief-stricken, exhausted, broke, burdened with student loans coming due, and fearful about the credit card debt we were racking up in order to pay for diapers and groceries. During the twenty-minute spurts of his nap times, I tapped out cover letters to schools in far off California and New England, and waded through the bureaucratic hell of unemployment. My caseworker, a former teacher himself, told me that in this economy I would be better off if the letters behind my name were GED instead of PhD.

Rebecca and I talked about how many months we had before we would have to ask my parents if they could put us up in their basement. They lived five hundred miles away, in Indiana, and the job prospects there were worse than in Nebraska. Rebecca's father was out of the picture, and her mother had passed away twenty years before, taken too young by breast cancer. We cashed in the small investments we had worked hard to accumulate and lived in fear of what new bills might arrive in the mail.

This was not how our lives were supposed to turn out. I should have had a job to support us, to at least get us the essentials. Rebecca should have had the chance to be the mother that she herself had only known for so long, the chance to be healed by love and loving. Our son should have known so many things: calm and comfort, the warmth of our arms, the wonder of a budding consciousness.

When we first decided to have him, I had been scared of everything that could go wrong: with his health, with Rebecca's health, with money and jobs. I did not know what kind of father I would be, and I worried I would lose my writing, my sense of self. I was anxious, too, over the fact that part of bringing a child into the world meant offering that child—and also myself, Rebecca—to the infinite variety of suffering life devises for us all. On our walks around the neighborhood with our dog, as we held hands and talked and made plans, I had a hard time imagining how I would feel as a father, and what would be different. In the mornings, as we lay in bed together—as I held Rebecca and cradled an arm around her growing belly—I wondered if I had made a huge mistake, if I would be found out as a fraud. At the same time, I knew how much Rebecca wanted this. Every night I watched her as she sat with her laptop, reading books on natural childbirth, buying baby clothes and slippers and BPA-free baby bottles, combing websites for tips, and making lists of all the other things we would need. Each time UPS brought a box to the door, she opened it and pulled out a prize to show me: alphabet flash cards to hang on his wall, a wrap for carrying him around, Sophie the teething giraffe.

If anything gave me the courage to face my fears about fatherhood it was the joy Rebecca felt preparing for his arrival. It was contagious. I began to imagine him, his soft weight on my shoulder some Saturday in the fall as I watched a college football game, the sighing up and down of his breath.

But that scene never played out. In the first eighteen months of his life, he fell asleep in our arms exactly three times (and then only out of exhaustion). I became angry, sullen, withdrawn. Jittery and lacking a good reaction time due to the sleep deprivation, Rebecca didn't feel safe on the road and stopped driving. Our walks with the dog got fewer and farther between. The toys and trinkets we bought before our son was born stayed in their boxes or were played with once and set aside. The night's adrenaline-spiked confusion left us hungover and wanting only to be alone between work and caretaking shifts, and in the mornings we did not hold each other. Instead we gradually became a family of shut-ins who only left the house when absolutely necessary, for work, groceries, the doctor. Any leftover energy Rebecca and I had went right back into our son's care.

Two months before his second birthday, I landed a phone interview with a school in New England and needed the house to myself for a few hours. Rebecca took him to the zoo. There was a train at the zoo, and she wanted to treat him to his first ride. But before they got to the train, he went ashen and started crying. She took him to the bathroom to change his diaper, and once she got his pants down he panicked, started screaming. Afraid of what the other women in the bathroom would think, Rebecca hurriedly pulled his clothes on and brought him out into the light of day. She took him to a park bench, held him, rocked him, offered him a sip of water, some animal crackers. He was confused and shrieking, and several times he tried to run away from her, but she held him tight, spoke to him in as soothing a voice as she could manage. Finally, when he still did not calm down, she walked him to the car, buckled him into his car seat, and drove around town, in tears herself, until she was sure my interview was over.

"I can't take my son to the zoo? To ride the goddamned train?" Back home she came in the door, angrier and more frantic than I had ever seen her. "I'm calling Tricia." Tricia was our new pediatrician, a woman I had known from one of my writing classes at school. She was writing a novel set on a ranch in western Nebraska.

"What's she supposed to do?" I said.

"She can get us a bed at Children's Hospital in Omaha. I'm calling her. I don't care if it's the ER. We're going."

"Hon—"

"We're going."

She stormed off to the bedroom to call Tricia, and I looked at our son where he sat on the floor. His eyes were puffy and red. He seemed a little dazed, out of it. Rebecca had convinced herself he had celiac or an intestinal blockage, *something* with the gut, and she wanted an endoscopy performed. I edged away from that. The thought of surgery scared me: a masked doctor leaning over our precious child.

I picked him up, stood in the doorway.

"Yes. Okay," Rebecca said.

She shouldered past me to the kitchen and wrote something on a piece of paper. I shifted him uneasily from one arm to the other. He was heavy, awkward. Finally she hung up the phone and turned to me.

"We've got a bed."

"For when?"

"Tonight." She went back to the bedroom and began packing an overnight bag for the three of us. "They may scope him."

I said I didn't understand. If he needed an endoscopy, why hadn't Tricia ordered one before? What had changed? He had a meltdown at the zoo? He had meltdowns every day. And what the hell were the doctors supposed to tell us that they had not already told us? No matter the symptoms we described or the photos and videos we brought in, he was meeting his physical and developmental milestones. And what if the scope proved as inconclusive as everything else had? What then?

"I don't care," Rebecca said.

There was a fierceness in her voice—she had made up her mind and nothing was going to change it. So I said nothing more. It was lunchtime anyway. I put him in his high chair, set about making his milk, dumping applesauce in a bowl. Rebecca put our bags by the door. The house was quiet.

All afternoon I worried about what would happen at the hospital. And if they didn't find anything wrong with him, what would they think of us for having brought him in? Out of my confusion the only reasonable thing seemed to be to talk to Tricia myself, to make sure we were in the right. So before we left for the hospital, I put in the call. I asked point-blank if she thought an endoscopy was necessary. No, she said, frankly, she did not. "Then why even get us a bed for the night?" I asked.

"For Mom's peace of mind."

"What?"

"Well, if we can make Mom feel better," she said, "that's probably what we should do. We should make Mom feel better."

I thanked her and hung up the phone, feeling sick to my stomach. She thought it was Rebecca—thought it was *us*. Part of me thought it was us, too. We *were* first-time parents without family nearby. We *were* under a tremendous amount of strain because of money. And even though we both feared something was wrong, he *did* have his good days. But I still could not get clear of the fact that if it were all in our heads, why could he not sleep for more than a few hours at a time? Why was he so fussy? Why did he shriek? Why was his belly distended? Why the alternating bouts of constipation and diarrhea? And why, no matter how we worked at his care, could we not comfort him?

When it was time for us to go to the hospital, we prepared—as we had learned to—down to the smallest detail. We packed the car with snacks, sippy cups, diapers, multiple changes of clothes, pillows, blankets, baby books, books to read, magazines, the iPod, Rebecca's laptop. On our way out of town, we picked up sandwiches and drove north to the interstate under an indelible powder-blue sky. Instead of our normal route, I took an ill-advised shortcut that ended in a barricade of flickering "Road Closed" signs. Rebecca stared out the window, silent, and I turned us around. We snaked through side streets and made our way to the outskirts of town, where houses and gas stations gave way to hot green cornfields rippling in the breeze. Up ahead, a rust-streaked grain elevator towered over a set of railroad tracks. No sooner had I spotted the crossing than bells sounded, red lights flashed. Here came the train—a freighter loaded with coal from Wyoming. It was huge and moving at a steady clip, and the roar as it approached and pounded down the tracks ate up every other sound. I pulled over to the side of the road, cut the engine. The rattling and clunking of its cars, the grinding screech of steel on steel: I felt it pulsing through me, from the hollow of my chest to the tips of my fingers. I thought maybe this was a sign. Maybe we shouldn't go. In the passenger's seat, Rebecca looked pale and overtired, as though that morning's flood of anger and determination had receded into the deep channel of weariness from which it had spilled. I asked her what she wanted to do. She shrugged, said she didn't know. In back, in his car seat, our son turned a Dr. Seuss book over and over in his little hands. I loved him so much. He was sick, and I did not want him to be sick.

I started the car and drove us home.

Paternal Authority Takes a Backseat

MARCO ROTH

I like to say that I dined out on the following story. Since no one really "dines out" on stories anymore, the way they did in eighteenth-century salons, where a well-told anecdote might earn you supper at some city merchant's table, what I mean is that I told it so I might continue to appear interesting to my friends, most childless then and many childless still. They're a conflicted group of fundamentally ambivalent folk, the kind of people who tend to argue earnestly about whether having children is morally unjustifiable: sometimes on utilitarian grounds (unfair to an overstretched and overheated world to add another mouth to feed), or, reversing the terms, they question how anyone could afflict a loved one with the prospect of growing up in such a downward spiraling, iniquitous, and unequal world as ours. They'd wrecked a number of relationships on the hard shoals of their scruples, but only a cynic would say they were still too young, too selfish to share their love with a third or a fourth, too eager to go from girlfriend to girlfriend, too self-centered not to be afraid of giving up years of their life to creatures who would probably be as demanding and as sensitive as they were. Everything in their lives they took seriously, more seriously than I took things, it seemed.

I could report to them from the land of breeders—having crossed over not because I had reasonable answers to their varied moral objections, but because I was prone to those moods where it seems like life is simply what happens to you, beyond your control, and one night, after my wife had brought up starting a family and we'd discussed ourselves into our usual stalemate about the pros and cons of having kids at that moment, while vanquishing a bottle of wine or two, I'd given myself over to one of them. Milling around at their glittering parties, after a friend greeted me with a polite "How's it going," I'd trap him in a tale of parenting, while he looked nervously toward the bar, where his girlfriend was waiting. At other moments, I thought I caught them taking sadistic "I told you so" pleasure in my little arias of fatherhood: the time I tried to whisk my two-year-old daughter into my arms as I thought she was about to toddle in front of an oncoming car, and she slipped from my grasp and fell, from the height of my knees, skinning and bruising, though thankfully not breaking, her elbow on the asphalt, the car passing several yards from us without threat and she, after the shock wore off, looking up at me and saying, "Why did you throw me, Daddy?" And my friends, most of whom, like me, had either been through some form of psychotherapy or read a quantity of Freud and Lacan in graduate school, would say, "See, it's always going to be your fault" or, making ironic eyebrows, "That elbow will heal, but the scar will never fade."

. . .

The story I want to tell took place a little while later, a month or so after my daughter's third birthday. I was picking her up at her day care, in an old stone church located at the western edge of the University of Pennsylvania campus. It was a tolerably anarchic sort of place, the best of a number of less-than-inspiring options, and convenient for my wife, whose tenure-track position in the humanities nevertheless did not come with free admission to the university's official day-care center, filled with the offspring of Wharton business school professors, administrators, and patent-generating chemists, and where we'd been informed that we should have put ourselves on the wait list two years before our daughter was even born. Our family planning not having been up to management school standards, we settled with relief for the more cooperative feel of St. Mary's. It was staffed by a few South Asian immigrants, a number of parent volunteers, some night school students in their twenties, and a guy with dreadlocks who played guitar to the kids, led a morning drum circle, and would, in two years, become my daughter's stepfather.

My wife and I were already separated when I drove out to West Philadelphia that afternoon, to fetch my daughter home. We were living a couple blocks apart, downtown, in those transitional apartments that divorcing couples with kids first move into. A dining area turns into a playroom turns into an office, a couch becomes your bed when your daughter sleeps in yours; the one table you salvaged from the division of goods is a multipurpose surface, hosting food, paperwork, and art projects, while the computer turns from work machine into "entertainment complex," multiplication of function as evidence of lack. "Transitional" was the operative adjective for just about everything then, learning to let go without entirely letting go. It was unsurprising, under those conditions, that "transitions"—so-called in therapized parentspeak—were often the most dramatic moments of our daughter's days. Dropping her off at the nursery often meant enduring a storm of tears, our daughter's features transformed into an uncannily accurate version of an ancient Greek tragic mask, leaving us with an image of deep human misery that, the staff assured us, passed about five or ten minutes after we'd gone. And it was true that by the time I picked her up, she was usually immersed in play with some other kids or in attentive pose at afternoon story time. In fact, taking her away often provoked another outburst, after she'd exhausted the more cunning ploys of hiding shoes and sweaters in far-flung corners. And then getting her into the car was one more challenge, equaled only by the difficulty of persuading her to get out of it once we'd arrived.

It didn't help that I was, by temperament, a gradualist and a lingerer when it came to goodbyes. If my daughter asked me to stay in the mornings and read to her in the nursery common room, I'd do it, even if she'd be encouraged by this display of her persuasive power to try to get me to stay longer, until, inevitably, the same drama of abandonment, the tears, the wailings, the holding on. Eventually we worked out a game where I'd deliver her to the guitar guy, her substitute father, just as her mother had to give her up to the attractive and caring woman who directed the day care. No other people were acceptable.

For the afternoons, I fortified myself with a series of bribes, or rewards: a fruit snack if she allowed herself to be peaceably strapped into the car seat, sometimes an additional cookie. How she hated the car seat! Emblem of societally enforced infantilism and disempowerment if ever there was one. I kind of saw things her way, despite the statistics about safety. On bad days, she'd hit out at me as I was holding her to strap her in, once delivering an accidental but perfectly executed head-butt to the bridge of my nose. To calm our rages, because the truth was that, in pain, I was barely in control of my own violence, and she could sense it, I inaugurated the tradition of playing the Smiths' "Is It Really So Strange?" during the ride home, "You can kick me / You can butt me / You can break my spine / But you can't change the way I feel / Cuz I love you." What better anthem to necessary parental obligation, I thought, than this cheery, major-chord hymn to teenage masochism? My daughter called it the "tantrum song" and began to request it even on good days.

The crucial moment happened on one of our better days. The pickup was going more or less smoothly. She'd been happy to see me, and the always half-playful chasing after clothes and shoes and tracking down the stuffed animal she'd brought with her in the morning, amid the overheated rooms of the church's upper floors, actually felt like play. She wanted to pretend to drive, for a bit, and I let her, until she honked the horn a few too many times for my eardrums, and I began to worry about who might come out to the parking lot to complain. She then clambered peaceably into the backseat, and I belted her in. At least the car seat wasn't one of those ridiculous backward-looking ones. I shared the chocolate croissant I'd brought, kissed her on top of her head, and climbed into the front. As I was about to turn the key in the ignition, I heard my daughter say clearly but insistently, without whining, "I want to sit next to you!" I tried telling her she was better off in the back, but she wasn't having it. "I want to sit next to you." I suppose I could have ignored her, started the car, and begun the slightly stressful process of reversing between the Scylla of a curbside lamppost and the Charybdis of a large dumpster, so that we could exit the narrow lot facing forward into oncoming traffic, but I didn't want her to start tantruming at a delicate moment.

Also, again, I wasn't unsympathetic. I often felt like a chauffeur or a taxi driver, alone in the front seat, only able to snatch occasional glances at my passenger in the rearview mirror. For some reason, the car seat only fit properly on the driver's side. With the music on, my daughter and I couldn't really hear each other well enough to talk. But I always imagined that the creeping drive homeward through Philadelphia's rush hour bottlenecks would feel less bleakly chore-like if we could really keep each other company. So I chickened out and tried to take the responsibility out of my hands.

"I'm sorry, baby. There's a law in Pennsylvania that children have to ride in car seats, in the back."

This explanation didn't sway her. She teared up more and asked again. A foot kicked out ominously against the back of my seat, in the region of my kidneys. Then I made it worse. "Even if I wanted to let you sit in the front, if a policeman saw us he could give me a ticket, or take me away from you—is that what you want?"

There was a short silence, as my words sunk in, and then, I heard a soft but clear voice, almost an adult's, one of those moments that seem so improbable to us when we read nineteenth-century novels with their clear-speaking, steady-voiced doomed children—Little Nell or Tiny Tim—stating, "You don't love me."

I was stunned. *Oh no, the heavy artillery is out early*, I thought at first. *Should I laugh it off, tell her not to be silly, that of course I love her, and it was precisely for that reason that I wouldn't want to expose her to the danger of sitting in the front?* That's what the law was about, after all. The state was on my side here, and being a good father meant setting limits, I understood that. But there was something else, maybe the seriousness of her tone, maybe a sudden influx from my own lonely childhood, or my own lonely-feeling fatherhood, the sense of isolation, of the unreality of the world when seen through automobile windows and windshields—whatever it was—I undid my seat belt and got out of the car, walked around to open the back passenger side door and climbed in.

"I think I'll sit next to you for a bit," I said. I stroked her hair. "You know I love you," I said, more statement than question.

"But why did you say you'd go away with the policeman?" she suddenly wailed out.

And in that moment, I thought I understood. She hadn't been exhibiting an improvisatory genius in the arts of emotional manipulation. This was more like "Why did you throw me, Daddy?" As far as she was concerned, I had been making up a story, just as I had made up "The Law" about kids having to ride in car seats. Since the law was just my story, the punishment was no less my invention. And what she understood me to be saying was "If you don't stay in the car seat, I'm going to leave you."

The damage was done. The question was how to begin repairing it. Maybe because I was frequently without any other adult company, I wanted to speak to my daughter without condescension, but soothingly. Maybe this was unwise, but I continued, "I don't make up the law," I said. "It's something outside me, out there, in the world. It doesn't come from me. And while you shouldn't worry about the policeman, I shouldn't have said that, I'm sorry. I really don't know what they might do if they saw me driving with you in the front seat."

We were looking each other in the eyes. She'd stopped crying, and her face was serious but composed. I had no idea how her mind would interpret what I'd just said, but at least I was changing the story so it was about something other than absolute paternal laws and threats. "It would be nice if I could control the world," I said, "but there are other drivers out there, too, and I don't know what they'll do. The car seat law is about that. So we're going to have to do this together, and it would really help me if you stayed in the backseat."

She nodded yes. Driving home, we were quiet, as though we both understood that something big had happened, without being able, either of us, to explain to each other what it was.

I don't mean to imply that this moment alone was transformative for us. In the short term, I certainly felt like I'd lost a bit of my daughter's respect. My aura was tarnished. She began to call me by my first name, a phase a lot of kids go through, and I didn't make an issue out of it, one way or the other. I liked that she did it with affection, not out of mischief or the sense of testing a taboo. There were certainly enough of those other moments: her ruses to get into the bathroom while I was peeing were hilarious and exhausting and almost convinced me that Freud was right about all the penis envy, Oedipal bullshit. But Freud hadn't written much about how children name their parents, and I decided that my daughter's use of my given name was a sign of hope. She'd understood that I was an individual with my own virtues and flaws rather than some omnipotent creature capable of compelling obedience and respect in the short term, but only at the cost of instilling later feelings of disappointment and betrayal.

Considering it later, it occurred to me that I'd disowned my paternal authority at the very instant I finally understood what it meant to be another human being's "reality." There are no doubt plenty of parents and psychoanalysts who'd like to reprove me: How could I be so unfair to my daughter to make it seem like we were sharing a responsibility that was mine alone! Shouldn't I just man up and make myself one with the law, the better to allow her to rebel against it later? In another sense, however, we'd stumbled our way through what seems a fairly paradigmatic crisis of contemporary fatherhood. The old patriarchal order, out of which developed Freudian and Lacanian identifications of the father with a stern, always distant lawgiver, really were not borne out by the facts of our lives. Social rules, whether expressed by the formulae of life insurance companies, legal formulas, or professional associations, all judged her mother to be a more symbolically powerful and valuable person than I was, a freelance critic and editor. The kinds of parental responsibilities once rigidly divided on gender lines were, in our case, all mixed up. On the days and nights my daughter stayed with me, I cooked for her, and filled her bath, sang to her at bedtime, and watched her at play, or joined in myself, in ways that would strike those with graver images of *paternitas* as a travesty. Rather than the strong absent father, which means always being there and never being available, I could be the weaker but present one.

In our situation, it probably made sense for me to act as if reality was something external to both of us. The more so because I couldn't be certain that I wanted my daughter to identify me with it. Having fathered a child ought not automatically make me one with a symbolic order that, among its imperfections, had evolved two sets of rules for two classes of persons, car seat laws and regressive taxes for little people like us, impunity for torturers and bailouts for misbehaving corporations. Maybe, the more I could signal my divorce from that present order of things, the more she and I might ultimately be able to shape our lives together as if that order was something we could change.

Zombie Father

BOB SMITH

My three-year-old son, Xander, after peeing in his grandma Sue's bathroom, returned to the living room and asked me, "Bob, do you have a penis?" The obvious answer would have been "You wouldn't be asking that question if I didn't have one." Instead, I laughed and nodded, "Yes."

Xander's question wasn't a criticism of his seven-year-old sister Madeline or his parents Chloe and Elvira or even of Grandma Sue. He adores his sister and loves his two moms and Grandma Sue, but he also relishes all the attention he receives as the only king in the castle at his home in Toronto. His inquiry was clearly a "Dude, awesome!" male-bonding moment.

I'm Xander's father, but I'm not his dad. I'm his Bob. I'm the deadbeat donor to Chloe and Elvira. Elvira and I have been friends for a long time, both of us working as stand-up comics; I met Chloe years later. We thoroughly discussed what my role would be in their lives and the lives of our children. I would be part of their family, but they were Maddie and Xander's parents. I'm not shirking the responsibilities of fatherhood, since the most important lesson any father can teach his children is that when a man makes a commitment, he should honor his agreement. Several times a year, I fly up from New York to visit Maddie and Xander and am welcomed like Santa Claus. In the three- or four-month intervals, the two blue-eyed blonds always seem to have become new children. Taller, more articulate, and with a striking new propensity to tell adults what they like and dislike.

I'm starting to feel that however many gifts my partner Michael and I bring, there's also a lump of coal that I leave in their stockings. Two years after Maddie was born, I was diagnosed with ALS, commonly called "Lou Gehrig's disease," because Americans need celebrity endorsements for everything, including life-threatening illnesses.

I have the sporadic form of ALS—not the familial version—so Maddie and Xander aren't stuck with a double-helix noose of my tarnished chromosomes. My kids have two cats and a big New-foundland dog, Bailey, but I sometimes feel like I'm their first dying pet. Now, that would be the saddest backyard burial imaginable, requiring a Cyclops-sized shoe box. The pet simile is particularly apt since, like a turtle or gerbil, I have no voice. ALS involves your motor neurons dying, which causes your muscles to atrophy and stop functioning. You're transformed into a Frankenstein monster, a collection of animate and inanimate body parts. My tongue and larynx gave their last gasps three years ago. That is partly why I love the TV series *The Walking Dead*. It's a dystopian fantasy about a world in which a virus has transformed most people into brainless, flesh-eating zombies and the few survivors into dinner. It's not nice, but I root for the zombies. The series is set in Georgia, and the walking dead are more intelligent than the right-wing conservatives who populate that state. So why shouldn't they snack on the talking stupid?

My disease isn't like that. My brain is sharper than ever, and I'm still walking. But my worst fear is that I'll be transformed into the Sitting Dead, stuck in a wheelchair with useless limbs, a corpse with a pulse. It would suck to be a zombie too weak and immobile to enjoy the cannibalistic satisfaction of dining on raw human intestines, since your hands are incapable of ripping flesh and you've lost the ability to swallow.

Oh, in case you're thinking I'm brain-straining for these metaphors about my own demise, you're wrong. Humorous writers don't struggle to be funny. We naturally view the world through rose-colored lenses, but that doesn't mean we're unaware of our thorny lives. Thinking of something funny and saying or writing it has been habitual with me since I was a little boy. My father always prepared the turkey for our Thanksgiving dinner, and when I was about eight or nine, he had his wrist and hand shoved in the bird and said, "I can't find the neck." I dryly commented, "Maybe you're looking in the wrong end." My dad stopped searching for the elusive body part to roar at my joke. It's a pivotal memory: the first time I can remember a sense of pride in making someone crack up.

Of course, I'm horribly distraught that I make Maddie cry instead of making her laugh. After our visits, she often sobs since she can remember when I could talk. She's told her parents that she's afraid I'm going to die. Xander can't remember when I could speak, and so he just comments, "Bob can't talk," without tears.

For years I was a successful stand-up comic. Losing my voice is an unoriginal O. Henry ending to my story. It's why I believe

God is a hack bestselling author whose one-hit wonder is never read for pleasure.

Anger combined with levity has been an important part of my survival; most ALS patients die within two to five years after their diagnosis. It's been six years since my diagnosis and eight years since my first symptoms. My fury is stoked by the thought that I might not see Maddie and Xander grow up, that I could become a snapshot memory like their kindergarten teachers. It infuriates me that I might not be there to help them. Their parents will be there for them, but the Bobs in our lives play important roles too.

For example, my father's sister, my aunt Ann, gave me a *National Geographic* subscription when I was a little boy, and also enrolled me in an after-school art class at a local college when I was in the second grade. My mom would pick me up with my brothers and sister in the car during the five o'clock shadow of a Buffalo winter. How did Aunt Ann figure out that I was a creative nature boy so early? I'll never know. She died of an aneurism when I was thirteen.

I don't want to be a closed book to Maddie and Xander. There are already so many unsolved mysteries in our lives that it can take a lifetime to figure out parent puzzles, and sibling riddles can be just as challenging. Parents and Bobs also have to grasp the brain twister of their children. They've inherited your DNA and, with it, a whole bunch of junk you didn't even know you had, like boxes you forgot in the back of the attic. Maddie is into her clothes and Xander loves his dance classes, and who knows where those passions came from. But they also love dinosaurs and books, two Bob passions.

Maddie and Xander are already avid readers, slowly learning that the great gift of literature is that someone else's tale becomes a chapter of your story. It's painful that I can't read Dr. Seuss to Maddie and Xander. It puts me in the position of Our Father Who Art in Heaven who recommends his good book, but doesn't talk. I would tell Maddie and Xander that the only rational explanation for God's lack of response to everyone's prayers must be that he has ALS. No one deserves ALS, except him. He's the one guy who should suffer from this horrible illness, since he created ALS and all the other diseases that don't afflict people universally, but punish people with different death sentences. The creator of the universe conceived of one way to be born, but let his imagination romp in devising millions of gruesome ways to die. His ingenuity in bumping off his children is clearly the artistic expression of a psychotic. Either that, or he's a fan of the Three Stooges and finds hilarity in all human suffering.

I want to discuss this with Maddie and Xander because I think the major flaw in most religions is a lack of humor. We worship a deity who regards all jokes, derisive remarks, and pointed questions about his gaping, loophole-filled master plan as a punishable blasphemy. I wouldn't want to spend a half hour listening to Old Testament Yahweh at a cocktail party, let alone be stuck with him yammering at me for an eternity. Listening to a pompous, know-it-all bore or burning in hell? Both sound equally cruel and unbearable.

I'm getting cranky, but I'd tell Maddie and Xander to read Thoreau and Emerson instead, since the American transcendentalists embraced wit and humor in their search for spirituality. God must have a sense of humor: he created the bluebird, which Thoreau brilliantly described as carrying the sky on its back, and also the lesula monkey, which carries the sky on its ass and testicles.

I'm not an atheist, but I believe that the Great Spirit animating our lives is love. I want Maddie and Xander to follow Emerson's advice and have an original relationship to the universe. If your religion was founded when people still thought slavery was okey-dokey, women were chattel, and witches should be burned, I'll bet your faith is filled with equally archaic beliefs. Maddie and Xander don't have to agree with me though. I think choosing a religion for your children is as outdated as when parents picked their kids' wives or husbands.

God implored us to love thy neighbors—a philosophy I embrace since my neighbors in Manhattan often see me struggling to swipe my subway card, and someone always asks, "Do you need help?" God watches us struggle, but I guess he doesn't need to nurture since he created nature. A father who doesn't do both isn't a father. He's a sperm donor.

Our Father Who Art in Heaven chooses to remain an anonymous donor. He gave us a cup of his light—all men think their spunk is radiant—but he refuses to identify himself as either Jehovah, Jesus, Allah, Krishna, or L. Ron Hubbard. He's not going to play an active role in our lives, so that means we're all living like lesbians. I would tell Maddie and Xander that their family isn't an anomaly, but is actually representative of every family on earth. We can be happy without an all-knowing/know-it-all father, but we have to woman up, be resourceful, and rely on our own love.

God plays the same role in our lives that I have in Maddie and Xander's lives. He visits several times a year, usually handing out gifts, such as the time Maude, the eleven-year-old daughter of our friends Jack Lechner and Sam Maser, decided to help me by raising money for ALS research. (Sam is a biological female. I don't want to give the impression my only close friends are fellow gays.)

Since Maude was asking adults to give up something dear to them—cash—she decided to reciprocate and give up something she treasured—her beautiful long brown hair. She shaved her head and raised eight grand. Maude's selflessness demonstrated that the first step toward the cure for all the diseases and problems that plague our lives is love.

Another example was the time I surprised Maddie with a visit to her preschool. She was in the playground, sitting on a step. When she saw and recognized me, her blue eyes flashed joy. She jumped up and ran over and hugged my thigh. Until that moment, I'd never understood that I had never been fully welcomed before.

As Maddie squeezed me, I remembered that when she was one month old, I went to visit her in Toronto and questioned whether I would feel a bond of love between us. I held her and she fell asleep on my stomach for over an hour, and as I looked at her adorable snoozing face, it seemed that she or God or both were letting me know that her company in my life was enough to create love. It's not a promise that the people you love won't occasionally aggravate you, but it was a revelation that love is about alleviating the loneliness of the hermit in our heads. Our thoughts reside in a bony cave, and we need someone to distract us from dwelling on that depressing notion for our entire lives.

The daily demonstration of caring in my life that I receive from my partner Michael keeps my heart beating to the rhythm of a love song. The list of things Michael does to help me every day is endless: helping put on my clothes, making me a protein shake, placing my man bag over my neck when I head out to acupuncture, writing checks and deposit slips since my handwriting now looks more childish than Xander's.

I want Maddie and Xander to experience the love I feel in my life. Not that love can't cause pain. The grimmest fact of life—that all parents avoid telling their children—is that adults play with their hearts like toys, and we all break them eventually.

Michael and I became a couple after Maddie was born, so he didn't contribute to our negotiations about trying to figure out the proper balance between donor dad and "bone her" dad. Michael loves his two nephews and niece and thought it was great that children were also a part of my life. In fact, when Elvira and Chloe asked me for a second cup of Joe or Josephine, after my doctor approved, Michael was all for it. It took just one donation to bring Xander into our lives, and Michael now proudly refers to me as "One-Shot Smith." (It's fortunate that I'm not heterosexual or there would be a trail of knocked-up women.)

It thrills me that Maddie and Xander love Michael. They both beam when they see him. Smiling children are night-lights that keep adults from being afraid of the full spectrum of darks, which come in a range of paint colors from Blackhead to Closed Coffin.

It's a relief when your kids love your partner, since their thumbs up or down tip the scales of your opinion about everyone and everything. If your son or daughter dislikes shredded wheat cereal, you might not agree with your child, but eventually dry and crusty will take precedence over healthy and wholesome.

On Michael's first visit to see Maddie—Xander wasn't born yet—we went to their cottage, named Treehab by Elvira. The cottage was a three-hour drive from Toronto on a lake that was picturesquely balanced among summer houses, bird nests, and rabbit burrows. As soon we arrived, Elvira and I took three-year-old Maddie for a canoe ride. Michael dove in the water and swam beside us. We stopped in a wild part of the lake, where Maddie and I hunted for frogs among the reeds. We caught a small green frog, which Maddie held in her palm for a second and then released. Holding a frog is a passing thrill, which our lives are filled with.

Maddie is a fashionista, and I usually buy her clothes. My selection is entirely based on whatever looks fun. A leopard-skin print dress for a four-year-old girl? Definitely. I dropped into a children's clothing shop called BeatNick and Nora near our apartment in Greenwich Village—the type of store where a Goth toddler can pick up black diapers that safety pin through her nose. I spotted a pair of green rubber boots that looked like two frogs with yellow eyes and bright red lips. They were in Maddie's size. The clerk, a middle-aged hipster, whose tattoo-painted arms were developing a craquelure of fine wrinkles, stepped forward. "We have stuff that goes with those boots." I bought an entire amphibious outfit for Maddie. A frog umbrella, frog backpack, along with a frog T-shirt and frog's leg leggings. When Maddie opened her gifts, she immediately chucked off her shoes and put on her frogs. She wore them for the rest of the day, and I was happy that she was happy. Your Happiness = My Happiness is the formula for all successful and satisfying relationships.

I hope that doesn't come across as sentimental, since my education about love has been grueling. It's deeply upsetting to go to a restaurant and drool more and be a messier eater than my three-year-old son. But Michael hands me a cloth napkin, and as I clean up, any doubts I have about being loved are wiped away. I want Maddie and Xander to understand that even while dealing with one of the most daunting diseases ever devised by Our Sperm Donor Who Art in Heaven, I've still been happy. Part of my resilience must be innate. I don't have the predisposition to depression that virtually all of my friends and my mother have and my sister had. I look up at night and admire the stars instead of pondering a universe that's more than half-empty. When I look at Maddie and Xander, I experience the same bewitching astonishment and the sense that we all stargaze on other people's lives. We might witness comet Shoemaker-Levy 9 hitting Jupiter or someone getting ALS, but we're unable to fully experience someone else's pain. The true marvel of children and novels is that they allow us to imagine someone else's hardships.

Being told you have a life-threatening illness forces you to read your autobiography and judge the merits of your story. I'm pretty happy with mine. I wanted to become a stand-up and a writer and did both. I performed at every benefit I was ever asked to do. I've never voted for any Republican presidential candidate. I've fallen in love, had my love returned, had my heart broken, and fallen in love again. Of all the things I've accomplished, nothing makes me happier or prouder than Maddie and Xander. Not that any father can take any credit for his children after they're born. Once they start talking and walking, they're individuals free to be happy or sad.

I still feel optimistic that I'm going to beat my ALS. There's research going on, and we can never predict our tomorrows. On our last visit to Toronto, Michael and I went for a walk with our family in a woodsy park with many ponds. We saw male red-winged blackbirds, and I identified and pointed out the brown females to Maddie and Xander. Maddie asked, "Why are the females plainer?" The four adults looked at one another. Michael said to Elvira and Chloe, "We'll let you explain that Mother Nature is sexist."

Elvira added, "Or she's a cougar." I explained to Maddie by iPad that the males use their bright colors to attract females, and the plainer females are less likely to be noticed by predators while they're nesting. I also told her that birds are different from people, where both males and females can be knockouts. "Good," she said, before running off to play with Xander.

Our conversation made me realize that good parents like Chloe and Elvira and good Bobs and Michaels are field guides for our children on how to live. Each volume contains its own expertise on making bad decisions, recovering from painful events, and identifying toxic, selfish assholes. I'm determined to stay in print.

The natural world has been such a source of joy in my life, and I want to preserve it for Maddie and Xander. I firmly believe that if you're a parent voting for anti-environmental, climate-change-denying conservatives who don't conserve anything, then Child Protective Services should put your kids in foster care, since you clearly don't care about their welfare.

After Xander confirmed that I have a penis, Maddie should have asked the important follow-up question, "Bob, are you a prick?"

I would have still laughed, then responded, "When it comes to my kids, I am."

Man, Dying

GARTH STEIN

I've been annexed to the outer boroughs. Ostracized. Usurped. On a family vacation, due to limited sleeping arrangements, I've been forced to share a bed with my wife and our five-year-old son, who has taken up position between us.

I think of Tristan and the lovely Isolde. How Tristan placed his sword between them as they shared a bed. How her father, the king, looked in on them during the night, suspicious that his favored protégé had less-than-honorable intentions for his virginal daughter. Upon seeing Tristan's sword lying between the young couple, symbolizing the honor with which Tristan treated the beautiful girl, the king was satisfied that no impropriety had been taken. Oh, how he was deceived!

I am jealous of my son. In the night, he rolls around luxuriously in the bed, upside down, sideways, arms and legs flopped every which way. He sleeps so soundly while I struggle fitfully, clinging to the edge, trying not to resent him. *I* should be the one burrowing my head into my wife's mane of hair. *I* should be hugging her tightly around her neck as he is. Matching her sleeping breaths, warming myself to her body heat. Yet I cede this pleasure to him, because he is my son.

My wife's first pregnancy miscarried. It's common, we were told, the first time around. I have to admit, I felt a flash of relief. Only a flash; I did not indulge in it. Still, for one moment I sighed and thought, *Well, at least we reset the clock a bit for now.*

My father once told me, "You don't really know someone until you've cleaned up his vomit."

He was referring to his time in the army, driving a tank around post–WWII West Germany, when motion sickness could be a problem. He also told me, "You don't really know who your friends are until you've spent a week living with them in a tank." I guess that's when the meaning of brotherly love really becomes apparent. I don't know. My father is not around for me to ask him to clarify. Old Marvin hurled his last chunks four years ago, yawned his final Technicolor yawn, departed this dreary world for the great vomitorium in the sky. But I often think of his words when I'm being vomited on. And, looking back on the years I've spent raising my three sons, I've been vomited on quite a bit; I know of which I speak.

Number One son was born the night Kerri Strug broke her foot but vaulted anyway, and the U.S. women's gymnastics team won gold. The doctors and nurses watched the TV in the room with us, as my wife slogged through her induced labor with a tube in her spine so she could bear the supercharged contractions caused by the Pitocin. When he was born, my son was slow to respond. He didn't do well on his Apgar test—maybe a bit *too much* Pitocin? They stuck him with vaccines practically before his first breath. Little did we know.

My father grew up in New York City; he couldn't swim. When I was a kid, he would take my sister and me to the community pool, and he would stand in the shallow end while my sister and I swam all over. They say fishermen in Alaska don't learn to swim for a reason: if their boat sinks, they hope to die quickly and get it over with, rather than bob around for hours, stewing in despair and regret until the ocean finally claims them. I don't know if my father had a reason for never learning to swim.

When I went to freshman orientation at Columbia University in New York City, they made us take a swimming test. We had to swim two lengths of the pool. If we failed, we would have to take swimming lessons. When we asked why we needed to swim to go to college, we were told, "Manhattan is an island; one day you may have to escape."

Number Two son was born the night the Yankees won the World Series, sweeping San Diego in four straight. The doctors and nurses all watched the game as my new son shot out of his mother's womb like he was in some kind of a race. Piece of cake, they said. How about that Chuck Knoblauch? Oh, and show the kid the needle . . .

. . .

I was a teenager when my mother told my sister and me that she was my father's second wife. That was a strange revelation. I was applying to colleges when my father told me he didn't have a college degree—deepening the mystery; I wondered what else he hadn't told me. He went to college for a while, he said, but then dropped out. He went to Oklahoma A&M, now Oklahoma State. A bit of an odd choice for a kid from New York whose own father worked as a waiter at Ratner's, a Jewish kosher dairy restaurant on Delancey Street. My father said one of his high school teachers had recommended Oklahoma. He said fellow students in Stillwater would take him home to meet their parents, who were fascinated to see a real Jew up close and personal. They were comforted when they felt his head and he didn't have horns. More Jew-myths debunked.

If you counted up the hours I've spent dancing to "Strangers in the Night," those hours would stretch three times around the equator. You see, our oldest had a dairy allergy. He was highly sensitive. But we didn't know that, so my wife followed doctor's orders: she drank lots of milk when she was nursing him. We had no idea that the reason for his gastrointestinal discomfort and constant vomiting after feeding was because her milk was contaminated with casein protein. "It'll pass in six weeks," they said. "It'll pass in twelve weeks." "Eighteen weeks, no question." Instead of finding the source of the problems in our world, we just try to make the symptoms go away. Or hope that they go away on their own. That's how we work. Don't ask, don't tell.

So I danced him for hours while my wife slept. I had a stack of rags standing by. I'd put one on my shoulder and dance him to Frank Sinatra songs as he spit up until the rag was soaked, then I'd get a dry one. For hours, until I felt like Jane Fonda in *They Shoot Horses, Don't They?*

My father had some kind of dairy issue when he was a baby, apparently. They gave him horse milk. I wonder if people do that anymore: give children horse milk? I know they still shoot horses.

So here's a funny story. My father's mother—please excuse the air of detachment; I only met her once because she used to beat my father with a wooden coat hanger and so he hated her; out of respect for my father, I can't really call her "Grandma"—anyway, she had hoped for a girl, since she already had two boys. When my father was born, she decided he could fill in for a girl, so she dressed him in dresses and frilly outfits and walked him around Brooklyn in a stroller. There was a fire station down the street, and whenever a new guy came on duty, the guys would call Mrs. Stein over to show off her baby. The new guy would admire the little girl, and the regulars would lift my father's dress to reveal his wiener.

I'm not sure how this affected my father later in life. Cross-dressing as an infant and having his mother parade his wiener about. Being beaten with a coat hanger. That's got to mess with a person's self-esteem.

Number Three son was born at home with midwives and doulas and meditation as the only method of pain relief—no epidurals hidden in the closet of our house. There were no sports on TV. He came out with one hand up by his head, thus making his head larger and prolonging the agony—sort of the ultimate dramatic entrance. As the midwives were cleaning up, one of them asked me if she could show the placenta to my older boys; they were fascinated by it. So was our dog.

It was strange birthing a baby at home. Strange in a good way. My memory of the first two boys was punctuated by two thoughts: Why do they give a Hepatitis B vaccine when a baby is one day old? And, is it good to stuff your day-old infant into a car seat?

Everything with Number Three was so . . . *normal.* He didn't see a car seat for weeks, I think. And nary a needle has punctured his tender skin.

When my father was drafted into the army, he was sent overseas on a military ship. He had to get a whole ration of vaccines, he told me, so he stood on line and got the shots.

"Next," the man said. "Stein."

"*I'm* Stein," my father said.

"You're Steed," the man observed.

"No, I'm Stein."

"Well, you just took Steed's shots, now you get Stein's shots."

So they dosed him again.

Many years later, my father was given the pneumococcal vaccine two years in a row, even though that is contra-indicated. He went to different doctors and forgot, he said. Of course there's no way to prove a causal link, but shortly after his second dose, he became quite ill. He tried to walk it off for weeks. Finally, my mother cajoled him into going to the emergency room. He never left the hospital. Six weeks later, he was dead.

Some people are just more sensitive than others. Sure. A few days after he received five vaccines at one time during his third course of antibiotics for a persistent ear infection, Number Two son, who had been ebullient and verbal, socially precocious and funny, stopped talking. He stopped making eye contact. He ate only cheese and crackers. He spent his days in front of the TV watching *Scooby-Doo*. He sucked his thumb so hard, a blood blister formed, then ruptured.

Our pediatrician said, "He appears to be in some distress."

Oh, but the vomiting! Don't let me forget to tell you about the vomiting!

Number One son struggled with ear infections, and you know, they have all sorts of liquid antibiotics for that. They don't even bother to check if the infection is viral or bacterial, they just push the drugs because that's the easiest way out, and it works for "most children." The medicines have funny names and they taste like pineapple or cherry. Yum! You use the dropper to get the stuff in his mouth. Wait for him to swallow. Within minutes, he will vomit all over you! I mean, this is awesome therapy for an ear infection! How can you go wrong when you can just drive over to the pharmacy and pick up another brand of antibiotic and make him vomit again? Is this not the greatest country in the world?

What did they do with ear infections before we had all these antibiotics? They used warm garlic-infused oil, maybe with a bit of rosemary extract mixed in. A gentle remedy that really works.

I had a feeling my father's condition was worse than we thought. The VPAP machines and CPAP machines. CNN always on the TV—twenty-four hours of nonstop-Wolf-Blitzer-party-rock. Of course, there's always a little fear involved. Usually you can suppress that, or at least hide it from sight. It's important to remain positive in a hospital setting. But those X-rays. They just never showed improvement.

Had he inhaled something? Had he been on any foreign trips? Had he cleaned out the garage recently? Shoveled a load of fertilizer? "No, of course not," my mother said. "Why do you ask?" They didn't want to use the term SARS yet, so they just shook their heads, perplexed, and said that something had assaulted his lungs and he wasn't recovering.

When they were gone, my mother quipped angrily: "I don't know why he got pneumonia in the first place. He took that damn vaccine . . . *twice!*"

I winced and looked over at my wife, who had warned me already: she was concerned the world was being vaccinated to death.

Okay, one time, Number One son ate an entire rack of baby back ribs all by himself. He was five. We were so proud of him. We cheered him on. What an appetite! Look at this kid put it away!

Well, he gave it all back, and more. That night, he sat up in bed and puked all over his comforter. And hands and feet and pajamas. I cleaned him up, hosed him down and remade his bed with fresh sheets, and tried very hard not to vomit, myself, when handling the foul-smelling effluvia.

My son and I repeated that sequence *three times* in two hours.

If my father were still alive, he would say I really got to know my son that night.

Then there was the time we were driving home from Whistler, where we had gone for a wintery break. North of Vancouver—still hours from home—Number Two son complained of his throat hurting. Throat pain? Drink some water. Suck on a hard candy. Could it be a cold? No, he insisted, it really hurt.

Hmm, my wife said. I wonder what it could be.

"It could be that he was trying to tell us he felt car sick," I would later say.

Shortly after complaining of "throat pain," Number Two went Linda Blair on us in the car. Seriously. Head spinning and the whole thing, spraying vomit on every possible surface, including the back of my head and every possible crack and crevice, of which there are many in a car. Fortunately, we happened upon a diner on the highway, so we didn't have to drip with vomit for long. My wife took the kids inside while I cleaned myself and the car as best I could, having begged a bucket of sudsy water and a couple of rolls of paper towels from the kitchen staff. And still, we had to cross the border to the U.S. and hope the agent didn't ask us about that terrible smell coming from the car.

· · ·

My wife does not suffer silently. She does not take things at face value. She doesn't go along with the expedient just to make life easier; if the right thing is to take the difficult path, she will always do the right thing. So she was in no mood to listen to the conventional wisdom of the doctors: there's nothing you can do to remedy this, they told us; you can only manage it. No. My wife refused to be a victim. She hit the phones, scoured the Internet, packed up the family and moved us to Seattle, found the people who could help and had our damaged kids shipshape in no time. Well, that's an exaggeration. It took a lot of time and a lot of energy and focus and an unwillingness to compromise, and a lot of it wasn't fun. A crazy diet for nearly three years. Alternative doctors. Detoxification. But she rescued our kids; they are both fully recovered from their vaccine-induced autism. And that's only part of why I love her.

I suppose I didn't think of my father as being immortal; I just thought of him as living forever. *I will show you fear in a handful of dust.* The concept that he would die just never occurred to me. And that surprises me, because, you know, I tend to be the kind of person who anticipates things. I see possibilities.

He was really struggling to breathe, even with the CPAP machine blowing oxygen into his lungs. It was a major effort and I could see it on his face. The doctor came in and spoke with him.

"You're having a pretty rough time of it, aren't you?"

My father nodded, looking distressed.

"We could intubate," the doctor said. "Would you like us to intubate?"

My father looked at me almost apologetically. Almost like he knew that intubation was the next step in an inevitable process.

He looked at the doctor and nodded.

"All right, then," the doctor said.

They put him under, opened his throat and slid a tube into his lungs, and plugged him into a machine that breathed for him. And that was his demise. I found out later that rarely does a patient who has sustained the kind of damage to the lungs my father had—from inhaling the mouse droppings he had never inhaled, or taking trips to the Sahara he had never taken—rarely does that patient get the tube removed.

Perhaps the most brutal vomit episode was in a hotel in Florida, and it led to a firmly enforced family rule: When vomiting, remain still and do not move about the cabin.

It was after a fine dinner at an Argentinian churrascaria, where the meat is sliced off long skewers onto your plate and an elaborate buffet of delicacies awaits. In the buffet line, Number One son complained of feeling nauseous. My wife asked him if he felt like he had to vomit—maybe he had picked up a virus or eaten some-thing that was a little off? No, he said. He toughed it out and ate his dinner. He awoke in the middle of the night, ready to get to work. It turns out, he had saved his vomit for later.

Vomiting on a comforter in a nice hotel room is not cool. But it is better—oh, so much better!—than vomiting on the comforter, on the rug, on the walls, on the door to the bathroom, on the bathroom floor, and on the bathroom walls en route to the toilet. I don't believe I need to get more graphic than that. Put it this way, remember the final scene of *Taxi Driver*, in which Travis Bickle, spurting blood from a gunshot wound to the neck, walks through the apartment building shooting bad guys in the face? Okay, replace the blood with vomit and you have a pretty clear picture of what our hotel room looked like.

Let me tell you again how well I know my children.

Can I tell you a secret? Every time my plane lands without exploding into a fireball, I think, *Another flight, and I did not die.*

Number Three son didn't understand. But then he was young enough that he didn't have a long history with Grandpa Marvin. Numbers One and Two, however, had spent a lot of time with Grandpa—playing baseball, badminton, soccer; going to the Museum of Flight, the waterfront for clams and chips, the park. And yet they didn't really understand either.

I remember feeling especially stressed one evening and getting into an argument with Number One, who was twelve years old at the time.

"Leave me alone!" I shouted. "My father is dying!"

"He is *not* dying!" my son shouted back.

We try to protect our children, but to what end?

So I took Number One and Number Two to visit Grandpa Marvin.

By that time, Marvin was in really bad shape. He'd picked up a nasty infection from the hospital which necessitated additional tubes to handle his emissions. His skin was pasty and gray. The respirator pumped him with air in a spastic, jerky rhythm, jolting his body with each breath. His legs were wrapped with pressure blankets that squeezed and released to keep the blood flowing. Grandma, at his side as usual, wore his suffering on her face as well.

We looked at him as if he were performance art. *Man, Dying.* My boys said nothing.

We didn't stay long. I took them out to lunch, I think. I don't remember. Maybe my mother came with us. Maybe not. But I remember riding in the elevator to the lobby, when Number Two looked down at his shoes. "I didn't realize it was that bad," he said.

So then they knew, too.

I was supposed to leave for Appleton, Wisconsin, the next day to give a talk. And then to Winnetka, Illinois. *Winnetka, I'm glad I met ya.* I went to the hospital as usual, after dropping the kids at school, and one of the doctors came over to me quickly and led me into my father's room. My mother and I liked this doctor; he was one of the good ones. It is my belief that to be a doctor, you must have a certain detachment from humanity. In order to cut open a body and remove a cancer, you must lack a little bit of empathy. And that's okay. I want my doctor to be able to cut into me without wincing. I want my doctor not to feel faint at the sight of blood. These are important qualities for a doctor, as they are for the guy who hits cows in the head with a sledgehammer to stun them before slitting their throats. But sometimes you get a doctor who is good at his work and also has full empathy. Those are the doctors you remember.

"I'm glad you got here before your mother did," he said. "Marvin took a bad turn last night. We had a real problem with his blood pressure; he's leaking blood internally, which isn't unexpected considering everything else that's going on. We gave him a transfusion, but . . ."

My father looked terrible. His skin was white and rubbery and bruised. His face was sallow. His cheeks were sunken, his mouth agape, and his tongue was black and swollen and sticking out of his mouth as if he were being strangled. And still, that machine jammed air into his lungs, wracking his body with every breath.

"If he ever recovers," the doctor said, "what kind of life will he lead? We believe he's suffered a stroke; there's likely brain damage, but his condition is too tenuous for us to move him for a CAT scan. His lungs just aren't recovering; he's too old for a lung transplant. . . ."

"What do you recommend?" I asked.

"We could make him more comfortable."

That sounded like a good option to me.

"How do we do that?" I asked. "How do we make my father more comfortable?"

"We turn up the morphine. His breathing slows. Soon his heart stops."

Ah. I understood. It's called palliative care. End-of-life scenario. They shoot horses, don't they.

"I'll have to talk to my mother," I said.

"I'm here if you need me," he replied.

I have no vomit stories for Number Three son. I've wracked my brain to think of one; I've come up with nothing. Because he doesn't vomit. When the other kids at school fall like dominoes with strep throat, Number Three son stands tall. As the whooping cough plague ravages the population, Number Three walks the halls as if he has some kind of force field around him. A force field of health.

Oh, I know the doubters and eye-rollers will pooh-pooh the thought that a holistic-alternative medical paradigm *actually works*. It's hocus-pocus, they will say. It's nonsense. If a doctor doesn't prescribe it, then it can't be true. But then a segment on NPR reports that removing chemical cleaners from a household and changing the diet of a child doesn't just alleviate the symptoms of asthma, it actually completely eliminates the asthma. Then the eye-rollers become head scratchers. When the hospitals say every dollar they spend on home asthma remediation saves $1.46 in hospitalizations and emergency room visits—when they reveal that healthy living is *profitable*—maybe the head scratchers become contemplative chin strokers. Maybe this "new" paradigm works after all.

Such is the progress of our civilization. The push-me pull-you of our society. For every voice of enlightenment hoping to bring change, there are five voices who insist the world is flat, and who will cling to those beliefs with great ferocity because it's easier to be angry than it is to listen to unfamiliar ideas and change one's mind. For each voice of enlightenment, there are ten voices who recite the narrative that has been fed to them by "the authorities"—*look at small pox, look at polio*—without looking into the facts themselves. Without examining the history with a whiff of skepticism, or questioning the gerrymandering of data and purposeful windowing of information employed by those in charge of the religion of medicine. Most people do more research when purchasing a car than they do when allowing their child to be given dozens of vaccine boosters that have never been proven safe or effective.

Sometimes it breaks my heart to think that the canaries in the coal mine of our world are not canaries at all. They are our children. They have an important message to tell us, but we don't seem to be listening.

My oldest son, who is sixteen, wants to own a record store. He wants to live in an apartment on Lake Union and play his guitar and have a dachshund named Bennett.

My middle son, fourteen but going on forty, who has dedicated his life to playing soccer at an elite level, has no idea if he wants to pursue a career in sports.

My youngest son, five and three-quarters years old, would like to transform into a Stone Warrior from the Lego Ninjago series. In fact, he's turning to stone now. He refuses to wear his jacket to school, because stones don't feel the cold. He makes me press on his stomach and admire his stone-like physique.

It is my job to facilitate the achievement of my sons' dreams. It is my job to do so selflessly and without prejudice. It is my job to catch my sons when they fall, but to remain as inconspicuous as possible until they do. It is my job to pick them up and dust them off and send them on their various ways, and to expect nothing in return. Not a thing. For only in the giving of oneself completely and without condition will one find joy.

I don't know when I got old. I certainly don't *feel* old; I feel like the rest of the world has gotten young around me.

I told the doctor we wanted to make my father more comfortable; the doctor obliged. There's a brass plaque on a wall at Evergreen Washelli, a cemetery in Seattle, attesting to that fact. It says April 21, 2009.

I don't know how I would like to die. A fiery ball at the end of a runway. A fatal dose of morphine administered by drip, with my wife by my side holding my hand. I suppose it doesn't matter; these are brief flickers in the vast histories of our souls.

But I know one thing. The older I get, the more I believe there is an afterlife. The more I am convinced. And that thought always makes me shake my head in wonder and amazement, because I anticipate all the joy we have yet to experience. I feel somehow uplifted by all the things we have yet to learn.

The Door

ANDRE DUBUS III

This was our first night home from the hospital, my wife recovering from her C-section, and something was wrong. Our baby cried right till dawn, only taking a breath to be fed when I carried him to his mother's breast in the darkness. Then I'd hold him to my shoulder and pat his tiny back, though he never burped or spit up. Instead, a labored grunting noise would come from his small mouth near my ear, and then he'd start crying again. What was strange was how he felt against me. I'd held babies before, most recently my youngest half sister, and in my arms she felt soft and pliant, too pliant, and I was always careful to cradle her head and neck against my palm. I did the same with our newborn son, too, except there was something about his torso; it was his stomach; it felt as hard and bloated as a wineskin about to burst.

Early the next morning I called my brother Jeb and told him I wouldn't be in till the afternoon. We were remodeling a house in

Charlestown. My younger brother, a far more skilled and experienced carpenter, was my boss.

"Everything all right?"

"Our baby needs a checkup."

"Already?"

I did not want to tell him that we feared something was wrong with our son. To say this would make it true.

Later that morning, his pediatrician examined him and told us he just needed to "pass gas."

I said: "Then why won't he?"

Our doctor shrugged. "Give him some time."

We took her at her word.

When my wife, Fontaine, got pregnant, we'd been married nearly three years. She's a modern dancer and choreographer, and those years she also worked as a part-time dance instructor and self-employed upholsterer of furniture. We lived north of Boston in a small apartment in the house of her former high school art teacher. In the basement, Fontaine had a workbench and a sewing machine and some nights when I came home from my own jobs as a carpenter and adjunct writing teacher, I'd find her down there tying down the springs of a wingback chair, or pulling buttons back through a frame to create diamond tufts in a brocaded fabric that often cost more per yard than we'd let ourselves spend on gas for our one car, an old VW. We never made much money, but it was enough.

It was a life of making things: a dance performance, a short story or novel, a chair, a deck, a new kitchen or bathroom which sometimes paid me a bonus that Fontaine and I would then blow at a restaurant with friends, many of whom spent their days making things, too. She and I made love quite often, and we ended up making this baby, Austin Christopher Dubus. The afternoon she told me she was pregnant, I was lying on the couch in our small living room trying to summon the will to get to my writing desk. It was early spring, a cold rain falling outside, and I'd already spent over eight hours demolishing a bathroom, hauling out the old sink, toilet, and bath, ripping horsehair plaster and lathe down to the studs, clearing between the bays the shredded newspapers used for insulation a hundred years ago. I wore a mask over my face for the lime dust, and I'd taken my flat bar and yanked every square-cut nail from each stud before ripping up the half-rotted floor planks over the joists, exposing ancient pipes for the plumber coming first thing in the morning.

That winter and spring I worked for Yaron. He was an Israeli who'd been in the army when the Egyptians bombed them in the desert. He had deep eyes, long black hair, and a mustache, and he would've been handsome if not for his shoulders, which were forever hunched as if he was still bracing himself to be blown to bits. He had a heavy accent, and his constant answer to any question about work or life was: "Why? It's not worth it. It's just not worth it."

Yaron was married and lived with his wife and two young daughters in a cul-de-sac in the north end of town, an antiseptic neighborhood of nearly identical houses with matching two-car garages. Every morning at six-forty-five he would pick me up in his Taurus (No truck. "It's not worth it," he'd say. "My materials are delivered."), and we'd ride to the job site together. I was thirty-two years old, and he was ten years older than that. One gray morning, both of us sipping from Styrofoam cups of hot coffee, he told me about the black-and-white photographs he used to take in

Europe, how he had an exhibition of them once in London, how that's what he'd thought his life would be, a life of art.

"What happened?"

"I fucked my wife and had two kids."

He shrugged and changed the subject. I couldn't imagine using that word when it came to making love with my wife, and he may have started talking about the job, about strapping and Sheetrock and electrical outlets, things that honestly bored me. I'd been doing construction work off and on since leaving college, but I never felt called to do it. Those years I wasn't even that good at it. When I began writing fiction in my early twenties, I made the decision to avoid jobs where there was room for advancement up some invisible ladder to greater responsibilities and more money. I was afraid they would define me and my life and would rob me of the time and energy I'd need to teach myself to write. Also, I preferred to write in the mornings, so I often took night jobs, working as a halfway house counselor, an office cleaner, a bartender, and for six months when I was twenty-two, I worked for a private investigator and bounty hunter.

The last job I'd had before I got married was as head bartender at an Irish pub in our small town on the Merrimack River. I worked four nights a week and had seven mornings to myself, but Fontaine's life happened during the day, and I did not want us to be on two different schedules, never seeing much of each other. I'd also just published my first book. It was a collection of short stories that very few people bought or read, though this did not surprise me or even disappoint me much; that manuscript had been rejected by more than thirty publishers, and I was happy just to hold that book in my hands. I was also happy trying to write the novel my agent was in his second year of sending around. And now I was trying to write another one, a better one, though lying on that couch after another day with unhappy Yaron doing unhappy work, my body tired and heavy, I was beginning to feel my work life had taken a wrong turn. Soon it would be dark, a time I associated with going to a job after I'd spent the day writing, but now I was giving the best part of each day to ripping out toilets or hauling away old kitchen cabinets or nailing roof shingles on the gable of some lawyer's guesthouse in a misty rain. There were far worse problems to have, I knew, but I could feel the novel I was working on begin to slip away like a boat whose bowline I no longer had the strength to hold with both hands. And that's the moment my wife walked into the living room from the bathroom, smiling, her long curly black hair held back in a loose ponytail, a turquoise scarf around her neck. She looked so beautiful to me then that I did not at first take in what she had just said.

"What?"

Her eyes filled. She held up something short and white. "You're a daddy."

My body seemed to move on its own. I was up off the couch, holding her and kissing her and telling her positive words I do not now remember, though I know I felt like a liar saying them; in no time I'd be Yaron, my life of art forever behind me as I drove slope-shouldered from one job site to another, sipping bad coffee, telling the young man beside me that nothing good is worth doing, "Believe me, it's just not worth it."

I was wrong, of course. If I've ever been more wrong about anything in my life, I do not know what it is. Almost immediately, within minutes of her telling me, it seemed, I could only see this big, new thing in our lives as good; I loved my wife, she loved me, and we would find a way to make room for this baby we'd made. I brewed coffee and opened my notebook and got to work.

Daddy. It's not something I ever thought of being. I had a hunch not many other men gave it much thought either. You fall in love, you make love, and one day or night your wife turns to you in bed and says, "I want a baby."

"You do?"

"Don't *you*?"

"If you do."

"But don't you?"

"It's just not something I've ever thought much about."

But in one way I had. Like too many people, I come from a broken family. When I met Fontaine (and the first time I saw her she was performing on stage), I knew I would marry her. This was not so much a wish of mine as a knowledge, as if what I felt for her was music and the only dance for it was marriage, an institution that pulled me back to a dark time, my mother and father yelling at each other, throwing pots and pans, swearing, crying, this going on for months and months till that early Sunday morning in November when we four kids in pajamas followed our father out to his car before he drove away. When I heard the word marriage, yes, I thought of kids—hurt kids, lost kids, kids believing if they'd only been better kids their mother and father would still be together, kids who pretended it wasn't their fault.

"I really want a baby, honey. I want to go off the pill, okay?"

"Okay."

A few days after she told me this, I drove to my father's nine miles east. He lived alone in a small house on a hill overlooking a two-lane road and the rise of a grassy slope, its ridge a thick stand of maple trees. Six years earlier my father had pulled over on the highway to help two people hurt in an accident, and he'd been run over and suffered thirty-four broken bones, one leg pulverized, the other so damaged it had to be amputated just below the knee. It was late afternoon, and I knew he'd be finished with his day's writing and working out, exercises he did with dumbbells from his wheelchair.

He met me at the door. His hair was wet and he was naked, a towel draped over his crotch and right stump. He was fifty-six years old and had wide shoulders and a deep chest, and he was smiling, his eyes lit with love for me. "Hey, man." He held up his arms. I leaned down and hugged him. He smelled like soap, clean hair, and skin.

Soon he was dressed, and we were out on his back deck. The sun was low over the ridge of maples, their branches still bare. It was cold and I was wearing my leather jacket, but my father sat there in a short-sleeved shirt and sweatpants the empty right leg of which he'd tied around his stump with a red bandana. He was lighting a cigarette with his Zippo, one hand cupped around the flame. The night before, I'd called him and asked if I could stop by just before supper; I had to ask him a question. He said, "Yeah, man. I'm here."

This was new, my going to him to ask for any advice. It was my mother who raised us four kids, moving us from one cheap rented house in one mill town after another. When we saw our father, it was for two hours on a Sunday when he'd pick us up and drive us to church or take us out to a movie or restaurant he could barely afford. There was the feeling he was relaxing with us, that we, his kids, were part of his recreation, and there was also the feeling that he was doing the best he could and if we were to ask for any more than that, he wouldn't be happy.

But that was years ago. Since then, he'd married and divorced two more times, having two daughters with his third wife, who was a year older than I was. She and my half sisters lived ten miles south, and he primarily saw them on weekends, the way he used to see us. Ever since I was old enough to sit in a bar with him, my father and I had had the easy rapport of drinking buddies; we sipped and talked about whatever came up: lifting weights, a good book, politics and women and dirty jokes. But I don't remember him ever asking me what I might want to do with my time on this planet. Once, at a party at his house when he still had legs, I overheard him tell a friend of his, "I never tell my kids what to do with their lives." This, in many ways, was fine with me. I seemed to prefer to learn everything on my own the hard way anyway. And I rarely, if ever, sought out teachers.

"What's on your mind, man?"

"Fontaine wants a baby."

"Of course she does."

"But isn't it irresponsible to have one when you're as broke as we are?"

My father was looking over the railing out at the trees and sky. He took a drag from his cigarette and shook his head. He told me that lack of money will always be a problem for most people, but that shouldn't stop anyone. "I just believe, son, when the woman wants a baby, then that's it. It's time to have that baby."

I found myself agreeing, nodding my head.

"Besides, all that shit work you have to do, when you know it's for diapers and food for your child, it makes all work holy."

Holy. This was one of my father's words. He was a Catholic, and I was not. He believed there was a God who loved him; I did not. He believed he was being watched over, while I felt strongly that I was entirely alone and the only good that would ever come to me would have to come from my own hard work and occasional good luck.

Still, driving away from my thrice-divorced father's house, I felt better, for I believed if my wife wanted a baby then that should be that. Women only had a few years to get this done, and who was I to say she could not?

Then she was pregnant, her belly growing by the week. It was a cold winter and it snowed a lot, and whenever we walked up the shoveled icy sidewalk to our apartment, I'd take Fontaine's arm and hold her close. I imagined her slipping and falling, she and the baby imperiled. I read books on nutrition for pregnant women and learned that if the fetus didn't get enough calcium, the mother's body would take it from her own bones. I made sure my wife ate yogurt and drank milk four to five times a day. When the baby began to kick, Fontaine would kneel in front of our record player, her curly black hair down around her shoulders, her back straight, and she'd place our stereo headphones against her protruding belly and play Mozart, Motown, and Stevie Wonder. From the couch, I watched her do this. It was like watching a panel open to a secret room you hadn't known was there. It was like watching a flower blossom into a shape you didn't see coming. We were beginning to feel less like two and more like three, and all I felt about this was joy.

Then there was the bright light of the operating room, a gloved nurse handing me our newborn son. His mother's labor had been hard and painful, more than twenty-eight hours long, her cervix never fully dilating, and now she lay conscious on the table with an oxygen mask over her nose and mouth, looking up at us, quietly weeping. Just below her breasts, there was a short curtain to keep her from seeing the surgeons sewing up her abdomen, but seconds earlier, the moment our son was born, I had looked over that curtain and watched him being lifted from the incision, his tiny face handsome and raging just before he blurred and my voice broke and I told Fontaine, "He's a boy. He's a *boy*." Wiping my eyes and staring at him, I thought, *It's you. It's you*, for I recognized him from some other time and place. How was this possible? But I did, I recognized him, and now I was carrying him behind the nurse to the warming table, his fine hair wet as he cried with all the air he could summon from his small, pink chest, the stub of his umbilical cord still attached to what would become his navel. I lay him under a warming lamp, and the nurse handed me a pair of shears. I opened the blades. I was afraid to get too close to his skin.

"A little more, honey," she said. "You won't hurt him."

Snipping my son's umbilical cord felt like cutting through coated wire, an act he didn't seem to notice. The nurse began to clean our baby with a warm sponge, and I couldn't stop staring at his eyes and nose and mouth and chin, his tiny chest and nipples, his rising and falling abdomen as he kept crying, his penis and thighs and ankles and feet. I couldn't stop crying either, and I leaned in and stroked the side of his head with my thumb. I told him I was his dad and everything was going to be all right. Everything. I promise.

I first noticed the blood when I was changing his diaper on the apron of the stage. This was at the high school where Fontaine taught dance, and I was there to pick her up and drive her home. The rehearsal had just ended, and while Fontaine was talking to one of the dancers and the rest chatted gleefully while drifting up the aisles of the dark theater, it was clear our four-week-old son's diaper needed changing so I laid him down on a blanket under the colored gel lights of the stage. Maybe if I had not done this in that hazy purple light I would not have seen what I saw, a thread of orange in our son's stool. I finished cleaning and dressing him, then carried him and his open diaper out to the lighted foyer. That thread of orange seemed to be gone, but then I looked closer and saw traces of what had to be only one thing.

When I showed Fontaine, she was concerned but calm. Like my father, she has a deep and private faith. But I was a boy again, living in a shabby house on a shabby street, getting chased down it by other boys out to get me, and now they were out to get my son, too, this sleeping infant against my shoulder I already somehow loved far more than I loved my own heartbeat, my own breaths that were shallow now as I rushed out of that theater to buckle him into his seat and drive him and Fontaine back home to where there was a phone.

Our doctor told us to bring him in first thing in the morning.

"But shouldn't we take him to the *emergency* room?"

"No, not yet."

Early the next morning, our doctor, a kind woman with six kids of her own, examined our infant son and said, "I still don't think this is serious, but we'll do a GI series to be sure."

I said: "Doesn't he have to drink *barium* for that?"

"Yes," she said. "He'll have to do it through his bottle."

Fontaine and I looked at each other. Her black hair was held back, and again, she looked calm. I picked up our nine-pound son.

He grunted against me, his belly more distended than it had ever felt before.

The upper and lower GI series was scheduled for the following morning. That week Jeb and I were in his shop, close to finishing the construction of custom cabinets, and his deadline for delivery was just days away; I'd be hurting his business if I did not go in to work that morning. Fontaine said she would call me just as soon as they had the results. She said this to me as we lay in bed, Austin swaddled and finally asleep in his baby basket on the floor beside us. I rose up on one elbow and peered down at him. His face was so small. On his head was the knit cap we put on him because we kept the heat low. Even in sleep, his expression was slightly strained, like he was never quite comfortable and when was someone going to *notice* this? I pictured being in Jeb's shop in Charlestown a few miles away from the Boston hospital where Fontaine and my son would be. It wasn't that far, but still, I imagined my wife having to feed our infant barium from a bottle by herself. This felt like abandonment to me; I was abandoning my family when they needed me most. But we also had to pay our bills, didn't we? I got paid by the hour—no work meant no money—and I couldn't let Jeb down either. Fontaine was beginning to drift off against me, but I climbed out of bed and wrote the phone number for Jeb's shop on a piece of paper. I placed it under her car keys on the kitchen table then knelt at Austin's basket. I leaned down and kissed him lightly on his small forehead. He smelled like clean skin and wool and something sweet I couldn't name.

Minutes later, lying in the dark beside my wife, I prayed for the first time. If I'd prayed even once in my life before this moment, I do not recall doing so. But now I was silently asking God to help our son. *Please, let this not be serious, and if it is serious, please—whoever you are, whatever you are—please heal our baby of it.*

I felt like a hypocrite. But as I closed my eyes I also felt just a little bit better, even if I did not believe anyone or anything was truly listening or cared.

When the call came the following afternoon, I was standing at the drill press, drilling identical holes one after another into medium-density fiberboard. On the other side of the shop, Jeb was gluing and clamping together cabinet boxes, a smoking cigarette between his lips, and his partner Bob, a quiet man with two grown kids and an ex-wife, had just finished ripping maple stiles on the table saw and switching it off, and that's when he heard what I did not, the black phone on the wall ring.

My job was simple, but the holes had to be perfect, and even though I seemed to be boring into the center of each penciled X my brother had drawn for me, I kept seeing Fontaine holding our son in her arms, trying to get him to drink some chemical element that probably tasted terrible—and then what?—was our baby put into some kind of X-ray machine? I didn't know, and it felt irresponsible to me that I didn't know.

"Andre?" Bob's deep voice, his hand on my shoulder. "Your wife's on the phone."

The telephone was in a corner of the shop. Taped to the wall was a sheet of emergency numbers, a water-stained bank calendar from three years earlier, a pencil stub hanging by a string. It's the image that comes when I hear again my wife's voice in my head, high and nearly breathless, as if she's running in the dark away or toward something and there isn't much time—*birth defect, malro-tated, life-threatening.*

"*What?* What do they fucking mean *life*-threatening?"

"Yes, they think—" She couldn't say the rest, and I couldn't hear anymore and then I was out of the shop and driving too fast through the streets of Boston toward my wife and son and the doctors who'd just given her this news.

Our four-week-old son needed emergency surgery to correct something called a malrotated upper bowel. It happens in about one out of six thousand births, and it had happened to Austin. In his tenth week of embryonic development, Austin's organs had finished developing outside what would become his torso. His spleen, liver, kidneys, and appendix then had to do a 270-degree revolution into the cavity that would hold them, finding their rightful place, the small and large intestines fanning out in that shape most perfectly suited to easy digestion. But with Austin that revolution never occurred. The organs, while functional, went into the wrong places, and the intestines twisted and bunched and never fanned out the way they should have. Most babies who experience this die, or the diagnosis comes so late their intestines no longer work, and then these children are hooked up to medical machinery for as long as they live.

I no longer see the face of the surgeon who told us all this; I only see his assistant, a man my age then or younger, tall and pale-faced and wearing black-framed glasses. I stood there in my carpentry sweatshirt, jeans, and work boots, sawdust feathered across my chest, and he nodded at me and said, as if I needed the language to be made simpler: "It's life-threatening."

Fontaine was holding Austin to her shoulder, patting his back and bouncing slightly. She looked pale and focused but calm, her faith rising up from wherever faith lives. But all I felt was flaming bees hurling through my veins, for I did not trust these men or this hospital. They were just other men who'd learned another trade, and what if they were wrong? But there was no time for a second opinion, and from whom would we get it? This was one of the best hospitals for children in the world. Wait any longer and our son might not make it, or his intestines might not, and he'd be attached to a machine the rest of his life. What was there to do *but* trust these men? Trust them and let go and have faith they could save our son?

Hours passed before they were ready to operate. There was a waiting room with a TV and magazines and deep chairs, black night outside the hospital windows. Austin kept crying and crying; because he was going into surgery, we were not allowed to feed him, and he hadn't eaten in hours. We took turns holding him, walking him back and forth. Sometimes he'd fall quiet, and then rage again, his piercing wail in my ear. He sounded betrayed, and I felt neglectful and cruel.

A nurse finally came in and told us they were ready. She pointed to a wing of the building where the operating rooms were, and Fontaine and I hurried in that direction, Austin against my chest and shoulder. This faster movement calmed him down, and he seemed to take in the swinging doors we passed through, then the empty, quiet corridor, only a third of its overhead lights on. Against the wall in the shadows were three or four gurneys. Their mattresses were stripped, and Austin stared at them. Fontaine and I just stood there. I heard the faint buzz of the fluorescent lights above, nothing else. Fontaine may have said something about us being in the wrong place, I'm not sure, but now there were voices, low and feminine and cheerful, then soft footsteps, two women in surgical blue coming around a corner toward us. They were smiling, and they both had their hair tucked up, cotton masks hanging beneath their chins.

They introduced themselves as our son's anesthesiologists. There was the shaking of hands, their eyes on Austin, and one of them took him from my arms while the other handed me a clipboard with a form on it.

"You just have to sign this, and we'll be off."

Fontaine and the doctors began to talk about Austin's curly hair, his handsome face, but I was reading the form as quickly as you'd run barefoot over smoking embers: *accidental death*, *not responsible*, *no liability*, etc. I signed and handed the clipboard to the one who wasn't holding Austin. Then they were walking away before I could kiss him or touch him, both women holding him between them, his small head erect on his neck, his tiny back straight as they carried him into deep shadows through another set of swinging doors that opened and closed swiftly behind them, Fontaine and I turning to each other, holding tight, our crying echoing down the hallway.

When Austin was two days old, his troubles undiagnosed, Fontaine slept all afternoon in the bedroom recovering, and I held him swaddled in my lap in a rocking chair I'd pulled over to the gable window. Outside it was snowing, the wind kicking up every few minutes and gusting against the glass. I'd turned the heat up, and now I was rocking gently back and forth, staring down at our son's small face and hands and fingers. Sometimes I'd look out the window at the snow but not for long. I couldn't stop staring at the sleeping face of this child we'd made, this child I somehow already loved more deeply than anyone I'd ever known or loved before.

A phrase came to me, words, it seemed, for what was happening to me that afternoon when nothing felt more important or pressing or essential than what I was doing at that very moment, holding our child, keeping him safe and warm: *State of Grace*. I don't know where these words came from, and I did not know what they meant, but they moved through me like notes from an old cello miles away.

Hours later, when Fontaine had woken and was breast-feeding Austin in bed beside her, I took down our dictionary and looked up that phrase. The first definition I read was this: "to be surrounded by God's love."

God. Part of me resisted this. And another part, well, it just did not.

Fontaine and I sat in that waiting room, and we waited. If there were other people there, I do not remember them. If any of our families came, I can no longer summon who they were. But I see the flat light of that room, my reflection in the night windows of the hallway I'd pace every ten or fifteen minutes. It was long and empty, and as I walked it, there was the heavy-shouldered, hollow-chested feeling that I was being punished for that late afternoon nearly a year earlier when I lay on our couch and Fontaine came into the room looking so beautiful and happy to tell me of this unspeakable gift coming to us, and my very first response, before all that came after, was to reject it.

The sins of the fathers are visited upon the sons. The Bible now, a book I'd never read and had no intention of reading. But I had no words for the limitless love I felt for our son, or the shadow side of this love, and I needed some. I remembered Hemingway: "When you have a child, the world forever takes a hostage." And there was Rilke, too: "Beauty is the beginning of terror which we are only just able to bear."

Through the waiting room window, I could see Fontaine sitting straight in her chair, her eyes closed, her lips moving almost imperceptibly.

The operation took hours. In my memory, it took all night, because when the doctor called us out to that corridor, his eyes bloodshot but warm, the early sun was shining outside the windows behind him. A cotton surgical mask still hung beneath his chin, the stubble there beginning to show. *Successful.* That's the word that comes. And *surgery.* And *no complications.* And *congratulations.* Fontaine and I holding each other, the doctor's face blurring, his big hand in mine, my hand squeezing his shoulder. And it may have been then or hours later or maybe even the next day that we got the full details of how they opened up our infant's belly. How they took out his appendix because if, years later, he ever had appendicitis the doctors would never know it because his appendix would be in the wrong place. How they could not move Austin's other organs, but they could and did save his intestines, which saved him, fanning them out the way they were supposed to be in the first place.

"And that's it?" I said. "He'll be all right?"

"He'll live a completely normal life."

Austin may have come home with us that day, or the next, I no longer know. All I know is that profound relief, joy, and gratitude were shooting heat through me like kisses from the gods, and I had to do something with it all; we had been given something so good, and I had to give something, too. I kissed Fontaine and told her I would be right back. I was half-walking, half-running down that hallway, looking for the first person who could tell me where I could give blood, anything. There were kind faces and helpful faces, men and women, fingers pointing to signs and elevators and closed rooms behind glass doors, all of this on a moving current of what I can only call love. Then I was sitting at a desk filling out a form, adding my name to all those willing to give the marrow of their bones to a stranger who one day might need it. A woman took a vial of my blood, but this did not feel like enough. I wanted to give something away right then, on the same day my son was spared. I kept looking for the blood bank but could not find it, and I wanted to get back to my wife and child. I wanted to hold him. I wanted to hold him close and never let go.

But we have to let go, don't we?

This was more than twenty years ago. Austin is now over six feet and two hundred twenty pounds and wears a size fifteen shoe. He lifts weights six days a week and reads and writes and loves serious films and good music and all sports with balls in them. When he was a baby, the scar on the right side of his abdomen was pale and an inch long. As he's grown, it's grown a bit longer and deeper, though now it's largely covered with dark hair. Every single time I see that scar, I feel only boundless gratitude.

Austin lives a thousand miles west of us, on his college campus in Ohio. He has an eighteen-year-old sister and a sixteen-year-old brother. With the birth of each, my capacity for love seemed to grow exponentially larger, opening up in me its attendant fear of loss but a deep reservoir of joy, too. So much joy, as if my deepest, truest life could only begin once I became a father.

Soon our daughter, Ariadne, a dancer and artist like her mother, will be moving to another campus, and not long after, Elias, an athlete and drummer, will want to do the same. Fontaine and I will be two again. Back to where we began, for we do not own these three people that came from us. We were simply given them to love and to guide and to set free. And even though I still do not believe in an all-powerful and loving God, I know I'll pray for my children's health and safety daily and nightly, as I do now, as I will until I am no longer on this earth, for *something* is here among us: something I cannot see but feel; something I cannot hear but sense; something I cannot smell but know; that one late afternoon, this life will bring you to a door your lover may walk through smiling, and just because you're tired and afraid and have little to no faith, you're supposed to lift your head and breathe and walk with joy and trembling right through it.

ABOUT THE CONTRIBUTORS

André Aciman was born in Alexandria, Egypt, and is an American memoirist, essayist, novelist, and scholar of seventeenth-century literature. His work has appeared in the *New Yorker*, the *New York Review of Books*, the *New York Times*, the *New Republic*, *Condé Nast Traveler*, the *Paris Review*, and *Granta*, as well as in many volumes of *The Best American Essays*. Aciman received his PhD in Comparative Literature from Harvard University and is chair and distinguished professor of Comparative Literature at the Graduate Center of the City University of New York. He is the author of the Whiting Award–winning memoir *Out of Egypt* (1995) and of three novels, *Harvard Square* (2013), *Eight White Nights* (2010), and *Call Me by Your Name* (2007), for which he won the Lambda Literary Award for Men's Fiction (2008). He is also the author of two essays collections, *False Papers* (2001) and *Alibis* (2011).

Chris Bachelder is the author of the novels *Bear v. Shark*, *U.S.!*, and *Abbott Awaits*. He teaches fiction writing at the University of Cincinnati.

David Bezmozgis, a writer and filmmaker, is the author of *Natasha and Other Stories* and *The Free World*.

Justin Cronin is the author of the *New York Times* and international bestsellers *The Passage* and *The Twelve*. His other books are *The Summer*

Guest and *Mary and O'Neil*, which received the PEN/Hemingway Award and the Stephen Crane Prize. A Distinguished Faculty Fellow in the Humanities at Rice University, he divides his time between Houston, Texas, and Cape Cod, Massachusetts.

Peter Ho Davies is the author of the novel *The Welsh Girl*, and the story collections *The Ugliest House in the World* and *Equal Love*. His work has appeared in *Harpers*, the *Atlantic*, *Granta*, and the *Paris Review*, and has been selected for *Prize Stories: The O. Henry Award* and *The Best American Short Stories*.

Anthony Doerr is the author of four books: *Memory Wall*, *The Shell Collector*, *About Grace*, and *Four Seasons in Rome*. His fiction has won four O. Henry Prizes, three Pushcart Prizes, the Rome Prize, the New York Public Library's Young Lions Award, the National Magazine Award, a Guggenheim Fellowship, the Story Prize, and the *Sunday Times* EFG Private Bank Short Story Award. His fifth book, a novel entitled *All the Light We Cannot See*, will be published in 2014.

Andre Dubus III is the author of six books, including the *New York Times* bestsellers *House of Sand and Fog*, *The Garden of Last Days*, and his memoir, *Townie*. Mr. Dubus has been a finalist for the National Book Award, has been awarded a Guggenheim Fellowship, the National Magazine Award for Fiction, and two Pushcart Prizes, and was a 2012 recipient of an American Academy of Arts and Letters Award in Literature. He teaches full-time at the University of Massachusetts Lowell, and he lives north of Boston with his wife, Fontaine, a modern dancer, and their three children. His latest book, *Dirty Love*, was published in the fall of 2013.

Steve Edwards lives in Massachusetts and teaches writing at Fitchburg State University. He is the author of *Breaking into the Backcountry*, a memoir of his seven months of "unparalleled solitude" as caretaker of a wilderness ranch in Oregon in 2001. At present he is at work on a nonfiction book about fatherhood, the writing life, and his grandfather, a soldier who on March 16, 1942, graced the cover of *LIFE* magazine and lent a human face to a war effort whose outcome was far from certain.

Karl Taro Greenfeld is the author of seven books, including the novel *Triburbia*, about a group of fathers in Tribeca.

Ben Greenman is a contributing writer at the *New Yorker* and elsewhere. He is the author of several acclaimed books of fiction, including *Superbad*, *Please Step Back*, and *What He's Poised to Do*. His most recent books are *The Slippage*, a novel, and *Mo' Meta Blues*, cowritten with Questlove.

Lev Grossman is the award-winning author of the *New York Times* bestselling novels *The Magicians* and *The Magician King*. He is the book critic at *Time* magazine and has also written for *Wired*, the *Believer*, the *Wall Street Journal*, the *Village Voice*, *Salon*, the *New York Times*, and NPR. He lives in Brooklyn, New York, with his wife and three children.

Dennis Lehane grew up in Boston. Since his first novel, *A Drink Before the War*, won the Shamus Award, he has published nine more novels with William Morrow & Co., which have been translated into more than thirty languages and become international bestsellers.

Three of his novels—*Mystic River, Gone, Baby, Gone*, and *Shutter Island*—have been adapted into award-winning films. Mr. Lehane was a staff writer on the acclaimed HBO series *The Wire* and is currently a writer-producer on the fourth season of HBO's *Boardwalk Empire*. He and his wife, Angie, divide their time between Boston and the Gulf Coast of Florida. His most recent book, *Live by Night*, won the Edgar Award for best novel.

Bruce Machart is the author of *The Wake of Forgiveness*, a novel, and a collection of short stories entitled *Men in the Making*. An assistant professor of English at Bridgewater State University, Machart lives in Hamilton, Massachusetts.

Rick Moody is the author of five novels, three collections of stories, a memoir, and, most recently, a volume of essays entitled *On Celestial Music*. Since 2009 he has written on music at the *Rumpus*. He teaches at New York University and Yale.

Stephen O'Connor is the author of two collections of short fiction, *Here Comes Another Lesson* and *Rescue*, and of two works of nonfiction, *Will My Name Be Shouted Out?*, a memoir, and *Orphan Trains*, biography/history. His fiction, essays, and poetry have appeared in numerous journals, including the *New Yorker*, the *New York Times*, the *Nation*, *Conjunctions*, *One Story*, and *Poetry Magazine*. He teaches in the MFA programs of Columbia and Sarah Lawrence.

Benjamin Percy is the author of three novels, *The Dead Lands* (forthcoming from Grand Central/Hachette in 2014), *Red Moon*, and *The Wilding*, as well as two books of short stories. His fiction and nonfiction have been published by *Esquire* (where he is a contributing editor), *GQ*, *Time*, the *Wall Street Journal*, *Men's Journal*, *Outside*, the *Paris Review*, and *Tin House*. His honors include a Whiting Writers' Award, an NEA Fellowship, two Pushcart Prizes, the Plimpton Prize, and inclusion in *The Best American Short Stories*.

Frederick Reiken is the author of three novels, most recently *Day for Night*, which was a finalist for the Los Angeles Times Book Prize in fiction. His debut novel, *The Odd Sea*, won the Hackney Literary Award for a first novel and was a finalist for the Barnes & Noble Discover Prize. His follow-up, *The Lost Legends of New Jersey*, was a national bestseller and a *New York Times* Notable Book. His short stories have appeared in publications including the *New Yorker*, *Glimmer Train*, *Gulf Coast*, and the *Western Humanities Review*, and his essays have appeared in the *Writer's Chronicle*. Formerly a news reporter and columnist, he teaches on the Creative Writing faculty at Emerson College. He lives in western Massachusetts with his wife and daughters.

Marco Roth is the author of *The Scientists: A Family Romance* (Farrar, Straus and Giroux, 2012) and a founding co-editor of the magazine *n+1*. He lives in Philadelphia with his daughter.

Bob Smith was the first openly gay stand-up comic to appear on *The Tonight Show* and have his own HBO special. His first book of comic essays, *Openly Bob*, won the Lambda Literary Award. His first novel, *Selfish and Perverse*, was one of three nominees for the Edmund White Award for Debut Fiction. His most recent novel, *Remembrance of Things I Forgot*, was picked by Amazon as one of Ten Best Gay and Lesbian Books of 2011, was short-listed for the Green Carnation Prize, won an Honor Award from the American Library Association, and was nominated for the Ferro-Grumley Award.

Matthew Specktor is the author of the novels *American Dream Machine* and *That Summertime Sound*, as well as a nonfiction book of film criticism. His writing has appeared or is forthcoming in the *Paris Review*, the *Believer*, *Tin House*, and other publications. He is a founding editor of the *Los Angeles Review of Books*.

Garth Stein is the author of three novels, including *The Art of Racing in the Rain*, a *New York Times* and international bestseller. He is the cofounder of Seattle7Writers, a nonprofit collective of Northwest authors working to foster a passion for the written word. He lives in Seattle with his family.

A recipient of a National Book Critics Circle Award, the Guggenheim Fellowship, the American Library Association Award, and numerous other prizes, the internationally bestselling writer **Darin Strauss** is the author of the novels *Chang & Eng*, *The Real McCoy*, and *More Than It Hurts You*, and the NBCC-winning memoir *Half a Life*. In addition, Darin has recently been named an opinion columnist at Al-Jazeera America, and he is the clinical associate professor of fiction at NYU's creative writing program. His work has been translated into fourteen languages and published in nineteen countries.

Alexi Zentner is the author of the novels *Touch* and *The Lobster Kings*. He has been short-listed for the 2011 Governor General's Literary Award, the Center for Fiction's 2011 Flahery-Dunnan First Novel Prize, the 2012 VCU Cabell First Novelist Award, and the 2011 Amazon.ca First Novel Award, and long-listed for the 2011 Scotiabank Giller Prize and the 2013 International IMPAC Dublin Literary Award. His short fiction has appeared in the *Atlantic*, *Tin House*, *Glimmer Train*, *Narrative*, and many other magazines, and he is the winner of both the O. Henry Prize and the Narrative Prize and has been short-listed for *The Best American Short Stories* and the Pushcart Prize. Alexi is an assistant professor at Binghamton University and a member of the faculty in the Sierra Nevada College low-residency MFA program. His website is alexizentner.com.

ACKNOWLEDGMENTS

First and foremost, I am grateful for my fierce agent and true friend, Erin Harris at Folio Literary Management, who has been my partner on this project from the very start. Thanks, Erin, for your tireless effort and boundless enthusiasm. This book wouldn't exist without you.

Andie Avila at Berkley Books trusted my vision from the moment we met and was always there to be my compass when I was unable to see the forest from the trees. I couldn't have asked for a better editor!

I am thankful for the wonderful and inspiring writing of all of the authors included in this collection, who opened their hearts and shared their experiences with such honesty and good humor. It's been a pleasure working with each of you.

This book would not have been possible without the gracious help and support of Jeremiah Chamberlin, Maria Gagliano, David Gates, Jenny Halper, Ann Hood, Celia Blue Johnson, Jeff Kleinman, Jonathan Lethem, Sara Lippmann, Michael Lowenthal, Polly Rosenwaike, Penina Roth, Karen Russell, Helen Schulman, Irene Skolnick, Linda Swanson-Davies, and Lynne Tillman. I owe you all so much.

Adam Bell (co-editor of *Anatomy of a Photographer*), John Donohue (editor of *Man with a Pan*), and Kim Perel (co-editor of *Wedding Cake for Breakfast*) provided expert advice. Thanks too to John Morgan for coaching me from the sidelines.

For lightening my spirit and sparking my creativity at every step, thanks to Lindsey Alexander, Patrick Callihan, Denis Hurley, Kyle Magill, Ryan Matthews, David Zweig, Miranda Beverly-Whittemore and David Lobenstine, Brittney Inman Canty and Tony Canty, Melissa Clark and Daniel Gercke, Cornelia Reiner and Laura Sedlock, Liz Sanders and Brendan Conheady, Kim Brockway and Zach Williamson. You guys rock.

Thanks to Catherine Connors and the excellent editors at *Babble* for encouraging my voice, especially Lindsay Hood.

Shout-out to all of my family and friends, in particular Pat Frik, Paul Gresko, and my mom and dad. Your support, encouragement, and levity helps me keep my sanity.

And most importantly, to Sara for putting up with me through all this and reading countless drafts and telling me again and again that I'm a great writer and a better dad than I give myself credit for. And to Felix too, for obvious reasons. Thanks and love.

ABOUT THE EDITOR

Brian Gresko is a writer and stay-at-home dad based in Brooklyn. At the heart of his work lies a fascination with culture, gender roles, and parenting. His essays and journalism have appeared on the *Huffington Post*, *Salon*, TheAtlantic.com, the *Daily Beast*, the *Paris Review Daily*, the *Rumpus*, the *Los Angeles Review of Books*, and *Poets & Writers*, among numerous others. In print, he has contributed to *Glimmer Train Stories* and *Slice* literary magazine. He writes a column about dads for *Babble* and is currently at work on a novel. You can find him online at briangresko.com.